Library of Southern Civilization

LEWIS P. SIMPSON, EDITOR

I'LL TAKE MY STAND

I'LL TAKE MY STAND

The South and the Agrarian Tradition

BY TWELVE SOUTHERNERS

Introduction by Louis D. Rubin, Jr.

Biographical Essays by Virginia Rock

LOUISIANA STATE UNIVERSITY PRESS

Baton Rouge

Louisiana Paperback Edition, 1977
06 05 04 03 02 01 00 99   14 13 12

LIBRARY OF CONGRESS CATALOGING IN PUBLICATION DATA

Main entry under title:
I'll take my stand.
    (Library of Southern civilization)
    Reprint of the ed. published by Harper, New York.
    1. Southern States—Civilization—Addresses, essays, lec-
tures.   I. Twelve southerners.
F209.137   1977   975   77-22101
ISBN 0-8071-0357-8

The paper in this book meets the guidelines for permanence and
durability of the Committee on Production Guidelines for Book
Longevity of the Council on Library Resources. (∞)

This book is dedicated
in love and admiration
to
WALTER L. FLEMING

Historian; Professor of History and Dean of the
Graduate School of Vanderbilt University; to whom some
of the contributors owe doctrine and example, and all
would offer this expression of perfect esteem.

CONTENTS

LOUIS D. RUBIN, JR.

INTRODUCTION

LIBRARY OF SOUTHERN CIVILIZATION EDITION (1977)
The symposium entitled *I'll Take My Stand: The South and the Agrarian Tradition* was first published by Harper in 1930, in a modest edition that was subsequently permitted to go out of print. Except for a small clothbound reprint brought out by Peter Smith, primarily for library use, the book was not again made available to the general public until thirty-two years after its first publication, when Harper reissued it as a paperback to their Torchbook series. For the latter edition I was commissioned to write an introduction. Now that the Agrarian symposium is once again to be reprinted, this time as a volume in LSU Press's Library of Southern Civilization series, I have the privilege of contributing another commentary.

Fifteen years have gone by since the 1962 edition. The South is no more an embattled minority section, attempting to adjust long-standing racial attitudes to the consequences of *Brown* v. *Board of Education*, while also working with great haste to catch up economically with the rest of the country. Racially the South has now integrated itself far beyond the most sanguine expectations of 1962, and to an extent that would have seemed inconceivable in 1930. Economically it has all but closed the gap, and there is now even a growing

(xi)

concern in some places about the way in which industries have been moving southward away from the northern and western industrial belt. With the development of air-conditioning, the more balmy climate of what is now called the Sun Belt rather than the Bible Belt has meant that longer production days and more attractive living conditions and recreational facilities are possible south of the Ohio and Potomac Rivers.

The transformation, it seems to me, was symbolized, during the closing weeks of the bicentennial year in the spectacle of the leading figures in the nation's political and economic establishment converging upon a small community in southwestern Georgia to offer advice about future federal policy to a former peanut farmer who had recently been elected president of the United States. Future historians may well agree that the election of 1976, in which a southern candidate was chosen for the nation's highest office with the strong support of a once-again Solid South and with overwhelming majorities among black voters in the cities of the Northeast and Midwest, in effect signaled the end of the Civil War. It meant an end, surely, to the single issue that had most set apart the states of the South from the nation: segregation, and the attempt to maintain it. Not that the racial issue had been resolved, or black-white tensions eliminated, but no longer were either the issue or the tensions principally a southern problem. Indeed, in important respects they had become less critical in the South than elsewhere, for the South would appear, to a much greater degree at least than most other places, to have achieved a notable measure of genuine public racial integration, without as much of the economic and social polarization that characterized other regions.

Now what has all this to do with a book published forty-seven years earlier, which took for its title words from a song that had once been the anthem of a would-be southern nation whose very reason for being had to do with the desire to maintain and, if possible, to enhance Negro slavery? A book whose announced thesis was opposition to industrialization and urbanization, and advocacy of an agrarian life—a book which was introduced by a statement of principles that deplored the falling off of younger southerners from the southern tradition and that declared itself against the tendency of the South to "join up behind the common or American industrial ideal"?

Surely it must be obvious that if such was the book's objective, then it failed in its objective. The South not only joined up; industrially it has been leading the country in recent years. Southern cities, with their vast suburbs, have grown by incredible proportions, while the rural hinterlands have been bound into the complexities of an industrial society to a degree that has thoroughly blurred the once sharp distinction between countryside and city. As for the retention of the "Southern tradition," to the extent that that tradition involved what it was once commonly thought to involve—one would be hard put to identify the South by any such rubric nowadays. Racially the South is the most genuinely integrated of all American regions.

So, if *I'll Take My Stand* continues to command an audience today, almost half a century after its publication, the first conclusion to be drawn is that the importance and the appeal of the Agrarian symposium must not have resided in the efficacy of its prescription of an nonindustrialized, unchanged South as the proper model for the region's future, but in something else. After all, both before and after its appearance in the Depression-bound year of 1930, there have been dozens and dozens of books, and many manifestos, whose economic, political, and racial prescriptions for the South have proved to be much more accurate. Yet most such books have long since been relegated to the shelves of the library stacks, whereas the "backward-looking," "cloud-cuckoo land" manifesto of the twelve southerners has remained alive and in print.

Perhaps a clue to this apparent paradox lies in a remark, quoted in part in my introduction to the 1962 edition, by a distinguished southern economist who had devoted much effort to demonstrating why an agrarian economy was emphatically what the South did *not* need. The Agrarians, he said, though "abominable" advisers on ways to achieve greater material well-being, had much to offer as humanists in suggesting how the fruits of economic progress could be used as a means to "the more spiritual side of a good, full and happy life." But the Agrarians were *not* economists. They were humanists, just as Allen Tate said when he envisioned the enterprise as a calculated defense of religious humanism. And the real values they were asserting in 1930 were not those of "material well-being" or of neo-Confederate nostalgia, but of thoughtful men who were very much concerned with the erosion of the quality of individual life by the forces of industrialization and the uncritical worship of material progress as an end in itself. It was not their assumption that one first achieved material well-being, then used it to further "the more spiritual side of a good, full and happy life"; on the contrary, they insisted that any attempt to divorce economics and labor from "the more spiritual side" of one's life brutalized the labor and cheapened the humanity.

They were writing squarely out of an old American tradition, one that we find imbedded in American thought almost from the earliest days, and that runs counter to yet another old American tradition. The tradition out of which they were writing was that of pastorale; they were invoking the humane virtues of a simpler, more elemental, nonacquisitive existence, as a needed rebuke to the acquisitive, essentially materialistic compulsions of a society that from the outset was very much engaged in seeking wealth, power, and plenty on a continent whose prolific natural resources and vast acres of usable land, forests, and rivers were there for the taking.

The particular pastorale they wrote, however, was given substance and urgency by their own historical situation. They were southerners, young men born into a society that had only belatedly experienced the full impact of the industrial dispensation, and which in their own lifetimes had become caught up in the surge of overwhelming social, economic, and political change, so that the contrasts between earlier ways and later were dramatically visible. Nor were they external observers; they felt the change within themselves, and knew at first hand the problems of definition involved, and could thus recognize and identify many of the alternatives. Moreover, there was an historical circumstance that bound them together in a community identity and led them to perceive the changes that were altering their community in terms of deeply felt historical loyalties and sectional self-defense. Thus their special version of pastoral rebuke possessed a concrete imagery and an historical depth that imbued it with drama and passion. They did more than merely admonish and prescribe: they "took their stand."

In the introduction to the 1962 edition of *I'll Take My Stand* I described Nashville agrarianism as a metaphor: "an extended metaphor, of which the image of the agrarian community is the figure, standing for and embodying something else. The something else is modern society. Of this society the South is a part, and, for the purposes of the metaphor, the correlative." The Agrarian symposium, I went on to say, was "the vision of poets, and carried with it certain convictions about living and dying that have held much imaginative appeal to Southerners and many non-Southerners as well." I still believe this is essentially true, but I must say that in certain respects the formulation was misleading. For one thing, it suggests a conscious literary strategy, and the extent to which the strategy was conscious and premeditated actually varied from essay to essay and from contributor to contributor. For some—Allen Tate certainly, John Crowe Ransom to an extent, Stark Young, John Wade and Andrew Lytle perhaps—there was at the time of writing a considerable awareness of the metaphoric element involved. But for others—Donald Davidson, Frank Owsley, H. C. Nixon, and (for very different reasons) Robert Penn Warren—it is obvious that at the time the book was being written the enterprise was envisioned as a literal and practical program, a specific course of action. Warren soon changed his mind; Ransom, stung by the criticisms of the venture's "impracticality," proceeded to get much more literally involved in agrarian economics.

Donald Davidson objected strongly to me about the metaphor formulation: "If you say that," he told me, "it's very easy, because you don't have to believe it at all." And that is true. But let it be admitted that, to a very real extent, that was precisely why I *did* describe it as a metaphor. For in the year 1962, when I wrote my original introduction, I was very much concerned with the way that the symposium might be received by the audience for which the Torchbook edition was designed: the academic, intellectual community north and south. There was the chance, even the likelihood, that, as in the early 1930s, the obvious impracticalities of a return to subsistence farming in the age of the tractor, the supermarket, and the television set, as well as the political sectionalism and the defense, implied and stated, of racial segregation, might serve to distract the symposium's readers from what was and is the book's real importance: its assertion of the values of humanism and its rebuke of materialism.

It will also be noted that in the 1962 introduction relatively little is said about racial segregation. So much had happened in the three decades since *I'll Take My Stand* first appeared that many of the racial assumptions in it no longer represented the views of Tate, Ransom, Warren, and certain other contributors to the symposium. It seemed important to me that issues which by 1962 were highly controversial, seen by many southerners then in very different ways than in 1930, should not be permitted to distort the real importance of what the Agrarians had written.*

But if stressing the "metaphoric" element of *I'll Take My*

*I did not, however, presume to make this decision alone. Before I forwarded my introduction to the publisher, I sent it to Allen Tate for his approval; and I was heartened when he expressed his entire agreement with what I had done.

Stand helped to prevent the anachronistic application of the racial attitudes of the 1960s to the unexamined assumptions of the 1920s, it also had the unfortunate effect of failing to give proper emphasis to the striking "practicality" of another aspect of the Agrarian symposium that not only accounted for much of its continued appeal, but nowadays looms as perhaps the book's most far-sighted and prophetic element. For the critique that *I'll Take My Stand* offered of the social effects of capitalism and industrialism and the dangers they posed to the quality of human life and to the natural environment has become increasingly relevant over the years. The words of John Ransom's essay "Reconstructed but Unregenerate" speak to our economic and our ecological situation with a clarity that can be recognized today as never before:

Progress never defines its ultimate objective, but thrusts its victims at once into an infinite series. Our vast industrial machine, with its laboratory centers of experimentation, and its far-flung organs of mass production, is like a Prussianized state which is organized strictly for war and can never consent to peace. . . . Our progressivists are the latest version of those pioneers who conquered the wilderness, except that they are pioneering on principle, or from force of habit, and without any recollection of what pioneering was for.

In the 1970s we have learned to worry about such things. We begin to realize that our continent and our planet do not constitute an inexhaustible supply center of natural resources. We are concerned over the destruction of what is left of our wild places, in the name of Progress. We note the economic and social chaos and hardship that result from even temporary dislocations within an industrial system so huge that it can take no cognizance whatever of the needs of individuals, or even of the plight of towns, cities, even regions. We are disturbed at the appetite of our industrialized, electrified, mechanized consumer society, its willingness to use up a disproportionate share of the world's energy at an alarming rate. We begin to suspect that our vaunted material standard of living is being purchased at the cost of others, who now begin to show signs of impatience at their exploitation. And we have the uneasy feeling that there is something to the notion that wars may have played a greater role in our economic well-being than we like to think. What it all means we are not sure, but we begin to perceive that there is more to progress and improvement than had once seemed apparent.

The Nashville Agrarians saw it coming long before most of us. Their critique of 1930, ridiculed at the time by knowing observers who declared smugly that the clock could not be turned back—that, to quote H. L. Mencken, "the South, in point of fact, can no more revive the simple society of the Jefferson era than England can revive that of Queen Anne"— constituted a prophetic warning of what might be in store if the headlong exploitation of natural resources and the unthinking mechanization and dehumanization that accompanied untamed industrialism were not honestly acknowledged and confronted. Doubtless, a return to a preindustrial farming society was unfeasible, but that was the least of what the Agrarians had to say. If not agrarianism, then what? The point was that it was not enough merely to deplore and then look away from unchecked industrialism. In the words of the conclusion to the symposium's Statement of Principles,

If a community, or a section, or a race, or an age, is groaning under industrialism, and well aware that it is an evil dispensation, it must find the way to throw it off. To think that this cannot be done is pusillanimous. And if the whole community, section, race, or age thinks it cannot be done, then it has simply lost its political genius and doomed itself to impotence.

What the Agrarians were saying, at a time when few Americans worried about such things, was that if the republic was to live up to its ideals and be what it could be, then it had better look long and hard at what it was in danger of becoming and devote conscious effort to controlling its own destiny, rather than continuing to drift along on the tides of economic materialism. As Allen Tate put it in his essay: "How may the Southerner take hold of his Tradition? The answer is, by violence." How, in other words, can the southerner, as modern American, keep to the heritage of the human community in which men exist as individuals, and thus control and abate the prevailing drift toward mass dehumanization and materialism that seemed to be happening all about him? By an act of resolute, considered will. By refusing to be determined by events rather than attempting to determine them. By thinking in terms of ultimate human values, and then ordering one's economic and social arrangements and one's political actions accordingly, instead of letting the foundations of our values and conduct go unexamined.

For there *was* a southern tradition worthy of preservation, and it had little or nothing to do with racial segregation, Protestant orthodoxy, or states' rights: it was that of the good society, the community of individuals, the security and definition that come when men cease to wage an unrelenting war with nature and enjoy their leisure and their human dignity. If never in the history of the South had that goal been fully realized, and however much it had been largely restricted to only a part of the population, it was not thereby rendered any the less desirable as a standard to be cherished. *At least it had been in men's thoughts*. At least the society had evolved that ideal out of its human circumstance. At least there was the tradition of that kind of human aspiration.

I'll Take My Stand, therefore, was and still is a prophetic book. Its very "impracticality" constituted its strength, for the refusal of the twelve southerners to be bound by what in 1930 was considered "practical" and "inevitable" enabled them to see beneath the surface of Progress and examine the largely unquestioned assumptions on which much of its rhetoric was based. The issue to which the Agrarians addressed themselves was not that of farms versus factories, mules versus tractors, rural play-parties versus radio; it was that of man versus the machine. Their tradition had made it possible for them to believe that human beings could *choose* their course of action.

But is it not possible that in pinning their hopes on the ability of the South somehow to retain the best of its manners and mores, to cherish and retain the humane virtues and refuse to surrender its identity, the Agrarians were not after all backing a lost cause? Is it not possible that the present enviable situation of the South *vis-à-vis* the nation as a whole has come about because in certain vital, nonmaterial respects it has refused to give up its old community identity? May not future historians decide that it was that very "backwardness," that insistence upon retaining the sense of community identity, which made racial integration so difficult at first, but which, once the walls were breached, made it a reality in a way that is now becoming the envy of places where the economic and social forces of an impersonal mass society cannot so readily work such things out on terms of human dignity and individuality?

And if so, then are not recent political developments a testimony to the soundness of what Stark Young was getting at in his essay in *I'll Take My Stand*, that "the South changing must be the South still," and that "in the shifting relation between ourselves and the new order lies the profoundest source for our living, I mean change in that almost mystical sense by which, so long as we are alive, we are not the same and yet remain ourselves"?

No matter. Such speculations are a dubious business. But this much does seem certain: *I'll Take My Stand*, as it appears in its third edition since its publication almost half a century ago, is very much what Allen Tate wrote to Donald Davidson about it in 1942: "I think it was and *is* a very great success; but then I never expected it to have any political influence. It is a reaffirmation to the humane tradition, and to reaffirm that is an end in itself. Never fear: we shall be remembered when our snipers are forgotten."

Among those who consider the South, what it has been and what it can be, a book entitled *I'll Take My Stand: The South and the Agrarian Tradition* has for thirty years been the center of constant controversy. Not a single writer about the modern South has failed to mention and discuss it. From the very beginning it has been singled out for praise or blame. Some critics have termed it reactionary, even semifascistic. Others have considered it a misguided, romantic attempt to re-create an idyllic utopia that never really existed. Still others have seen it as a voice crying in the wilderness. Ridiculed, condemned, championed, it has been everything except ignored, for that it cannot be by anyone who wants to understand a complex American region.

Published in 1930 in a single printing with a moderate press run, *I'll Take My Stand* has been out of print for most of its history. Now that it becomes available once again it is not amiss to examine this remarkable set of essays with a view toward determining what has kept it so much in the public eye, and held the interest of so many persons at a time when, in order to read it, one has had to borrow a copy from a library or carefully scan the rare book lists until a copy came up for sale. What has given *I'll Take My Stand* its continuing life? What, thirty years and more after publication, does it still have to say about the South and the nation that is worth listening to?

I'll Take My Stand was written by a group of twelve Southerners, many of them associated in some way with Vanderbilt University in Nashville, Tennessee. At the center of the group were four poets who during the early 1920's had been active in one of the most important and influential literary groups ever to exist in American letters, the Nashville Fugitives. For several years this little association of poets published a magazine, *The Fugitive,* whose impact on American writing was far wider than its circulation list. In *The Fugitive,* and in other periodicals of the 1920's, John Crowe Ransom, Allen Tate, Robert Penn Warren and Donald Davidson published the poetry and the criticism of poetry that, along with the work of such writers as Eliot, Pound, Blackmur, Crane and certain others, was to revolutionize the craft of poetry in America.

During the early 1920's, the Fugitives were not particularly interested in their identity as Southerners. Rebelling from the United Daughters of the Confederacy tradition in Southern letters, they found sectional self-consciousness a hindrance to their own literary development. But in the late years of the decade, as they reassessed the role of poetry and the arts in American life, their attitude toward the South changed. The United States of the 1920's seemed increasingly devoted to material things, dedicated to a boom-or-bust economy. Artistic taste was being debased to accommodate the needs of mass culture. Industrial and commercial preoccupations were reducing the fine arts to the status of diversionary, non-essential activities. So overwhelmingly was postwar American life given over to the pursuit of profits that aesthetic and religious considerations were all but ignored.

It was at this point that the four leading Fugitive poets looked to the South. For as. poets they were given to the metaphor, and they instinctively resorted to an image for their critique of American society. They saw in the history of their own section the image of a region which had clearly resisted the domination of the machine, persisting in its agricultural ways, even after military defeat, well into the present century, and only now beginning to capitulate fully to the demands of American industrial society.

When measured by the dominant American ideal, the pre-industrial South had been backward, but it had evolved a society, they felt, in which leisure, tradition, aesthetic and religious impulses had not been lost in the pursuit of economic gain. Only now was the South 're-entering the Union'; only now were its old values and beliefs being cast aside as of little use in the rush to industrialize.

Yet in thus bartering away its tranquil ways for the gaudy benefits of industrial American life the South, they felt, was surrendering spiritual sustenance for dubious material gain. What was wrong with the South was not that it was backward and agricultural, but that it was failing to cherish its own highly civilized customs and attitudes. For it was the South, not the industrial Northeast, that still retained a manner of living in which grace, leisure, spirtual, and aesthetic experience were possible. As such it might furnish a needed corrective to America's head-long materialism, and provide an image of the good life. "Suddenly we realized to the full,"

Donald Davidson has written, "what we had long been dimly feeling, that the Lost Cause might not be wholly lost after all. In its very backwardness the South had clung to some secret which embodied, it seemed, the elements out of which its own reconstruction—and possibly even the reconstruction of America—might be achieved."

Thus the Fugitives became Agrarians. Ransom, Tate, Davidson and Warren were joined by a brilliant group of men with similar ideas about Southern and American life. Two were or would soon be novelists, Stark Young and Andrew Nelson Lytle. Another was a poet, John Gould Fletcher. One was a professor of English, John Donald Wade. Frank Lawrence Owsley and Herman Clarence Nixon were historians, Henry Blue Kline a journalist, Lyle Lanier a psychologist. In 1930, just as the American economy was slumping into the great Depression, they published their Agrarian manifesto.

In the years that followed *I'll Take My Stand*'s publication, the South and the nation cannot be said to have heeded its economic, political and social counsels to any startling effect. The industrialization of the South proceeded apace, with the Depression years representing only a temporary setback in the drive to increase manufactures and commerce. The importance of farm life in the South has steadily diminished, while the cities and towns have expanded relentlessly, until today one-half of all Southerners live in an urban environment. The question that Ransom raised in his essay, of whether the South would let industrialism destroy its traditional identity, or would instead "accept industrialism, but

with a very bad grace, and manage to maintain a good deal
of her traditional philosophy," has been answered, on the
economic plane at any rate, in a most un-agrarian fashion.
The South has thrown its lot squarely with the machines and
factories; agrarianism as a general pattern of life is largely a
dead letter. Today the suburbs of Nashville, Richmond,
Charleston, and Mobile are scarcely distinguishable from
those of Buffalo, Trenton, Indianapolis, and Hartford. Andrew Lytle's suggestion that the Southern farmer "throw out
the radio and take down the fiddle from the wall" has not
been followed; instead the radio has been replaced by a television set. Even politically the Solid South is no more; not
in 16 years has it voted as a unit. Ransom's proposal that the
Democratic Party be renovated in terms of "agrarian, conservative, anti-industrial" principles can hardly be said to
have worked out.

In still another respect aspects of *I'll Take My Stand* seem
very dated today. For the past decade the chief social issue
in the South has been that of Negro rights. While industrialization has steadily gone forward, remodeling the Southern
landscape, the attention of most Southerners has been
focussed on the desegregation issue. The 1954 decision of the
Supreme Court in *Brown v. Board of Education* has resulted
in widespread disturbance to countless Southern communities. On this momentous question, the attitude embodied in
some of the essays of *I'll Take My Stand* has seemed, to many
at least, quite outmoded. Robert Penn Warren's essay on the
Negro, entitled "The Briar Patch," was, in his own description, "a defense of segregation," but not only Warren but
many other Southerners have changed their minds. A poll

taken nowadays might find the surviving Agrarians sharply divided on the desegregation issue. For many of them, and for many Southerners, the attitudes of 1930 will not suffice at all.

If in its economic and social counsel *I'll Take My Stand* has been so little heeded by the South, and if in several important respects its attitude toward crucial issues does not provide a guide for many Southerners, then what accounts for the book's continued influence? Why must every commentator on the region devote paragraphs and pages to a consideration of its arguments? Why do symposia continue to be held about its contents? And why, thirty years later, has this new edition come into being?

For answer, we may turn back to what has already been remarked about this book's genesis. It was a book written, not by economists and sociologists, but by men of letters, of whom the moving spirits were poets. We have noted that as poets they were given to the *image*—the image, as Ransom remarks elsewhere, which is by nature "marvellous in its assemblage of many properties, a manifold of properties, like a mine or a field, something to be explored for the properties."

Just so. For this book of essays, and the vision of an agrarian South depicted within it, can best be considered as an extended metaphor, of which the image of the agrarian community is the figure, standing for and embodying something else. The something else is modern society. Of this society the South is a part, and, for the purposes of the metaphor, the correlative. But this book is about something far more generally important and essential than the economic and social well-being of any one region. It is about man, what he is, what he should be, what he must be. Written in a time when not only the South but the nation seemed given over to a frantic struggle for material possessions, it held up to examination some of the most widely-accepted assumptions of our time.

Man, it said, far from being a godlike genius of unlimited potentialities, is a fallible, finite creature, who functioned best in a society that took account of his limitations. In his zeal for the benefits of modern scientific civilization, he was placing so high a value on material gain that he ignored his own spiritual welfare and his moral obligations to society. Properly controlled, the benefits of science and industry might bolster his human dignity. As it was, he was turning the contrivances of the new industrialism into the objective itself. In place of beauty and truth he had erected a new ideal, Progress. Where properly controlled the benefits of science and industry might bolster his human dignity, he was turning the contrivances of the new industrialism into the objective itself. Caught up in a race to exploit the natural world through applied science, man was becoming an automaton, his entire effort directed toward highly specialized and narrow activities designed to secure immediate material profit.

Man was losing contact with the natural world, with aesthetic and religious reality; his machines were brutalizing and coarsening him, his quest for gain blinding him to all that made life worth living. The tenuous and frail spiritual insights of western civilization, achieved so arduously over the course of many centuries, were being sacrificed. The result, if unchecked, could only be dehumanization and chaos.

This headlong race for mastery over nature, called Progress by some and Industrialism by others, stifled the aesthetic impulse, rendered impotent the religious impulse, and converted man's days into a frantic and frenzied drive for the often tawdry conveniences of modernism. Such, felt the men who wrote *I'll Take My Stand*, was the ruling tendency of American life in the third decade of the twentieth century. As men of letters, dedicated not to Progress but to humanistic values, they felt impelled to protest against it.

The Agrarians were not only men of letters, however; they were Southerners. And in the life of their own region they saw the dehumanizing process going on in a particularly attenuated form. For industrialism had been late in coming to their region, and only now was its impact being felt in full force. In the difference between what the South had been, and the new South that was coming into being, they perceived an image of what had happened to American society. And to indicate the kind of life that they felt Americans should desire, they held up the image of the Old South. Here was what America might have become, but had not. As Robert Penn Warren said of his part in *I'll Take My Stand*, "for me it was a protest . . . against a kind of dehumanizing and disintegrative effect on our notion of what an individual person could be . . . The past is always a rebuke to the present; . . . it's a better rebuke than any dream of the future. It's a better rebuke because you can see what some of the costs were, what frail virtues were achieved in the past by frail men."

The image of the old agrarian South in *I'll Take My Stand* was the image of a society that perhaps never existed, though it resembled the Old South in certain important ways. But it was a society that *should* have existed—one in which men could live as individuals and not as automatons, aware of their finiteness and their dependence upon God and nature, devoted to the enhancement of the moral life in its aesthetic and spiritual dimensions, possessed of a sense of the deep inscrutability of the natural world.

Through their vision of an agrarian community, the authors of *I'll Take My Stand* presented a critique of the modern world. In contrast to the hurried, nervous life of cities, the image of the agrarian South was of a life in which human beings existed serenely and harmoniously. Not driven by lust for gain, they could live free of the tumultuous pace of the modern industrial community. "A farm is not a place to grow wealthy," Andrew Nelson Lytle wrote in his essay, "it is a place to grow corn."

It was the vision of poets, and carried with it certain convictions about living and dying that have held much imaginative appeal to Southerners and many non-Southerners as well.

This, I think, is the essential function of *I'll Take My Stand,* and accounts for the book's continuing hold on the Southern imagination. It is a rebuke to materialism, a corrective to the worship of Progress, and a reaffirmation of man's aesthetic and spiritual needs. And because the South has come so late into the industrial world, it appeals to the lingering memory within the Southerner's mind of the tranquil and leisurely Southern life that existed before the machines and superhighways came. As such the book constitutes both a reminder and a challenge. *What are you losing that you once possessed?* it says to the modern Southerner. *Are you quite sure that you want to discard it entirely?*

That such a life was doomed, that in many respects it was impossible, that many of its actual attributes were neither necessary nor desirable, is not important. What matters is the vision of a more harmonious, aesthetically and spiritually rewarding kind of human existence that the book holds up. That towns have become cities and farms have become suburbs, that fewer Southerners than ever exist on agriculture, matters very little in this respect. *I'll Take My Stand* is not a treatise on economics; it is not a guide to political action; it is not a sociological blueprint. It is a vision of what the good life can be.

Thus the essays in the book that are most appealing now are those that best evoke this image. John Ransom's portrait of the reconstructed but unregenerate Southerner holding fast to his leisurely ways; Donald Davidson's mirror for artistic activity in which he prophetically shows the value of the regional image for the creative artist; Allen Tate's cogent analysis of what religion should mean for the Southerner and the American, and what is wrong with what it now means; Stark Young's definitive commentary on the meaning of manners and customs; above all, John Donald Wade's beautiful sketch of the history of a Southern gentleman whose whole career embodies the good and satisfying life—these and other essays do not date, for what they have to say to the Southerner and to the American is perennially valid. Each of them preaches the gospel of religious humanism, in a compelling metaphor of agrarian life that serves as a rebuke and reminder to the busy modern man who is so caught up in specialization and money-making that he begins to lose sight of what he is living *for*. These essays are the heart of *I'll Take My Stand;* their meaning goes far deeper than the transient issues of economics, politics, social adjustment.

A recent commentator on this book, after castigating the Agrarians at great length for being "abominable advisers on the means of achieving greater material well-being" for the Southern economy, remarks that "as humanists, however, they had (and still have) much to offer in showing all of us how to use the fruits of economic progress, once achieved, as a means to the more spiritual side of a good, full and happy life." As if that were not the whole point of the book! What the Agrarians were telling the South and the nation was a way of life that omits or deemphasizes the "more spiritual side" of existence is necessarily disastrous to *all* phases of life. The Agrarians refused to divide man's life into isolated segments; there was no such thing, they insisted, as economic man, political man, social man; there was only *man,* and his various activities must be considered as parts of one human life. To think and act otherwise was to make him less than human, producing fragmentation, division, chaos.

Some have said that the impact of *I'll Take My Stand* might have been greater, and the amount of misunderstanding reduced, if the book had not been so closely tied in with the South. Indeed, at the time of its preparation several of the contributors wanted to give it a more general title. Tate wished to label it plainly as a defense of religious humanism; Warren proposed it be called *Tracts Against Communism*. Perhaps a more broadly aimed volume might have enjoyed a wider readership, and its purposes been better grasped by readers.

Perhaps so. Yet it is doubtful, I think. For once again, these men were poets, men of letters, to whom the *image* was central. And it is the tangible image of the South that gives the book so much of its compelling quality, its visible, palpable reality. A more abstractly conceived book might have been less topically identified with one region's particular economic and social problems, and therefore less immediately limited, but a great deal of the dramatic power of the book would have been lost. The image of the agrarian South provided the esayists with a rich, complex metaphor, giving body to their arguments, anchoring their perceptions in time and place. To dissociate *I'll Take My Stand* from the South is neither possible nor desirable.

Grounded firmly in the history and social life of one American region, the best essays in this book speak as vividly and as importantly today as ever before. The verdict they pronounce on modern American life has since been echoed by commentator after commentator. What the Agrarians warned about our business civilization is constantly reinforced by such social analysts as Riesman, White, Packard, Warburg, and many others, who nowadays point to the yawning discrepancies between the glittering American social ideal and the human misuse that lies behind it. These men are saying now what the contributors to *I'll Take My Stand* were saying three decades earlier.

One should read this prophetic book, then, not as a treatise on economics and politics, not as a guide to regional social structuring, but as a commentary on the nature of man— man as Southerner, as American, as human being. What the men of letters who composed it said about what man is and where he belongs is for the most part neither outdated nor unimportant. As a human document it is still very much alive; the concerns of 1930 are the concerns of 1962, and will very likely be concerns in the year 2000. They will be so unless human nature changes a great deal in the decades to come. One of the things *I'll Take My Stand* tells us is that human nature never changes very much, and that whatever we do and wherever we live, we had better accept the fact that it doesn't.

INTRODUCTION:

A STATEMENT

OF PRINCIPLES

THE authors contributing to this book are Southerners, well acquainted with one another and of similar tastes, though not necessarily living in the same physical community, and perhaps only at this moment aware of themselves as a single group of men. By conversation and exchange of letters over a number of years it had developed that they entertained many convictions in common, and it was decided to make a volume in which each one should furnish his views upon a chosen topic. This was the general background. But background and consultation as to the various topics were enough; there was to be no further collaboration. And so no single author is responsible for any view outside his own article. It was through the good fortune of some deeper agreement that the book was expected to achieve its unity. All the articles bear in the same sense upon the book's title-subject: all tend to support a Southern way of life against what may be called the American or prevailing way; and all as much as agree that the best terms in which to represent the distinction are contained in the phrase, Agrarian *versus* Industrial.

But after the book was under way it seemed a pity if the contributors, limited as they were within their special subjects, should stop short of showing how close their agreements really were. On the contrary, it seemed that they ought to go on and make themselves known as a group already consolidated by a set of principles which could be stated with a good deal of particularity. This might prove useful for the sake of future reference, if they should undertake any further joint publication. It was then decided to prepare a general introduction for the book which would state briefly the common convictions of the group. This is the statement. To it every one of the contributors in this book has subscribed.

Nobody now proposes for the South, or for any other community in this country, an independent political destiny. That idea is thought to have been finished in 1865. But how far shall the South surrender its moral, social, and economic autonomy to the victorious principle of Union? That question remains open. The South is a minority section that has hitherto been jealous of its minority right to live its own kind of life. The South scarcely hopes to determine the other sections, but it does propose to determine itself, within the utmost limits of legal action. Of late, however, there is the melancholy fact that the South itself has wavered a little and shown signs of wanting to join up behind the common or American industrial ideal. It is against that tendency that this book is written. The younger Southerners, who are being converted frequently to the industrial gospel, must come back to the support of the Southern tradition. They must be persuaded to look very critically at the

advantages of becoming a "new South" which will be only
an undistinguished replica of the usual industrial community.

But there are many other minority communities opposed
to industrialism, and wanting a much simpler economy to
live by. The communities and private persons sharing the
agrarian tastes are to be found widely within the Union.
Proper living is a matter of the intelligence and the will,
does not depend on the local climate or geography, and is
capable of a definition which is general and not Southern
at all. Southerners have a filial duty to discharge to their
own section. But their cause is precarious and they must
seek alliances with sympathetic communities everywhere.
The members of the present group would be happy to be
counted as members of a national agrarian movement.

Industrialism is the economic organization of the collective American society. It means the decision of society to
invest its economic resources in the applied sciences. But the
word science has acquired a certain sanctitude. It is out of
order to quarrel with science in the abstract, or even with
the applied sciences when their applications are made subject to criticism and intelligence. The capitalization of the
applied sciences has now become extravagant and uncritical; it has enslaved our human energies to a degree now
clearly felt to be burdensome. The apologists of industrialism do not like to meet this charge directly; so they often

take refuge in saying that they are devoted simply to science! They are really devoted to the applied sciences and to practical production. Therefore it is necessary to employ a certain skepticism even at the expense of the Cult of Science, and to say, It is an Americanism, which looks innocent and disinterested, but really is not either.

The contribution that science can make to a labor is to render it easier by the help of a tool or a process, and to assure the laborer of his perfect economic security while he is engaged upon it. Then it can be performed with leisure and enjoyment. But the modern laborer has not exactly received this benefit under the industrial regime. His labor is hard, its tempo is fierce, and his employment is insecure. The first principle of a good labor is that it must be effective, but the second principle is that it must be enjoyed. Labor is one of the largest items in the human career; it is a modest demand to ask that it may partake of happiness.

The regular act of applied science is to introduce into labor a labor-saving device or a machine. Whether this is a benefit depends on how far it is advisable to save the labor. The philosophy of applied science is generally quite sure that the saving of labor is a pure gain, and that the more of it the better. This is to assume that labor is an evil, that only the end of labor or the material product is good. On this assumption labor becomes mercenary and servile, and it is no wonder if many forms of modern labor are accepted without resentment though they are evidently brutalizing. The act of labor as one of the happy functions of human life has been in effect abandoned, and is practiced solely for its rewards.

Even the apologists of industrialism have been obliged to admit that some economic evils follow in the wake of the machines. These are such as overproduction, unemployment, and a growing inequality in the distribution of wealth. But the remedies proposed by the apologists are always homeopathic. They expect the evils to disappear when we have bigger and better machines, and more of them. Their remedial programs, therefore, look forward to more industrialism. Sometimes they see the system righting itself spontaneously and without direction: they are Optimists. Sometimes they rely on the benevolence of capital, or the militancy of labor, to bring about a fairer division of the spoils: they are Coöperationists or Socialists. And sometimes they expect to find super-engineers, in the shape of Boards of Control, who will adapt production to consumption and regulate prices and guarantee business against fluctuations: they are Sovietists. With respect to these last it must be insisted that the true Sovietists or Communists—if the term may be used here in the European sense—are the Industrialists themselves. They would have the government set up an economic super-organization, which in turn would become the government. We therefore look upon the Communist menace as a menace indeed, but not as a Red one; because it is simply according to the blind drift of our industrial development to expect in America at last much the same economic system as that imposed by violence upon Russia in 1917.

Turning to consumption, as the grand end which justifies the evil of modern labor, we find that we have been deceived. We have more time in which to consume, and many more products to be consumed. But the tempo of our labors communicates itself to our satisfactions, and these also become brutal and hurried. The constitution of the natural man probably does not permit him to shorten his labor-time and enlarge his consuming-time indefinitely. He has to pay the penalty in satiety and aimlessness. The modern man has lost his sense of vocation.

Religion can hardly expect to flourish in an industrial society. Religion is our submission to the general intention of a nature that is fairly inscrutable; it is the sense of our rôle as creatures within it. But nature industrialized, transformed into cities and artificial habitations, manufactured into commodities, is no longer nature but a highly simplified picture of nature. We receive the illusion of having power over nature, and lose the sense of nature as something mysterious and contingent. The God of nature under these conditions is merely an amiable expression, a superfluity, and the philosophical understanding ordinarily carried in the religious experience is not there for us to have.

Nor do the arts have a proper life under industrialism, with the general decay of sensibility which attends it. Art depends, in general, like religion, on a right attitude to nature; and in particular on a free and disinterested observation of nature that occurs only in leisure. Neither the creation nor the understanding of works of art is possible in an industrial age except by some local and unlikely suspension of the industrial drive.

The amenities of life also suffer under the curse of a strictly-business or industrial civilization. They consist in such practices as manners, conversation, hospitality, sympathy, family life, romantic love—in the social exchanges which reveal and develop sensibility in human affairs. If religion and the arts are founded on right relations of man-to-nature, these are founded on right relations of man-to-man.

Apologists of industrialism are even inclined to admit that its actual processes may have upon its victims the spiritual effects just described. But they think that all can be made right by extraordinary educational efforts, by all sorts of cultural institutions and endowments. They would cure the poverty of the contemporary spirit by hiring experts to instruct it in spite of itself in the historic culture. But salvation is hardly to be encountered on that road. The trouble with the life-pattern is to be located at its economic base, and we cannot rebuild it by pouring in soft materials from the top. The young men and women in colleges, for example, if they are already placed in a false way of life, cannot make more than an inconsequential acquaintance with the arts and humanities transmitted to them. Or else the understanding of these arts and humanities will but make them the more wretched in their own destitution.

The "Humanists" are too abstract. Humanism, properly speaking, is not an abstract system, but a culture, the whole way in which we live, act, think, and feel. It is a kind of imaginatively balanced life lived out in a definite social tradition. And, in the concrete, we believe that this, the genuine humanism, was rooted in the agrarian life of the older South and of other parts of the country that shared in such a tradition. It was not an abstract moral "check" derived from the classics—it was not soft material poured in from the top. It was deeply founded in the way of life itself—in its tables, chairs, portraits, festivals, laws, marriage customs. We cannot recover our native humanism by adopting some standard of taste that is critical enough to question the contemporary arts but not critical enough to question the social and economic life which is their ground.

The tempo of the industrial life is fast, but that is not the worst of it; it is accelerating. The ideal is not merely some set form of industrialism, with so many stable industries, but industrial progress, or an incessant extension of industrialization. It never proposes a specific goal; it initiates the infinite series. We have not merely capitalized certain industries; we have capitalized the laboratories and inventors, and undertaken to employ all the labor-saving devices that come out of them. But a fresh labor-saving device introduced into an industry does not emancipate the laborers in that industry so much as it evicts them. Applied at the expense of agriculture, for example, the new processes have reduced the part of the population supporting itself upon the soil to a smaller and smaller fraction. Of course no single labor-saving process is fatal; it brings on a period of unemployed labor and unemployed capital, but soon a new industry is devised which will put them both to work again, and a new commodity is thrown upon the market. The laborers were sufficiently embarrassed in the meantime, but, according to the theory, they will eventually be taken care of. It is now the public which is embarrassed; it feels obligated to purchase a commodity for which it had expressed no desire, but it is invited to make its budget equal to the strain. All might yet be well, and stability and comfort might again obtain, but for this: partly because of industrial ambitions and partly because the repressed creative impulse must break out somewhere, there will be a stream of further labor-saving devices in all industries, and the cycle will have to be repeated over and over. The result is an increasing disadjustment and instability.

It is an inevitable consequence of industrial progress that production greatly outruns the rate of natural consumption. To overcome the disparity, the producers, disguised as the pure idealists of progress, must coerce and wheedle the public into being loyal and steady consumers, in order to keep the machines running. So the rise of modern advertising—along with its twin, personal salesmanship—is the most significant development of our industrialism. Advertising means to persuade the consumers to want exactly what the applied sciences are able to furnish them. It consults the happiness of the consumer no more than it consulted the happiness of the laborer. It is the great effort of a false economy of life to approve itself. But its task grows more difficult every day.

It is strange, of course, that a majority of men anywhere could ever as with one mind become enamored of industrialism: a system that has so little regard for individual wants. There is evidently a kind of thinking that rejoices in setting up a social objective which has no relation to the individual. Men are prepared to sacrifice their private dignity and happiness to an abstract social ideal, and without asking whether the social ideal produces the welfare of any individual man whatsoever. But this is absurd. The responsibility of men is for their own welfare and that of their neighbors; not for the hypothetical welfare of some fabulous creature called society.

Opposed to the industrial society is the agrarian, which does not stand in particular need of definition. An agrarian society is hardly one that has no use at all for industries, for professional vocations, for scholars and artists, and for the life of cities. Technically, perhaps, an agrarian society is one in which agriculture is the leading vocation, whether for wealth, for pleasure, or for prestige—a form of labor that is pursued with intelligence and leisure, and that becomes the model to which the other forms approach as well as they may. But an agrarian regime will be secured readily enough where the superfluous industries are not allowed to rise against it. The theory of agrarianism is that the culture of the soil is the best and most sensitive of vocations, and that therefore it should have the economic preference and enlist the maximum number of workers.

These principles do not intend to be very specific in proposing any practical measures. How may the little agrarian community resist the Chamber of Commerce of its county seat, which is always trying to import some foreign industry that cannot be assimilated to the life-pattern of the community? Just what must the Southern leaders do to defend the traditional Southern life? How may the Southern and the Western agrarians unite for effective action? Should the agrarian forces try to capture the Democratic party, which historically is so closely affiliated with the defense of individualism, the small community, the state, the South? Or must the agrarians—even the Southern ones—abandon the Democratic party to its fate and try a new one? What legislation could most profitably be championed by the powerful agrarians in the Senate of the United States? What anti-industrial measures might promise to stop the advances of industrialism, or even undo some of them, with the least harm to those concerned? What policy should be pursued by the educators who have a tradition at heart? These and many other questions are of the greatest importance, but they cannot be answered here.

For, in conclusion, this much is clear: If a community, or a section, or a race, or an age, is groaning under industrialism, and well aware that it is an evil dispensation, it must find the way to throw it off. To think that this cannot be done is pusillanimous. And if the whole community, section, race, or age thinks it cannot be done, then it has simply lost its political genius and doomed itself to impotence.

I'LL TAKE MY STAND

JOHN CROWE RANSOM

RECONSTRUCTED
BUT UNREGENERATE

I

IT IS out of fashion in these days to look backward rather than forward. About the only American given to it is some unreconstructed Southerner, who persists in his regard for a certain terrain, a certain history, and a certain inherited way of living. He is punished as his crime deserves. He feels himself in the American scene as an anachronism, and knows he is felt by his neighbors as a reproach.

Of course he is a tolerably harmless reproach. He is like some quaint local character of eccentric but fixed principles who is thoroughly and almost pridefully accepted by the village as a rare exhibit in the antique kind. His position is secure from the interference of the police, but it is of a rather ambiguous dignity.

I wish now that he were not so entirely taken for granted, and that as a reproach he might bear a barb and inflict a sting. I wish that the whole force of my own generation in the South would get behind his principles and make them an ideal which the nation at large would have to reckon with. But first I will describe him in the light of

NOTE.—This article is made up largely from articles of the author's that have appeared in the *Sewanee Review* and *Harper's Magazine*.

(1)

the position he seems now to occupy actually before
the public.

His fierce devotion is to a lost cause—though it grieves
me that his contemporaries are so sure it is lost. They are
so far from fearing him and his example that they even
in the excess of confidence offer him a little honor, a little
petting. As a Southerner I have observed this indulgence
and I try to be grateful. Obviously it does not constitute a
danger to the Republic; distinctly it is not treasonable. They
are good enough to attribute a sort of glamour to the
Southern life as it is defined for them in a popular tradition. They like to use the South as the nearest available
locus for the scenes of their sentimental songs, and sometimes they send their daughters to the Southern seminaries.
Not too much, of course, is to be made of this last gesture,
for they do not expose to this hazard their sons, who in our
still very masculine order will have to discharge the functions of citizenship, and who must accordingly be sternly
educated in the principles of progress at progressive institutions of learning. But it does not seem to make so much
difference what principles of a general character the young
women acquire, since they are not likely to be impaired by
principles in their peculiar functions, such as virtue and
the domestic duties. And so, at suitable seasons, and on
the main-line trains, one may see them in some numbers,
flying south or flying north like migratory birds; and one
may wonder to what extent their philosophy of life will be
affected by two or three years in the South. One must
remember that probably their parents have already made
this calculation and are prepared to answer, Not much.

The Southerner must know, and in fact he does very well know, that his antique conservatism does not exert a great influence against the American progressivist doctrine. The Southern idea today is down, and the progressive or American idea is up. But the historian and the philosopher, who take views that are thought to be respectively longer and deeper than most, may very well reverse this order and find that the Southern idea rather than the American has in its favor the authority of example and the approval of theory. And some prophet may even find it possible to expect that it will yet rise again.

I will propose a thesis which seems to have about as much cogency as generalizations usually have: The South is unique on this continent for having founded and defended a culture which was according to the European principles of culture; and the European principles had better look to the South if they are to be perpetuated in this country.

II

The nearest of the European cultures which we could examine is that of England; and this is of course the right one in the case, quite aside from our convenience. England was actually the model employed by the South, in so far as Southern culture was not quite indigenous. And there is in the South even today an Anglophile sentiment quite anomalous in the American scene.

England differs from America doubtless in several respects, but most notably in the fact that England did her pioneering an indefinite number of centuries ago, did it well enough, and has been living pretty tranquilly on her

(3)

establishment ever since, with infrequent upheavals and re-placements. The customs and institutions of England seem to the American observer very fixed and ancient. There is no doubt that the English tradition expresses itself in many more or less intangible ways, but it expresses itself most importantly in a material establishment; and by this I mean the stable economic system by which Englishmen are content to take their livelihood from the physical en-vironment. The chief concern of England's half-mythical pioneers, as with pioneers anywhere, was with finding the way to make a living. Evidently they found it. But for-tunately the methods they worked out proved transmis-sible, proved, in fact, the main reliance of the succeeding generations. The pioneers explored the soil, determined what concessions it might reasonably be expected to make them, housed themselves, developed all their necessary trades, and arrived by painful experiment at a thousand satisfactory recipes by which they might secure their ma-terial necessities. Their descendants have had the good sense to consider that this establishment was good enough for them. They have elected to live their comparatively easy and routine lives in accordance with the tradition which they inherited, and they have consequently enjoyed a leisure, a security, and an intellectual freedom that were never the portion of pioneers.

The pioneering life is not the normal life, whatever some Americans may suppose. It is not, if we look for the mean-ing of European history. The lesson of each of the Eu-ropean cultures now extant is in this—that European opinion does not make too much of the intense practical enterprises, but is at pains to define rather narrowly the practical effort which is prerequisite to the reflective and æsthetic life. Boys are very well pleased to employ their muscles almost exclusively, but men prefer to exercise their minds. It is the European intention to live materially along the inherited line of least resistance, in order to put the surplus of energy into the free life of the mind. Thus is engendered that famous, or infamous, European conservatism, which will appear stupid, necessarily, to men still fascinated by materialistic projects, men in a state of arrested adolescence; for instance, to some very large if indefinite fraction of the population of these United States.

I have in mind here the core of unadulterated Europeanism, with its self-sufficient, backward-looking, intensely provincial communities. The human life of English provinces long ago came to terms with nature, fixed its roots somewhere in the spaces between the rocks and in the shade of the trees, founded its comfortable institutions, secured its modest prosperity—and then willed the whole in perpetuity to the generations which should come after, in the ingenuous confidence that it would afford them all the essential human satisfactions. For it is the character of a seasoned provincial life that it is realistic, or successfully adapted to its natural environment, and that as a consequence it is stable, or hereditable. But it is the character of our urbanized, anti-provincial, progressive, and mobile American life that it is in a condition of eternal flux. Affections, and long memories, attach to the ancient bowers of life in the provinces; but they will not attach to what is always changing.

(5)

Americans, however, are peculiar in being somewhat averse to these affections for natural objects, and to these memories.

Memories of the past are attended with a certain pain called nostalgia. It is hardly a technical term in our sociology or our psychiatry, but it might well be. Nostalgia is a kind of growing-pain, psychically speaking. It occurs to our sorrow when we have decided that it is time for us, marching to some magnificent destiny, to abandon an old home, an old provincial setting, or an old way of living to which we had become habituated. It is the complaint of human nature in its vegetative aspect, when it is plucked up by the roots from the place of its origin and transplanted in foreign soil, or even left dangling in the air. And it must be nothing else but nostalgia, the instinctive objection to being transplanted, that chiefly prevents the deracination of human communities and their complete geographical dispersion as the casualties of an insatiable wanderlust.

Deracination in our Western life is the strange discipline which individuals turn upon themselves, enticed by the blandishments of such fine words as Progressive, Liberal, and Forward-looking. The progressivist says in effect: Do not allow yourself to feel homesick; form no such powerful attachments that you will feel a pain in cutting them loose; prepare your spirit to be always on the move. According to this gospel, there is no rest for the weary, not even in heaven. The poet Browning expresses an ungrateful intention, the moment he shall enter into his reward, to "fight onward, there as here." The progressivist H. G. Wells has outlined very neatly his scheme of progress, the only disheartening feature being that he has had to revise it a good many times, and that the state to which he wants us to progress never has any finality or definition. Browning and Wells would have made very good Americans, and I am sure they have got the most of their disciples on this side of the Atlantic; they have not been good Europeans. But all the true progressivists intend to have a program so elastic that they can always propose new worlds to conquer. If his Utopia were practicable really, and if the progressivist should secure it, he would then have to defend it from further progress, which would mean his transformation from a progressivist into a conservative. Which is unthinkable.

The gospel of Progress is a curious development, which does not reflect great credit on the supposed capacity of our species for formulating its own behavior. Evidently the formula may involve its practitioners in self-torture and suicide just as readily as in the enjoyment of life. In most societies man has adapted himself to environment with plenty of intelligence to secure easily his material necessities from the graceful bounty of nature. And then, ordinarily, he concludes a truce with nature, and he and nature seem to live on terms of mutual respect and amity, and his loving arts, religions, and philosophies come spontaneously into being: these are the blessings of peace. But the latter-day societies have been seized—none quite so violently as our American one—with the strange idea that the human destiny is not to secure an honorable peace with nature, but to wage an unrelenting war on nature. Men, therefore, determine to conquer nature to a degree which is quite beyond reason so far as specific human advantage

(7)

is concerned, and which enslaves them to toil and turnover. Man is boastfully declared to be a natural scientist essentially, whose strength is capable of crushing and making over to his own desires the brute materiality which is nature; but in his infinite contention with this materiality he is really capitulating to it. His engines transform the face of nature—a little—but when they have been perfected, he must invent new engines that will perform even more heroically. And always the next engine of his invention, even though it be that engine which is to invade the material atom and exploit the most secret treasury of nature's wealth, will be a physical engine; and the man who uses it will be engaged in substantially the same struggle as was the primitive Man with the Hoe.

This is simply to say that Progress never defines its ultimate objective, but thrusts its victims at once into an infinite series. Our vast industrial machine, with its laboratory centers of experimentation, and its far-flung organs of mass production, is like a Prussianized state which is organized strictly for war and can never consent to peace. Or, returning to the original figure, our progressivists are the latest version of those pioneers who conquered the wilderness, except that they are pioneering on principle, or from force of habit, and without any recollection of what pioneering was for.

III

Along with the gospel of Progress goes the gospel of Service. They work beautifully as a team.

Americans are still dreaming the materialistic dreams of

their youth. The stuff these dreams were made on was the illusion of preëminent personal success over a material opposition. Their tone was belligerence, and the euphemism under which it masqueraded was ambition. But men are not lovely, and men are not happy, for being too ambitious. Let us distinguish two forms under which ambition drives men on their materialistic projects; a masculine and a feminine.

Ambitious men fight, first of all, against nature; they propose to put nature under their heel; this is the dream of scientists burrowing in their cells, and then of the industrial men who beg of their secret knowledge and go out to trouble the earth. But after a certain point this struggle is vain, and we only use ourselves up if we prolong it. Nature wears out man before man can wear out nature; only a city man, a laboratory man, a man cloistered from the normal contacts with the soil, will deny that. It seems wiser to be moderate in our expectations of nature, and respectful; and out of so simple a thing as respect for the physical earth and its teeming life comes a primary joy, which is an inexhaustible source of arts and religions and philosophies.

Ambitious men are belligerent also in the way they look narrowly and enviously upon one another; and I do not refer to such obvious disasters as wars and the rumors of wars. Ambition of the first form was primary and masculine, but there is a secondary form which is typically feminine, though the distribution between the sexes may not be without the usual exceptions. If it is Adam's curse to will perpetually to work his mastery upon nature, it is

(9)

Eve's curse to prompt Adam every morning to keep up with the best people in the neighborhood in taking the measure of his success. There can never be stability and establishment in a community whose every lady member is sworn to see that her mate is not eclipsed in the competition for material advantages; that community will fume and ferment, and every constituent part will be in perpetual physical motion. The good life depends on leisure, but leisure depends on an establishment, and the establishment depends on a prevailing magnanimity which scorns personal advancement at the expense of the free activity of the mind.

The masculine form is hallowed by Americans, as I have said, under the name of Progress. The concept of Progress is the concept of man's increasing command, and eventually perfect command, over the forces of nature; a concept which enhances too readily our conceit, and brutalizes our life. I believe there is possible no deep sense of beauty, no heroism of conduct, and no sublimity of religion, which is not informed by the humble sense of man's precarious position in the universe. The feminine form is likewise hallowed among us under the name of Service. The term has many meanings, but we come finally to the one which is critical for the moderns; service means the function of Eve, it means the seducing of laggard men into fresh struggles with nature. It has special application to the apparently stagnant sections of mankind, it busies itself with the heathen Chinee, with the Roman Catholic Mexican, with the "lower" classes in our own society. Its motive is missionary. Its watchwords are such as Protestantism, Individualism, Democracy, and the point of its appeal is a discontent, generally labeled "divine."

Progress and Service are not European slogans, they are Americanisms. We alone have devoted our lives to ideals which are admirable within their proper limits, but which expose us to slavery when pursued without critical intelligence. Some Europeans are taken in by these ideals, but hardly the American communities on the whole. Herr Spengler, with a gesture of defeat, glorifies the modern American captain of industry when he compares his positive achievements with the futilities of modern poets and artists. Whereupon we may well wish to save Europe from even so formidable a European as Spengler, hoping that he may not convert Europe to his view. And it is hardly likely; Europe is founded on a principle of conservatism, and is deeply scornful of the American and pioneer doctrine of the strenuous life. In 1918 there was danger that Europe might ask to be Americanized, and American missionaries were quite prepared to answer the call. But since then there has been a revulsion in European opinion, and this particular missionary enterprise confronts now an almost solid barrier of hostility. Europe is not going to be Americanized through falling suddenly in love with strenuousness. It only remains to be seen whether Europe may not be Americanized after all through envy, and through being reminded ceaselessly of our superior prosperity. That is an event to be determined by the force of European magnanimity; Europe's problem, not ours.

IV

The Southern states were settled, of course, by miscellaneous strains. But evidently the one which determined the peculiar tradition of the South was the one which came out of Europe most convinced of the virtues of establishment, contrasting with those strains which seem for the most part to have dominated the other sections, and which came out of Europe feeling rebellious toward all establishments. There are a good many faults to be found with the old South, but hardly the fault of being intemperately addicted to work and to gross material prosperity. The South never conceded that the whole duty of man was to increase material production, or that the index to the degree of his culture was the volume of his material production. His business seemed to be rather to envelop both his work and his play with a leisure which permitted the activity of intelligence. On this assumption the South pioneered her way to a sufficiently comfortable and rural sort of establishment, considered that an establishment was something stable, and proceeded to enjoy the fruits thereof. The arts of the section, such as they were, were not immensely passionate, creative, and romantic; they were the eighteenth-century social arts of dress, conversation, manners, the table, the hunt, politics, oratory, the pulpit. These were arts of living and not arts of escape; they were also community arts, in which every class of society could participate after its kind. The South took life easy, which is itself a tolerably comprehensive art.

But so did other communities in 1850, I believe. And

doubtless some others do so yet; in parts of New England, for example. If there are such communities, this is their token, that they are settled. Their citizens are comparatively satisfied with the life they have inherited, and are careful to look backward quite as much as they look forward. Before the Civil War there must have been many such communities this side of the frontier. The difference between the North and the South was that the South was constituted by such communities and made solid. But solid is only a comparative term here. The South as a culture had more solidity than another section, but there were plenty of gaps in it. The most we can say is that the Southern establishment was completed in a good many of the Southern communities, and that this establishment was an active formative influence on the spaces between, and on the frontier spaces outlying, which had not yet perfected their organization of the economic life.

The old Southern life was of course not so fine as some of the traditionalists like to believe. It did not offer serious competition against the glory that was Greece or the grandeur that was Rome. It hardly began to match the finish of the English, or any other important European civilization. It is quite enough to say that it was a way of life which had been considered and authorized. The establishment had a sufficient economic base, it was meant to be stable rather than provisional, it had got beyond the pioneering stage, it provided leisure, and its benefits were already being enjoyed. It may as well be admitted that Southern society was not an institution of very showy elegance, for the so-called aristocrats were mostly home-made

(13)

and countrified. Aristocracy is not the word which defines this social organization so well as squirearchy, which I borrow from a recent article by Mr. William Frierson in the *Sewanee Review*. And even the squires, and the other classes, too, did not define themselves very strictly. They were loosely graduated social orders, not fixed as in Europe. Their relations were personal and friendly. It was a kindly society, yet a realistic one; for it was a failure if it could not be said that people were for the most part in their right places. Slavery was a feature monstrous enough in theory, but, more often than not, humane in practice; and it is impossible to believe that its abolition alone could have effected any great revolution in society.

The fullness of life as it was lived in the ante-bellum South by the different social orders can be estimated today only by the application of some difficult sociological technique. It is my thesis that all were committed to a form of leisure, and that their labor itself was leisurely. The only Southerners who went abroad to Washington and elsewhere, and put themselves into the record, were those from the top of the pyramid. They held their own with their American contemporaries. They were not intellectually as seasoned as good Europeans, but then the Southern culture had had no very long time to grow, as time is reckoned in these matters: it would have borne a better fruit eventually. They had a certain amount of learning, which was not as formidable as it might have been: but at least it was classical and humanistic learning, not highly scientific, and not wildly scattered about over a variety of special studies.

V

Then the North and the South fought, and the consequences were disastrous to both. The Northern temper was one of jubilation and expansiveness, and now it was no longer shackled by the weight of the conservative Southern tradition. Industrialism, the latest form of pioneering and the worst, presently overtook the North, and in due time has now produced our present American civilization. Poverty and pride overtook the South; poverty to bring her institutions into disrepute and to sap continually at her courage; and a false pride to inspire a distaste for the thought of fresh pioneering projects, and to doom her to an increasing physical enfeeblement.

It is only too easy to define the malignant meaning of industrialism. It is the contemporary form of pioneering; yet since it never consents to define its goal, it is a pioneering on principle, and with an accelerating speed. Industrialism is a program under which men, using the latest scientific paraphernalia, sacrifice comfort, leisure, and the enjoyment of life to win Pyrrhic victories from nature at points of no strategic importance. Ruskin and Carlyle feared it nearly a hundred years ago, and now it may be said that their fears have been realized partly in England, and with almost fatal completeness in America. Industrialism is an insidious spirit, full of false promises and generally fatal to establishments since, when it once gets into them for a little renovation, it proposes never again to leave them in peace. Industrialism is rightfully a menial, of almost miraculous cunning but no intelligence; it needs to be strongly governed or it will destroy the economy of the household. Only a community of tough conservative habit can master it.

The South did not become industrialized; she did not repair the damage to her old establishment, either, and it was in part because she did not try hard enough. Hers is the case to cite when we would show how the good life depends on an adequate pioneering, and how the pioneering energy must be kept ready for call when the establishment needs overhauling. The Southern tradition came to look rather pitiable in its persistence when the twentieth century had arrived, for the establishment was quite depreciated. Unregenerate Southerners were trying to live the good life on a shabby equipment, and they were grotesque in their effort to make an art out of living when they were not decently making the living. In the country districts great numbers of these broken-down Southerners are still to be seen in patched blue-jeans, sitting on ancestral fences, shotguns across their laps and hound-dogs at their feet, surveying their unkempt acres while they comment shrewdly on the ways of God. It is their defect that they have driven a too easy, an unmanly bargain with nature, and that their æstheticism is based on insufficient labor.

But there is something heroic, and there may prove to be yet something very valuable to the Union, in their extreme attachment to a certain theory of life. They have kept up a faith which was on the point of perishing from this continent.

Of course it was only after the Civil War that the North and the South came to stand in polar opposition to each other. Immediately after Appomattox it was impossible for the South to resume even that give-and-take of ideas which had marked her ante-bellum relations with the North. She was offered such terms that acquiescence would have been abject. She retired within her borders in rage and held the minimum of commerce with the enemy. Persecution intensified her tradition, and made the South more solid and more Southern in the year 1875, or thereabouts, than ever before. When the oppression was left off, naturally her guard relaxed. But though the period of persecution had not been long, nevertheless the Southern tradition found itself then the less capable of uniting gracefully with the life of the Union; for that life in the meantime had been moving on in an opposite direction. The American progressive principle was like a ball rolling down the hill with an increasing momentum, and by 1890 or 1900 it was clear to any intelligent Southerner that it was a principle of boundless aggression against nature which could hardly offer much to a society devoted to the arts of peace.

But to keep on living shabbily on an insufficient patrimony is to decline, both physically and spiritually. The South declined.

VI

And now the crisis in the South's decline has been reached.

Industrialism has arrived in the South. Already the local chambers of commerce exhibit the formidable data of Southern progress. A considerable party of Southern opinion, which might be called the New South party, is well pleased with the recent industrial accomplishments of the South and anxious for many more. Southerners of another school, who might be said to compose an Old South party, are apprehensive lest the section become completely and uncritically devoted to the industrial ideal precisely as the other sections of the Union are. But reconstruction is actually under way. Tied politically and economically to the Union, her borders wholly violable, the South now sees very well that she can restore her prosperity only within the competition of an industrial system.

After the war the Southern plantations were often broken up into small farms. These have yielded less and less of a living, and it said that they will never yield a good living until once more they are integrated into large units. But these units will be industrial units, controlled by a board of directors or an executive rather than a squire, worked with machinery, and manned not by farmers living at home, but by "labor." Even so they will not, according to Mr. Henry Ford, support the population that wants to live on them. In the off seasons the laborers will have to work in factories, which henceforth are to be counted on as among the charming features of Southern landscape. The Southern problem is complicated, but at its center is the farmer's problem, and this problem is simply the most acute version of that general agrarian problem which inspires the despair of many thoughtful Americans today.

The agrarian discontent in America is deeply grounded in the love of the tiller for the soil, which is probably, it must be confessed, not peculiar to the Southern specimen, but one of the more ineradicable human attachments, be the tiller as progressive as he may. In proposing to wean men from this foolish attachment, industrialism sets itself against the most ancient and the most humane of all the modes of human livelihood. Do Mr. Hoover and the distinguished thinkers at Washington see how essential is the mutual hatred between the industrialists and the farmers, and how mortal is their conflict? The gentlemen at Washington are mostly preaching and legislating to secure the fabulous "blessings" of industrial progress; they are on the industrial side. The industrialists have a doctrine which is monstrous, but they are not monsters personally; they are forward-lookers with nice manners, and no American progressivist is against them. The farmers are boorish and inarticulate by comparison. Progressivism is against them in their fight, though their traditional status is still so strong that soft words are still spoken to them. All the solutions recommended for their difficulties are really enticements held out to them to become a little more coöperative, more mechanical, more mobile—in short, a little more industrialized. But the farmer who is not a mere laborer, even the farmer of the comparatively new places like Iowa and Nebraska, is necessarily among the more stable and less progressive elements of society. He refuses to mobilize himself and become a unit in the industrial army, because he does not approve of army life.

I will use some terms which are hardly in his vernacular. He identifies himself with a spot of ground, and this ground carries a good deal of meaning; it defines itself for him as nature. He would till it not too hurriedly and not too mechanically to observe in it the contingency and the infinitude of nature; and so his life acquires its philosophical and even its cosmic consciousness. A man can contemplate and explore, respect and love, an object as substantial as a farm or a native province. But he cannot contemplate nor explore, respect nor love, a mere turnover, such as an assemblage of "natural resources," a pile of money, a volume of produce, a market, or a credit system. It is into precisely these intangibles that industrialism would translate the farmer's farm. It means the dehumanization of his life.

However that may be, the South at last, looking defensively about her in all directions upon an industrial world, fingers the weapons of industrialism. There is one powerful voice in the South which, tired of a long status of disrepute, would see the South made at once into a section second to none in wealth, as that is statistically reckoned, and in progressiveness, as that might be estimated by the rapidity of the industrial turnover. This desire offends those who would still like to regard the South as, in the old sense, a home; but its expression is loud and insistent. The urban South, with its heavy importation of regular American ways and regular American citizens, has nearly capitulated to these novelties. It is the village South and the rural South which supply the resistance, and it is lucky for them that they represent a vast quantity of inertia.

Will the Southern establishment, the most substantial exhibit on this continent of a society of the European and historic order, be completely crumbled by the powerful acid of the Great Progressive Principle? Will there be no more looking backward but only looking forward? Is our

New World to be dedicated forever to the doctrine of newness?

It is in the interest of America as a whole, as well as in the interest of the South, that these questions press for an answer. I will enter here the most important items of the situation as well as I can; doubtless they will appear a little over-sharpened for the sake of exhibition.

(1) The intention of Americans at large appears now to be what it was always in danger of becoming: an intention of being infinitely progressive. But this intention cannot permit of an established order of human existence, and of that leisure which conditions the life of intelligence and the arts.

(2) The old South, if it must be defined in a word, practiced the contrary and European philosophy of establishment as the foundation of the life of the spirit. The ante-bellum Union possessed, to say the least, a wholesome variety of doctrine.

(3) But the South was defeated by the Union on the battlefield with remarkable decisiveness, and the two consequences have been dire: the Southern tradition was physically impaired, and has ever since been unable to offer an attractive example of its philosophy in action; and the American progressive principle has developed into a pure industrialism without any check from a Southern minority whose voice ceased to make itself heard.

(4) The further survival of the Southern tradition as a detached local remnant is now unlikely. It is agreed that the South must make contact again with the Union. And in adapting itself to the actual state of the Union, the

Southern tradition will have to consent to a certain industrialization of its own.

(5) The question at issue is whether the South will permit herself to be so industrialized as to lose entirely her historic identity, and to remove the last substantial barrier that has stood in the way of American progressivism; or will accept industrialism, but with a very bad grace, and will manage to maintain a good deal of her traditional philosophy.

VII

The hope which is inherent in the situation is evident from the terms in which it is stated. The South must be industrialized—but to a certain extent only, in moderation. The program which now engages the Southern leaders is to see how the South may handle this fire without being burnt badly. The South at last is to be physically reconstructed; but it will be fatal if the South should conceive it as her duty to be regenerated and get her spirit reborn with a totally different orientation toward life.

Fortunately, the Southern program does not have to be perfectly vague. There are at least two definite lines, along either of which an intelligent Southern policy may move in the right general direction; it may even move back and forth between them and still advance.

The first course would be for the Southern leaders to arouse the sectional feeling of the South to its highest pitch of excitement in defense of all the old ways that are threatened. It might seem ungrateful to the kind industrialists to accept their handsome services in such a churlish spirit.

But if one thing is more certain than another, it is that these gentlemen will not pine away in their discouragement; they have an inextinguishable enthusiasm for their rôle. The attitude that needs artificial respiration is the attitude of resistance on the part of the natives to the salesmen of industrialism. It will be fiercest and most effective if industrialism is represented to the Southern people as—what it undoubtedly is for the most part—a foreign invasion of Southern soil, which is capable of doing more devastation than was wrought when Sherman marched to the sea. From this point of view it will be a great gain if the usually-peaceful invasion forgets itself now and then, is less peaceful, and commits indiscretions. The native and the invader will be sure to come to an occasional clash, and that will offer the chance to revive ancient and almost forgotten animosities. It will be in order to proclaim to Southerners that the carpet-baggers are again in their midst. And it will be well to seize upon and advertise certain Northern industrial communities as horrible examples of a way of life we detest —not failing to point out the human catastrophe which occurs when a Southern village or rural community becomes the cheap labor of a miserable factory system. It will be a little bit harder to impress the people with the fact that the new so-called industrial "slavery" fastens not only upon the poor, but upon the middle and better classes of society, too. To make this point it may be necessary to revive such an antiquity as the old Southern gentleman and his lady, and their scorn for the dollar-chasers.

Such a policy as this would show decidedly a sense of

what the Germans call *Realpolitik*. It could be nasty and it could be effective.

Its net result might be to give to the South eventually a position in the Union analogous more or less to the position of Scotland under the British crown—a section with a very local and peculiar culture that would, nevertheless, be secure and respected. And Southern traditionalists may take courage from the fact that it was Scottish stubbornness which obtained this position for Scotland; it did not come gratuitously; it was the consequence of an intense sectionalism that fought for a good many years before its fight was won.

That is one policy. Though it is not the only one, it may be necessary to employ it, with discretion, and to bear in mind its Scottish analogue. But it is hardly handsome enough for the best Southerners. Its methods are too easily abused; it offers too much room for the professional demagogue; and one would only as a last resort like to have the South stake upon it her whole chance of survival. After all, the reconstruction may be undertaken with some imagination, and not necessarily under the formula of a literal restoration. It does not greatly matter to what extent the identical features of the old Southern establishment are restored; the important consideration is that there be an establishment for the sake of stability.

The other course may not be so easily practicable, but it is certainly more statesmanlike. That course is for the South to reënter the American political field with a determination and an address quite beyond anything she has exhibited during her half-hearted national life of the last half a century. And this means specifically that she may pool her own stakes with the stakes of other minority groups in the Union which are circumstanced similarly. There is in active American politics already, to start with, a very belligerent if somewhat uninformed Western agrarian party. Between this party and the South there is much community of interest; both desire to defend home, stability of life, the practice of leisure, and the natural enemy of both is the insidious industrial system. There are also, scattered here and there, numerous elements with the same general attitude which would have some power if united: the persons and even communities who are thoroughly tired of progressivism and its spurious benefits, and those who have recently acquired, or miraculously through the generations preserved, a European point of view—sociologists, educators, artists, religionists, and ancient New England townships. The combination of these elements with the Western farmers and the old-fashioned South would make a formidable bloc. The South is numerically much the most substantial of these three groups, but has done next to nothing to make the cause prevail by working inside the American political system.

The unifying effective bond between these geographically diverse elements of public opinion will be the clean-cut policy that the rural life of America must be defended, and the world made safe for the farmers. My friends are often quick to tell me that against the power of the industrial spirit no such hope can be entertained. But there are some protests in these days rising against the industrial ideal, even from the centers where its grip is the stoutest; and this would indicate that our human intelligence is beginning again to assert itself. Of course this is all the truer of the European countries, which have required less of the bitter schooling of experience. Thus Dean Inge declares himself in his Romanes Lecture on "The Idea of Progress":

> I believe that the dissatisfaction with things as they are is caused not only by the failure of nineteenth-century civilization, but partly also by its success. We no longer wish to progress on those lines if we could. Our apocalyptic dream is vanishing into thin air. It may be that the industrial revolution which began in the reign of George the Third has produced most of its fruits, and has had its day. We may have to look forward to such a change as is imagined by Anatole France at the end of his *Isle of the Penguins*, when, after an orgy of revolution and destruction, we shall slide back into the quiet rural life of the early modern period. If so, the authors of the revolution will have cut their own throats, for there can be no great manufacturing towns in such a society. Their disappearance will be no great loss. The race will have tried a great experiment, and will have rejected it as unsatisfying.

The South has an important part to play, if she will, in such a counter-revolution. But what pitiful service have the inept Southern politicians for many years been rendering to the cause! Their Southern loyalty at Washington has rarely had any more imaginative manifestation than to scramble vigorously for a Southern share in the federal pie. They will have to be miraculously enlightened.

I get quickly beyond my depth in sounding these political possibilities. I will utter one last fantastic thought.

No Southerner ever dreams of heaven, or pictures his Utopia on earth, without providing room for the Democratic party. Is it really possible that the Democratic party can be held to a principle, and that the principle can now be defined as agrarian, conservative, anti-industrial? It may not be impossible, after all. If it proves possible, then the South may yet be rewarded for a sentimental affection that has persisted in the face of many betrayals.

A MIRROR FOR ARTISTS

WHAT is the industrial theory of the arts? It is
something to which industry has not turned its
corporate brains in any large measure. Yet however un-
formulated, there seems to be the phantom of a theory in
the air; perhaps it may materialize into some formidable
managerial body which will take care of the matter for us
—a United States Chamber of Art or a National Arts
Council, with a distinguished board of directors and local
committees in every state. In the absence of the reassuring
information which it would undoubtedly be the function of
such a body to collect and disseminate, I must beg leave to
define the industrial theory of the arts as best I can.

Whenever it is attacked for dirtying up the landscape and
rendering human life generally dull, mechanical, standardized, and mean, industrialism replies by pointing out
compensatory benefits. In the field of the arts, these are
the benefits that a plodding Mæcenas might think about
without greatly agitating his intellect: When material prosperity has finally become permanent, when we are all rich,
when life has been reduced to some last pattern of efficiency,
then we shall all sit down and enjoy ourselves. Since nice,
civilized people are supposed to have art, we shall have art.
We shall buy it, hire it, can it, or—most conclusively—
manufacture it. That is a sufficient answer to the whole

question, so far as the industrial Mæcenas is concerned—and he does not, of course, realize what a strange part he plays in the rôle of Mæcenas. The *nouveau riche* is never sensible of his own errors. If the industrial Mæcenas were alone to be considered, I should not be writing this essay. Other people, some of them persons of learning and thoughtfulness, hold essentially the same theory. They talk of "mastering the machine" or "riding the wild horses" of industrial power, with the idea that industrialism may furnish the basis for a society which will foster art. It is a convenient doctrine, and a popular one.

The contention of this essay is that such theories are wrong in their foundation. Industrialism cannot play the rôle of Mæcenas, because its complete ascendancy will mean that there will be no arts left to foster; or, if they exist at all, they will flourish only in a diseased and disordered condition, and the industrial Mæcenas will find himself in the embarrassing position of having to patronize an art that secretly hates him and calls him bad names. More completely, the making of an industrialized society will extinguish the meaning of the arts, as humanity has known them in the past, by changing the conditions of life that have given art a meaning. For they have been produced in societies which were for the most part stable, religious, and agrarian; where the goodness of life was measured by a scale of values having little to do with the material values of industrialism; where men were never too far removed from nature to forget that the chief subject of art, in the final sense, is nature.

It is my further contention that the cause of the arts,

thus viewed, offers an additional reason among many reasons for submitting the industrial program to a stern criticism and for upholding a contrary program, that of an
agrarian restoration; and that, in America, the South, past
and present, furnishes a living example of an agrarian
society, the preservation of which is worth the most heroic
effort that men can give in a time of crisis.

Let us recall the song of the sirens, which Sir Thomas
Browne ventured to say was not beyond conjecture. I dare to
make the conjecture, though well knowing how we moderns have shattered all myths in our wish to flood our
brows with the light of reason, and how lightly we hold
the wisdom of untruths or double truths in which the
ancients often shadowed their greatest mysteries. Whatever
the words and melody, the song of the sirens must have
had this meaning: "You shall enjoy beauty without the
toil of winning it, if you will forsake your ship and dwell
with us." It was an alluring promise, and few of those
who yielded thought of the condition on which it was
made. They were attracted by the first clause and forgot
the second, which implied, yet revealed not that alien shore
where the bones of victims littered the rocks. For the sirens
were cannibals; their embrace was death.

Industrialism makes the promise of the sirens, though of
course with no real malignancy—rather with a mild innocence which we could forgive if it were not so stupid.
Industrialism wants to take a short-cut to art. Seeing the
world altogether in terms of commodities, it simply proposes to add one more commodity to the list, as a conces-

(30)

sion to humanity's perfectly unaccountable craving, or as just one more market—why not? It will buy art, if any fool wants art. And industrialism is quite unconscious that the bargain (which the Middle Ages would have described as a devil's bargain, ending in the delivery of the soul to torment) involves the destruction of the thing bargained for. The takers of the bargain, if there are any, are likely to be equally unconscious of what is happening to them, except as they are vaguely aware of being somehow betrayed. Hence results a situation that might be put into a dialogue:

"Incompetent wretch," says the industrialist, "is this sorry product what I bargained for? Have I not endowed you with leisure and comfort in which to produce your masterpieces? Do I not reward you with great wealth and provide you with all the proper facilities in all manner of institutions? Yet you perform no great works, but oddly prefer to indulge in maudlin ravings that no sensible person can understand or in obscene scoldings that no right-minded citizen can approve."

"You do not understand the nature of genius," the artist answers, haughtily. "I am what I am. I do not expect to be appreciated in my lifetime, anyway, and certainly not by vulgar persons unlearned in the modern theories of art. Art makes its own rules, which are not the rules of commerce. If you want to play my game, you must play it by my rules."

The industrialist, reorganizing society according to theories of material progress, avows his good intentions. He naturally expects the arts to flourish as a matter of course, perhaps even more joyously and quickly than in the past.

For he thinks his dispensation sets men free to use the blessings of art, however minor and incidental these may be in his cosmic scheme. The artist, who is in spirit dissociated from the industrialist's scheme of society but forced to live under it, magnifies his dissociation into a special privilege and becomes a noble exile.

Do the arts require leisure for their creation and enjoyment? The industrialist claims that he increases the sumtotal of human leisure through machines that save labor; furthermore, that this leisure is more widely distributed than ever before in history, and that the proportion of leisure to labor and the extent of its distribution are bound to increase as industrialism waxes mightier and ever more efficient. With leisure goes physical security—greater length of life, freedom from disease and poverty, increase of material comforts. If, under this benevolent dispensation, men do not spontaneously devote themselves to art, then the further presumption is that industrial philanthropy will be equal to the emergency, for its accumulations of surplus capital can be used for promoting the "finer things of life."

Through his command over nature the modern man can move his art about at will. Literary masterpieces, chosen by the best critics that can be hired, can be distributed once a month to hundreds of thousands of disciples of culture. Symphony concerts, heavily endowed and directed by world-famous experts, can be broadcast to millions. Much as the Red Cross mobilizes against disease, the guardians of public taste can mobilize against bad art or lack of art; one visualizes caravans of art, manned by regiments of lecturers, rushed hastily to future epidemic centers of barbarism when some new Mencken discovers a Sahara of the Bozart. Or, *vice versa*, modern man can move himself to t⁺ₑ place where art is—to the Louvre, to the cathedrals, to the pagodas, to meetings of the Poetry Society of America. Through power of accumulated wealth, in public or private hands, he can bring precious canvasses and sculptures together for multitudes to stare at. He can build immense libraries or put little libraries on wheels—the flying library may be looked for eventually. The millionaire can retain an expert to buy his gallery of Corots—or of the newest, surest masters declared by modern dealers. Or, as wealth trickles down to humbler hands, the shop girl can get a ten-cent print of Corot to hang above her dressing-table, or buy her dollar edition of Shakespeare, with an introduction by Carl Van Doren. Between the shop girl and the millionaire will of course be a universal art-audience of all the people, introduced to the classics through schemes of mass-education and trained from babyhood (in nursery schools) in all varieties of art-appreciation.

In short, the artist is to have a freer and fuller opportunity than he has ever known before. With leisure to enjoy art, with command over the materials of art, with remarkable schemes for communicating, distributing, manufacturing, and inculcating art—how can the creative spirit fail to respond to the challenge? Why not a golden age of the arts, wherein ideal cities, grandiosely designed, shelter a race of super-beings who spend all their unemployed moments (destined to be numerous, when production is finally regulated) in visiting art museums, reading immortal

(33)

works, and dwelling in beautiful homes adorned with designs approved by the best interior decorators?

What a shame if, with all this tremendous array of compulsions, the stubborn pig still refuses to get over the stile! Yet that is what happens. The arts behave with piggish contrariness. They will not budge, or they run crazily off into briar patches and mud puddles, squealing hideously.

It is common knowledge that, wherever it can be said to exist at all, the kind of leisure provided by industrialism is a dubious benefit. It helps nobody but merchants and manufacturers, who have taught us to use it in industriously consuming the products they make in great excess over the demand. Moreover, it is spoiled, as leisure, by the kind of work that industrialism compels. The furious pace of our working hours is carried over into our leisure hours, which are feverish and energetic. We live by the clock. Our days are a muddle of "activities," strenuously pursued. We do not have the free mind and easy temper that should characterize true leisure. Nor does the separation of our lives into two distinct parts, of which one is all labor —too often mechanical and deadening—and the other all play, undertaken as a nervous relief, seem to be conducive to a harmonious life. The arts will not easily survive a condition under which we work and play at cross-purposes. We cannot separate our being into contradictory halves without a certain amount of spiritual damage. The leisure thus offered is really no leisure at all; either it is pure sloth, under which the arts take on the character of mere entertainment, purchased in boredom and enjoyed in utter

(34)

passivity, or it is another kind of labor, taken up out of a sense of duty, pursued as a kind of fashionable enterprise for which one's courage must be continually whipped up by reminders of one's obligation to culture.

The premise of distribution is equally deceptive. One thing has obviously happened that nobody counted on when industrialism first appeared as Messiah. It has been generally assumed that the art to be distributed will naturally be good art. But it is just as easy to distribute bad art—in fact, it is much easier, because bad art is more profitable. The shop-girl does not recite Shakespeare before breakfast. Henry Ford's hired hands do not hum themes from Beethoven as they go to work. Instead, the shop-girl reads the comic strip with her bowl of patent cereal and puts on a jazz record while she rouges her lips. She reads the confession magazines and goes to the movies. The factory hand simply does not hum; the *Daily Mirror* will do for him, with pictures and titles that can be torpidly eyed. The industrialists in art—that is, the Hollywood producers, the McFadden publications, the Tin Pan Alley crowd, the Haldeman-Julius Blue Books—will naturally make their appeal to the lowest common denominator. They know the technique of mass-production, which, if applied to the arts, must invariably sacrifice quality to quantity. Small margins of profit, large sales, the technique of forcing the market through salesmanship and high-pressure advertising, will all work havoc; nor have we much reason to hope that the ravages will eventually be limited to the vulgar enterprises I have named, of which the movies offer perhaps the most convincing example.

(35)

What have we to hope for when eminent critics sell their prestige and ability to book clubs whose entire scheme of operations is based on the technique of mass-production; when publishers begin to imitate the methods of William Wrigley and Lydia E. Pinkham? What but a gradual corruption of integrity and good taste, a preference for the mediocre and "safe," if not for the positively bad. The magnificent possibilities for distributing art become appalling opportunities for distributing bad art. One has only to glance at magazines of large circulation, at the advertising columns of reviews (if not at the articles themselves), at the general critical confusion of New York, to see what inroads have already been made.

At this point somebody might argue that the lower classes never produced or enjoyed good art, anyway; and the number of persons of good taste is steadily increasing.

This objection would ask us to view good art as an aristocratic affair. It cannot be granted without ignoring history, which shows that art in its great periods has rarely been purely aristocratic. It has generally been also "popular" art in a good sense and has been widely diffused. The "popular" art that has survived for inspection is good art, certainly as compared with the McFadden publications. Furthermore, this objection would at once subtract from consideration one of the major claims of industrialism, which proposes to enlarge and not to diminish the audience of the artist—even to make his audience universal. And even if there should be proved to be, by actual census, a larger number of people who enjoy good art through the agency of industrialism than in past times, I should still suspect the validity of the process by which they achieved good taste. For good taste cannot be had by simply going into the market for it. It will be but a superficial property, the less valued because it was easily got; and it will be dangerous to society if society is merely gilded with culture and not permeated. Such an aristocracy, if it could be achieved, would reign very insecurely; and it would always be more likely that its manners would be perverted by the "lower" class than that the manners of the "lower" class would be raised.

Education, we are told, should deal with such matters as this. In the long run we shall educate everybody, and good art will win because only good art will be taught.

Under ideal circumstances education can probably accomplish a great deal, and even under the worst handicaps it produces intangible results in which we can well afford to rejoice. However, again we encounter the old difficulty. Education can do comparatively little to aid the cause of the arts as long as it must turn out graduates into an industrialized society which demands specialists in vocational, technical, and scientific subjects. The humanities, which could reasonably be expected to foster the arts, have fought a losing battle since the issue between vocational and liberal education was raised in the nineteenth century. Or, they have kept their place by imitating the technique of their rivals, so that one studies the biology of language, the chemistry of drama, the evolution of the novel, and the geological strata or fossil forms of literature and the fine arts. That is, they abdicate the function by which they were formerly able to affect the tone of society. So

(37)

far as they still maintain this function, they still face a dilemma. Either they will appear as decorative and useless to the rising generations who know that poetry sells no bonds and music manages no factories, and hence will be taken under duress or enjoyed as a pleasant concession to the softer and more frivolous side of life. Or, the more successfully they indoctrinate the student with their values, the more unhappy they will make him. For he will be spoiled for industrial tasks by being rendered inefficient. He will not fit in. The more refined and intelligent he becomes, the more surely will he see in the material world the lack of the image of nobility and beauty that the humanities inculcate in him. The product of a humanistic education in an industrial age is most likely to be an exotic, unrelated creature—a disillusionist or a dilettante. Lastly, there is the almost overwhelming difficulty of communicating the humanities at all under systems of education, gigantic in their scope, that have become committed to industrial methods of administration—the entire repulsive fabric of standards, credits, units, scientific pedagogy, over-organization. The sign of these difficulties is found in the great confusion and argument that exists today in the educational profession itself. On the whole, though we may allow that some institutions, notably some colleges and universities, are oases hospitable to the arts—oases that might become centers of leadership—the educational situation offers more cause for discouragement than for hope.

As to art museums and other philanthropic schemes for promoting art, I do not speak against them in any denunciatory sense. Yet one cannot help but fear that they too only serve to emphasize the discrepancy between our life and our art. Alone, they can hardly supply the impulses which a thousand other influences are negating and destroying. It is futile to imagine that the arts will penetrate our life in exact proportion to the number of art galleries, orchestras, and libraries that philanthropy may endow. Rather it is probable that a multiplication of art galleries (to take a separate example) is a mark of a diseased, not a healthy civilization. If paintings and sculptures are made for the purpose of being viewed in the carefully studied surroundings of art galleries, they have certainly lost their intimate connection with life. What is a picture for, if not to put on one's own wall? But the principle of the art gallery requires me to think that a picture has some occult quality in itself and for itself that can only be appreciated on a quiet anonymous wall, utterly removed from the tumult of my private affairs.

The art gallery or art museum theory of art to which philanthropists and promoters would persuade us views art as a luxury quite beyond the reach of ordinary people. Its attempt to glorify the arts by setting them aside in specially consecrated shrines can hardly supply more than a superficial gilding to a national culture, if the private direction of that culture is ugly and materialistic—Keyserling would say, animalistic. The proposition is as absurd as this: Should we eat our meals regularly from crude, thick dishes like those used in Greek restaurants, but go on solemn occasions to a restaurant museum where somebody's munificence would permit us to enjoy a meal on china of the most delicate design? The truly artistic life is surely that in which the æsthetic experience is not curtained off but is mixed up with all sorts of instruments and occupations pertaining to the round of daily life. It ranges all the way from pots and pans, chairs and rugs, clothing and houses, up to dramas publicly performed and government buildings. Likewise public libraries, which tend ever to become more immense and numerous, pervert public taste as much as they encourage it. For the patrons are by implication discouraged from getting their own books and keeping them at home. Their notion is that the state —or some local Mæcenas—will take care of their taste for them, just as the police take care of public safety. Art galleries and libraries are fine enough in their way, but we should not be deceived into putting our larger hope in them.

The final evidence of the false promise of industrialism is in the condition of the arts themselves. That they have in our time a real excellence as arts I should be the last to deny. I am, however, not so much concerned with defining that excellence as with discovering their general status in relation to the profound changes which industrialism has brought into human society. Those who study the modern arts seriously and disinterestedly are obliged to note that their excellence is maintained somewhat desperately and defiantly. It has a back-against-the-wall heroism. It has the fierce courage that flares up when one is cornered by an overwhelming adversary, or it has the malaise of defeat. The arts are subject to exactly the same confusion of purpose that Matthew Arnold once attributed to the English Romantic poets. Their work, he said, was "premature," largely because they did not participate in a "current of ideas in the highest degree animating and nourishing to the creative power"—such a "current of ideas" or a "national glow of life and thought" as Sophocles or Pindar enjoyed. Arnold thus put his finger on the difficulty that beset not only the Romantic poets, but Arnold himself and the Victorian writers in general, and that is exaggerated rather than diminished today.

For Arnold's "premature," however, I should substitute "belated." Romantic writers, from William Blake to T. S. Eliot, are not so much an advance guard leading the way to new conquests as a rear guard—a survival of happier days when the artist's profession was not so much a separate and special one as it is now. Romantic writers—and modern writers, who are also romantic—behave like persons whose position is threatened and needs fresh justification. The rebellion against tradition, so marked in some kinds of Romanticism, is thus an abandonment of one untenable fortress in order to take a new position that the artist hopes will be unassailable. In turn it too is besieged, and a new manœuvre must be attempted. Yet every time it is not merely Neoclassic art or Victorian art that is invaded. It is art itself, as art, that is being attacked by an enemy so blind and careless that he does not know what citadel he is approaching.

Mr. Babbitt, Mr. More, and other critics of the Humanist school have dragged the weaknesses of Romantic art into the light, but seemingly fail to realize that if there is to be any art at all under the conditions of modern life, it must probably be Romantic art, and must have the weaknesses of Romantic art, with such excellences as may be allowed

(41)

to the unvictorious. It is alarming and somewhat tragic to witness a Humanist attack upon the retiring outposts of the army whose ancient generals they are pleased to commend. The fury and ridicule that young men of letters, like Edmund Wilson, have heaped upon the Humanist program must be at least partly due to their awareness that the Humanists, in their bombardment of all modernisms, are demolishing the walls of Troy in order to admit the wooden horse.

Mr. Eugene O'Neill may have every wish to be Sophocles, but he cannot be Sophocles in a New York skyscraper, any more than Mr. Thornton Wilder can be God by sending his astral body to Peru. The Humanists commend us to Sophocles and God, *in vacuo*. Their thinking stops where it should begin, with social conditions that shape the artist's reaction. Like Arnold they imagine that culture will conquer Philistinism and have faith that the "best" ideas will prevail over the false ideas or no-ideas of the great Anarch. In Arnold's time it was reasonable to entertain such a hope. Today it is the academic equivalent of Y. M. C. A. "leadership."

Unpredictable though the great artist may be, no study of the past can fail to reveal that social conditions to a large extent direct the temper and form of art. And many though the varieties of Romanticism may be, their origin is probably always in an artificial or maladjusted relation between the artist and society. We shall not be far wrong if we describe Romanticism somewhat in the terms that Mr. Harold J. Laski has used for Rousseau: "He (Rousseau) never lost the sense of anger against an order the tradition

of which forced him at every step to fight for himself.
. . . He was driven by the law of his being to deny the
foundations of the world he had hoped to conquer. He saw
between himself and its spirit a fundamental contradiction
of principle which neither compromise nor recognition
could bridge."

Eighteenth Century society, which pretended to classicism
artistically and maintained a kind of feudalism politically,
was with all its defects a fairly harmonious society in which
the artist was not yet out of place, although he was already
beginning to be. But in the middle of the eighteenth century, democracy and the industrial revolution got under
way almost simultaneously. The rise of the middle classes
to power, through commercial prosperity, prepared the way
for the one; scientific discovery, backed by eighteenth century rationalism, prepared for the other, and society speedily
fell into a disharmony, where it has remained. Political
democracy, as Mr. Laski has shown, left social democracy
unrealized. The way was clear for the materialistic reorganization of society that in effect brought a spiritual disorganization.

Thus arise the works of the Romantic school, in which
the artist sets forth "the fundamental contradiction of principle" between himself and society. The artist is no longer
with society, as perhaps even Milton, last of classicists, was.
He is *against* or *away from* society, and the disturbed relation becomes his essential theme, always underlying his
work, no matter whether he evades or accepts the treatment of the theme itself. His evasion may consist in nostalgia for a remote past, mediæval, Elizabethan, Grecian, which

he revives imaginatively or whose characteristic modes he appropriates. He has thus the spiritual solace of retreating to a refuge secure against the doubtful implications of his position in contemporary society. His retreat is a psychological compensation, but there is also an appeal to something that has survival value. He does not so much rebel against a crystallized tradition (the misleading notion of Lowes' "convention and revolt") as retire more deeply within the body of the tradition to some point where he can utter himself with the greatest consciousness of his dignity as artist. He is like a weaponless warrior who plucks a sword from the tomb of an ancient hero.

Or with greater hardihood the artist may defy the logic of circumstances. Individuality being imperilled, he reaffirms the sacredness of the individual. In Romantic poetry we have from the beginning a vast increase in lyric poetry, personal and subjective, with the objective practically ruled out. The poet sings less and less for the crowd in whose experiences he no longer shares intimately. The lonely artist appears, who sings for a narrower and ever diminishing audience; or having in effect no audience, he sings for himself. He develops not only a peculiar set of ideas, more and more personal to himself, but a personal style that in time becomes the "unique" style demanded of modern poets, highly idiomatic, perhaps obscure.

Likewise he exaggerates feeling at the expense of thought. The works of sensibility emerge. Shelley's skylark and Keats's nightingale are not birds, but causes, stimuli, barely tangible perceptions that start a flow of feeling which the poets struggle almost vainly to declare. Later the Imagists

(44)

repeat the Romantic mode in a slightly different pattern. Their art is exclamatory and personal; it avoids synthesis and meaning. Other modern poets retreat into a still more impregnable world of feeling—the bristling and rugged metaphysical world of Donne, where every approach is labyrinthean, and the tender soul of the poet goes armored in an array of blossoming thorns. There are more and more poems about the difficulty of writing poetry; such a one is "The Waste Land."

The more combative and critical artist may prefer a different method. Turning upon what has foiled him, he proposes to reform and change it. Thus occur—most frequently in the novel or the drama—works of social criticism and protest. The history of the novel reveals how rapid has been the shift from objective narrative to the problematic, the satirical, and the critical. The shift occurred, in fact, almost as soon as the eighteenth-century novel was born, and it has continued until pure story is now relegated to minor types of fiction, and serious novels are, by and large, those that tell us how wrong the world is.

The last choice for the artist is to accept the disturbed state of society as something which cannot be altered by him or as promising an altogether new kind of society that will require to be interpreted in some wholly new kind of art. The enemy is too strong for him; so he joins the enemy, hoping thus to secure the integration that otherwise is denied him. The disturbing element, which is science pure and applied, offers methods, attitudes, subjects that he determines to appropriate.

Perhaps he becomes a realist. Without a hint of moralizing, and disdaining escape and protest, he merely observes, classifies, reports. But the works of realists which ought—if science has merit in art—to disclose the beauty that is truth more often reveal the truth that is ugliness or injured beauty. The realist turns out to be a historian rather than an artist, and, at that, a historian of calamities. Or the more he verges toward art, the more he will be found to depart from scientific method, which is a negation of art to begin with. In any case, no matter what his pretensions, the realist succeeds no better than the romanticist in avoiding the ill relation between the artist and society. Although he may seem definitely to enlarge the field of art and get hold of new materials, he is singularly ill at ease in his rôle of reporter. Having accepted the valuations of science along with its method, he finds himself confronted with a purposeless world of men and things whose lack of meaning he must honestly reveal. His honesty, however, is quite uncheerful and it is not objective. Tragedy may be impossible, in a world where men behave as their glands make them behave; but painful literature remains to exhibit the repugnance of the scientific-artist toward the rôle he has chosen.

Wordsworth's hope that the objects of science—such as, presumably, dynamos, atoms, skyscrapers, knitting-machines, and chemical reactions—might one day become materials of art, when they are as familiar as trees and rocks, seems as far from realization as ever. The attempt to sublimate them, which has something of the attitude of the realist without his method, does not yet show much promise of success. The objects appear in art, of course, but that art is already conditioned by the social trends that machines and scientific theories have caused. They become a part of the background of artistic interpretation or they furnish motives, but their rôle is mainly Satanic. Since their influence on humanity is to dehumanize, to emphasize utilitarian ends, to exalt abstraction over particularity and uniformity over variety, the artist tends to view them as evil. He cannot accept them as offering an approach to some "new" art unless he adopts the resolution of Satan, "Evil, be thou my good!" A world committed to some hypothetical and as yet unheard-of form of art-science can today be visioned only as a monstrous and misshapen nightmare which we pray we may not survive to witness. Whether or not science and art are actually hostile to each other, as I have argued, it is certainly true that they have no common ground; they are as far apart as science and religion.

In short, the condition of the arts themselves, in whatever field, gives little ground for thinking that they are actually cherished in an industrial civilization. The sporadic vitality that they show is probably not a mark of abundant health, but of a lingering and lusty capacity to survive every disaster and disease short of complete extinction. The ultimate disaster of extinction must honestly be faced—unless the arts accept a rôle inferior to anything they have previously enjoyed, so greatly in contrast to their old state as to make them appear slavish and parasitical.

In his *Portrait of the Artist as American* Matthew Josephson has shown to what an astonishing extent the careers of American artists have been distorted and erratic. Rarely if ever in America do we find a great artist slowly maturing his powers in full communion with a society of which he is an integral part. Instead we have seclusionists like Emily Dickinson, retiring within a narrow subjective cell; or at the other extreme exiles like Henry James and Lafcadio Hearn who sought salvation in flight. Van Wyck Brooks has tended, in such cases, to blame the insufficiency of the artists themselves—that is, Mark Twain should not have let himself be gentled; Henry James should have drawn strength from his native earth. Rightly, I think, Mr. Josephson finds that American society was to blame, and not the artists, for their defeatism was but a corollary of their dislocated relation to society. The rule of mechanism, though it began early in America, promised for a while to be checked by the New England group who might have established a society hospitable to the arts. But New England idealism failed in the débâcle of the Civil War that it egged on. Thenceforth industrialism, which had been long resisted by the agrarian South and its old ally, the West of the transition period, held strong sway. The schism between the artist and society, already foreshadowed in the inherent weaknesses of New England, became more and more exaggerated until today France and England harbor veritable colonies of expatriates, while at home new tribes of artists repeat the subjective tragedy of Emily Dickinson or Poe, or with a vain assurance attempt like Whitman to adumbrate the glory of a democratic, muscular future that forever recedes in mists of retreating hope.

Mr. Josephson makes a strong case, but states it too narrowly. His America is New England or New York; he is blissfully oblivious to the agrarian South, past and present. He does not realize that the malady he pictures appears in the United States only in its most exaggerated and obvious form. Geographically, it covers Western civilization wherever industrialism has fully entered. Historically, its ravages may be studied throughout the nineteenth century. The long list from Byron to Tennyson to Eliot, from Hugo to the Symbolists, from Goethe to the Expressionists, will reveal the lamentable story of dissociation and illustrate profusely, with examples of exile, distortion, sensibility, Mr. Josephson's dictum, "Under mechanism, the eternal drama of the artist becomes *resistance to the milieu.*"

It is significant, as I have previously indicated, that the Romanticism which could be defined under this principle begins almost simultaneously with the industrial revolution. Democracy began its great rule at the same time; but we should do wrong to blame democracy too much, as Mr. Josephson does, for the bad estate of the artist. Democracy did not, after all, disturb society unduly. It was a slow growth, it had some continuity with the past, and in an agrarian country like pre-Civil War America it permitted and favored a balanced life. Industrialism came suddenly and marched swiftly. It left a tremendous gap. Only as democracy becomes allied with industrialism can it be considered really dangerous, as when, in the United States, it becomes politically and socially impotent; or, as in the extreme democracy of the Soviets, where, converted into equalitarianism within class limits, it threatens the existence of man's humanity. Democracy, if not made too acquisitive by industrialism, does not appear as an enemy to the arts. Industrialism does so appear, and has played its hostile rôle for upwards of a hundred and fifty years. As socialism in its various forms may be considered the natural political antitoxin that industrialism produces, Romanticism is the artistic antitoxin and will appear inevitably if the artist retains enough courage and sincerity to function at all. To yield to industrialism means to surrender the artistic function, to play the clown at Dives' feast, to become a kind of engineer—which is, for example, just what the architects of skyscrapers have become. Not to yield means to invite and even to exploit the unbalance that is a unique characteristic of modern Romanticism, all the more marked because of the modern tendency to exalt the separate rôle of the artist as artist and to make art itself sacrosanct and professional.

There is but one other possibility. The supremacy of industrialism itself can be repudiated. Industrialism can be deposed as the regulating god of modern society.

This is no doubt a desperate counsel. But the artist may well find in it more promise for his cause than in all the talk of progressivists about "mastering the machine." Mastery of the machine, he will reflect, can only begin with a despisal of the machine and the supposed benefits it offers. He has no reason to hope that those who hold the machine in awe will ever subdue it. Lonely exile though he be, he must be practical enough to distrust the social philosophers who promise him a humble corner in the Great Reconstruction that they are undertaking to produce for our age.

Harmony between the artist and society must be regained; the dissociation must be broken down. That can only be done, however, by first putting society itself in order. In this connection we must realize that discussions of what is good or bad art, no matter how devoted or learned, cannot avail to reëstablish the arts in their old places. Criticism, for which Arnold and others have hoped so much, is futile for the emergency if it remains wholly aloof from the central problem, which is the remaking of life itself. We are drawn irresistibly toward social criticism, as the Victorian artists were. But we cannot hope, as they did, that we can win men to beauty by simply loving the beautiful and preaching its merits as they are revealed to us in an admirable body of tradition. We cannot have much faith in, though we may respect, Mr. Frank Jewett Mather's suggestion that we civilize from the top down; for our whole powerful economic system rests on mass motives—the motives of society's lowest common denominator. This counsel leads us toward fastidiousness, dilettantism, at best a kind of survival on sufferance.

As in the crisis of war, when men drop their private occupations for one supreme task, the artist must step into the ranks and bear the brunt of the battle against the common foe. He must share in the general concern as to the conditions of life. He must learn to understand and must try to restore and preserve a social economy that is in danger of being replaced altogether by an industrial economy hostile to his interests.

For strategic purposes, at least, I feel he will ally himself with programs of agrarian restoration. Out of conviction he should do so, since only in an agrarian society does there remain much hope of a balanced life, where the arts are not luxuries to be purchased but belong as a matter of course in the routine of his living. Again, both strategy and conviction will almost inevitably lead him to the sections of America that are provincial, conservative, agrarian, for there only will he find a lingering preference for values not industrial. The very wilderness is his friend, not as a refuge, but as an ally. But he does not need to go into the wilderness. There are American communities throughout the country from the West, even to the fringes of the industrialized East, that are in the industrial sense backward, and are naturally on his side. Negatively to his advantage are the discontent and confusion in the heart of industrialism itself.

The largest and most consistent exhibit of such communities is in the South. For a century and a half the South has preserved its agrarian economy. On one occasion it fought to the death for principles now clearly defined, in the light of history, as representing fundamentally the cause of agrarianism against industrialism. The South lost its battle. What was worse for the nation, it lost the peace— first in the Reconstruction, second by temporarily conforming, under the leadership of men like Walter H. Page and Henry W. Grady, to "new South" doctrines subversive of its native genius. Yet the agrarian South did not vanish. Only at this late day has it given any general promise of following the industrial program with much real consent. The danger of such consent is real. So far as industrialism triumphs and is able to construct a really "new" South, the South will have nothing to contribute to modern issues. It will merely imitate and repeat the mistakes of other sec-

tions. The larger promise of the South is in another direction. Its historic and social contribution should be utilized.
It offers the possibility of an integrated life, American in the older rather than the newer sense. Its population is homogeneous. Its people share a common past, which they are not likely to forget; for aside from having Civil War battlefields at their doorsteps, the Southern people have long cultivated a historical consciousness that permeates manners, localities, institutions, the very words and cadence of social intercourse. This consciousness, too often misdescribed as merely romantic and gallant, really signifies a close connection with the eighteenth-century European America that is elsewhere forgotten. In the South the eighteenth-century social inheritance flowered into a gracious civilization that, despite its defects, was actually a civilization, true and indigenous, well diffused, well established. Its culture was sound and realistic in that it was not at war with its own economic foundations. It did not need to be paraded loudly; it was not thought about particularly. The manners of planters and countrymen did not require them to change their beliefs and temper in going from cornfield to drawing-room, from cotton rows to church or frolic. They were the same persons everywhere. There was also a fair balance of aristocratic and democratic elements. Plantation affected frontier; frontier affected plantation. The balance might be illustrated by pairings; it was no purely aristocratic or purely democratic South that produced Thomas Jefferson and Andrew Jackson, Robert E. Lee and Stonewall Jackson, John C. Calhoun and Andrew Johnson, Poe and Simms. There was diversity within unity.

(53)

There were also leisureliness, devotion to family and neighborhood, local self-sufficiency and self-government, and a capacity, up through the 'sixties, for developing leaders.

Above all, the South was agrarian, and agrarian it still remains very largely. Whether it still retains its native, inborn ways is a question open to argument in the minds of those who know the South mainly from hearsay. In the South itself, especially in its scattering and deluded industrial centres, there is much lip-service to progress—the more because industrialism makes a very loud noise, with all its extravagant proclamations of better times; and the South has known hard times only too well. Yet probably the secret ambition of most Southern city-dwellers, especially those in apartment houses, is to retire to the farm and live like gentlemen. There are still plenty of people who find the brassy methods of tradesmen a little uncouth. The Southern tradition is probably more vital than its recent epitaphists have announced. If it were not alive, even in the younger generations, this book would never be written. But these are considerations which are touched upon elsewhere. My business is to consider to what extent it offers the kind of society we are looking for.

One must allow that the South of the past, for all its ways of life, did not produce much "great" art. An obvious retort to such a criticism would be, "Neither did the rest of America." Also I might say, as it is frequently said, that the long quarrel between Southern agrarianism and Northern industrialism drove the genius of the South largely into the political rather than the artistic field. A good case might be made out, indeed, for political writing itself as a kind of art in which the South excelled, as in forensic art.

Yet this is not the whole story. So far as the arts have flourished in the South, they have been, up to a very recent period, in excellent harmony with their milieu. The South has always had a native architecture, adapted from classic models into something distinctly Southern; and nothing more clearly and satisfactorily belongs where it is, or better expresses the beauty and stability of an ordered life, than its old country homes, with their pillared porches, their simplicity of design, their sheltering groves, their walks bordered with boxwood shrubs. The South has been rich in the folk-arts, and is still rich in them—in ballads, country songs and dances, in hymns and spirituals, in folk tales, in the folk crafts of weaving, quilting, furniture-making. Though these are best preserved in mountain fastnesses and remote rural localities, they were not originally so limited. They were widespread; and though now they merely survive, they are certainly indicative of a society that could not be termed inartistic. As for the more sophisticated arts, the South has always practised them as a matter of course. I shall not attempt to estimate the Southern contribution to literature with some special array of names; the impassioned scholars who are busily resurrecting Chivers, Kennedy, Byrd, Longstreet, Sut Lovengood, and such minor persons, in their rediscovery of American literature, will presently also get around again to Cooke, Page, Cable, Allen, and the like. What I should particularly like to note is that the specious theory that an "independent" country ought to originate an independent art, worthy of its national greatness, did not originate in the South. Emerson fostered such a theory, Whitman tried to practice it, and the call for the "great American novel" has only lately died of its own futility. Since the day when Southerners read Mr. Addison or got Mr. Stuart to paint grandfather's portrait, they have not, on the whole, been greatly excited over the idea that America is obliged to demonstrate its originality by some sharp divorce from the European tradition.

What might have happened, had not the Civil War disrupted the natural course of affairs, I cannot venture to say. Certainly an indigenous art would have had a good chance to spring up in the South, as the inevitable expression of modes of life rather favorable to the arts. What kind of art it might have been, or whether it would have been "great," I do not know. We should, however, recognize that the appearance or non-appearance of a "great" art or a "great" artist can hardly be accepted as a final criterion for judging a society. That is a typically modern view, implying that society merely exists to produce the artist, and it is wrong. Certainly the "great" art cannot be made by fiat; it probably hates compulsion. But an artistic life, in the social sense, is achievable under right conditions; and then, probably when we least expect it, the unpredictable great art arrives. If art has any real importance in life, it is as a significant and beautiful way of shaping whatever there is to be shaped in life, secular and religious, private and public. Let me go back to my thesis. I do not suggest that the South itself is about to become the seat of some grand revival of the arts—though such might happen. I do suggest that the South, as a distinct, provincial region, offers terms of life favorable to the arts, which in the last analysis are a by-product anyway and will not bear too much self-conscious solicitude.

Our megalopolitan agglomerations, which make great ado about art, are actually sterile on the creative side; they patronize art, they merchandise it, but do not produce it. The despised hinterland, which is rather carefree about the matter, somehow manages to beget the great majority of American artists. True, they often migrate to New York, at considerable risk to their growth; they as often move away again, to Europe or some treasured local retreat. Our large cities affect a cosmopolitan air but have little of the artistic cosmopolitanism that once made Paris a Mecca. They do not breed literary groups; the groups appear in the hinterland. We have only to examine the biographies of our artists to learn how provincial are the sources of our arts. The Mid-Western excitement of some years ago was a provincial movement, as is today the Southern outburst. Zona Gale, Robert Frost, James Branch Cabell, Julia Peterkin, Sherwood Anderson, Willa Cather, and many others are provincialists. The Little Theater movement is provincial; it has decentralized dramatic art and broken the grip of Broadway.

And certainly the provincial artist ought to enjoy special blessings. More nearly than his big-city colleague, he should be able to approximate a harmonious relation between artist and environment. Especially to his advantage is his nearness to nature in the physical sense—which ought to mean, not that he becomes in the narrow sense an artist "of the soil," dealing in the picturesque, but that nature is an eternal balancing factor in his art, a presence neither

(57)

wholly benign nor wholly hostile, continually reminding him that art is not a substitute for nature. Likewise he is far from the commercial fury and the extreme knowingness of the merchandising centers. He works unaware of critical politics; he is ignorant of how this or that career was "put over," he does not have to truckle and wear himself out at drinking bouts and literary teas, he is not obliged to predict cleverly the swings of the artistic pendulum before they fairly begin to swing.

Even so, he cannot escape the infection of the cities by mere geographical remoteness. The skepticism and malaise of the industrial mind reach him anyway, though somewhat subdued, and attack his art in the very process of creation. Unself-conscious expression cannot fully be attained. It is conditioned by the general state of society, which he cannot escape. It is inhibited by the ideals of the market place, which are, after all, very powerful.

In the South today we have artists whose work reveals richness, repose, brilliance, continuity. The performance of James Branch Cabell has a consistency that might have been more flickering and unstable if it had originated in some less quiet region than Virginia. The novels of Ellen Glasgow have a strength that may come from long, slow prosecution by a mind far from nervous. Yet these and others have not gone untainted. Why does Mr. Cabell seem so much nearer to Paris than to Richmond, to Anatole France than to Lee and Jefferson? Why does Miss Glasgow, self-styled the "social historian" of Virginia, propagate ideas that would be more quickly approved by Oswald Garrison Villard than by the descendants of first families? Why are

DuBose Heyward's and Paul Green's studies of negro life so palpably tinged with latter-day abolitionism? Why does T. S. Stribling write like a spiritual companion of Harriet Beecher Stowe and Clarence Darrow?

The answer is in every case the same. The Southern tradition in which these writers would share has been discredited and made artistically inaccessible; and the ideas, modes, attitudes that discredited it, largely not Southern, have been current and could be used. One has to look closely at the provincial Southern artists to discover traces of the indigenous Southern. Some would argue that this is as it should be. Perhaps they should not be expected to perform like Southerners, but like artists, and in that case we could do no better than to admonish them to be artists without regard to geography. Still it remains astonishing that they should adopt somebody else's geography and contrarily write like Northerners—at that, like Northerners made sick by an overdose of their own industrialism.

We should not here fall into the typically American mistake of imagining that admonition will succeed in getting the Southern artist to perform more like a Southerner and a provincial. For many reasons the Southern tradition deserves rehabilitation, but not among them is the reason that it would thus enable Southern artists to be strictly Southern artists. If the Southern tradition were an industrial tradition, it would deserve to be cast out rather than cherished. It happens, however, to be an agrarian tradition. And so it needs to be defined for the present age, as a mode of life congenial to the arts which are among the things we esteem as more than material blessings. In the emergency it needs, in fact, to be consciously studied and maintained by artists, Southern or not, as affording a last stand in America against the industrial devourer—a stand that might prove to be a turning-point.

The artist should not forget that in these times he is called on to play the part both of a person and of an artist. Of the two, that of person is more immediately important. As an artist he will do best to flee the infection of our times, to stand for decentralization in the arts, to resist with every atom of his strength the false gospels of art as a luxury which can be sold in commercial quantities or which can be hallowed by segregation in discreet shrines. But he cannot wage this fight by remaining on his perch as artist. He must be a person first of all, even though for the time being he may become less of an artist. He must enter the common arena and become a citizen. Whether he chooses, as citizen-person, to be a farmer or to run for Congress is a matter of individual choice; but in that general direction his duty lies.

FRANK LAWRENCE OWSLEY

THE IRREPRESSIBLE CONFLICT

I

FROM 1830 to 1861 the North and South quarreled with a savage fury that was unknown in the history of any country whose sections had been bound together by voluntary agreement. Finally war came, and the war which came was a war such as history had never recorded until that date. Over three millions of men from first to last marched forth to deadly combat, and nearly a million went down. This, out of a population of little more than twenty-five millions of white men meant that nearly one man in every six went to war. Europe first smiled contemptuously at the armed mobs of civilian soldiers who ran from one another at first Manassas, but stood pop-eyed with wonder and awe when Anglo-Saxons stood within ten paces of one another at Chickamauga and fired point-blank, mowing down one-third of the combatants, or marched up Cemetery Ridge at Gettysburg as on dress parade, or charged twenty deep at Cold Harbor with their addresses pinned to their backs, so that their dead bodies might be identified after being torn by artillery at close range.

Seldom has there been such a peace as that which followed Appomattox. While Sherman, Sheridan, and Grant

(61)

had allowed their armies to harry and plunder the population of the invaded country all too much, using churches, universities, and state capitols with their archives as stables for horses and mean men, General Grant could pause long enough during the deadly Spotsylvania Courthouse campaign to remove his hat at the house where Stonewall Jackson had died the year before and say, "General Jackson was a gallant soldier and a Christian gentleman." And Grant and Sherman were generous enough to refuse to take the side-arms and horses from the Southern soldiers who surrendered. But after the military surrender at Appomattox there ensued a peace unique in history. There was no generosity. For ten years the South, already ruined by the loss of nearly $2,000,000,000 invested in slaves, with its lands worthless, its cattle and stock gone, its houses burned, was turned over to the three millions of former slaves, some of whom could still remember the taste of human flesh and the bulk of them hardly three generations removed from cannibalism. These half-savage blacks were armed. Their passions were roused against their former masters by savage political leaders like Thaddeus Stevens, who advocated the confiscation of all Southern lands for the benefit of the negroes, and the extermination, if need be, of the Southern white population; and like Charles Sumner, whose chief regret had been that his skin was not black. Not only were the blacks armed; they were upheld and incited by garrisons of Northern soldiers, by Freedman's Bureau officials, and by Northern ministers of the gospel, and at length they were given the ballot while their former masters were disarmed and, to a large extent, disfranchised. For ten

(62)

years ex-slaves, led by carpetbaggers and scalawags, continued the pillages of war, combing the South for anything left by the invading armies, levying taxes, selling empires of plantations under the auction hammer, dragooning the Southern population, and visiting upon them the ultimate humiliations.

After the South had been conquered by war and humiliated and impoverished by peace, there appeared still to remain something which made the South different—something intangible, incomprehensible, in the realm of the spirit. That too must be invaded and destroyed; so there commenced a second war of conquest, the conquest of the Southern mind, calculated to remake every Southern opinion, to impose the Northern way of life and thought upon the South, write "error" across the pages of Southern history which were out of keeping with the Northern legend, and set the rising and unborn generations upon stools of everlasting repentance. Francis Wayland, former president of Brown University, regarded the South as "the new missionary ground for the national school-teacher," and President Hill of Harvard looked forward to the task for the North "of spreading knowledge and culture over the regions that sat in darkness." The older generations, the hardened campaigners under Lee and Jackson, were too tough-minded to reëducate. They must be ignored. The North must "treat them as Western farmers do the stumps in their clearings, work around them and let them rot out," but the rising and future generations were to receive the proper education in Northern tradition.

The South, in the days after the so-called Reconstruction,

was peculiarly defenseless against being educated by the North. Many leaders of the Civil War days were politically disfranchised or so saddened and depressed that they drew within themselves. From 1865 to 1880 the father of one of Alabama's later Governors refused to read a newspaper. His was only an extreme case of what was a general tendency, for the reading of the "news" was nothing but the annals of plunder, rape, murder, and endless injustices. Such old Spartans, living thus within themselves in order that they might live at all, built up around themselves a shell which cut them off spiritually from all that was going on about them. This, too, when many of them were still in their prime and fitted for many years of leadership. These were the men whom the Northern intellectual and spiritual plowmen were to plow around like stumps until they rotted out. Their older sons had been in the war. They adjusted themselves, if only to a degree. Their younger sons and daughters between 1865 and 1876 or later grew up wild and uncouth, either unable to attend school or too proud to attend school in company with their former slaves.

Hence, for thirty years after the Civil war the intellectual life of the South was as sterile as its own rocky uplands and sandy barrens. The rising generations read Northern literature, shot through with the New England tradition. Northern textbooks were used in Southern schools; Northern histories, despite the frantic protests of local patriotic organizations, were almost universally taught in Southern high schools and colleges,—books that were built around the Northern legend and either completely ignored the South or insisted upon the unrighteousness of most of its history and its philosophy of life. One would judge from the average history text and from the recitations conducted by the Northern schoolma'am that the Puritans and Pilgrim fathers were the ancestors of every self-respecting American. Southern children spoke of "our Puritan fathers." No child ever heard of the Southern Puritan fathers—the great horde of Scotch-Irish Presbyterians and German Lutherans and other strict and puritanical peoples who had pushed to the Mississippi River and far North of the Ohio before the New England population had got a hundred miles west of Boston.

In short, the South either had no history, or its history was tainted with slavery and rebellion and must be abjured. There was for the Southern child and youth until the end of the nineteenth century very little choice. They had to accept the Northern version of history with all its condemnations and carping criticisms of Southern institutions and life, with its chanting of "John Brown's Body," its hanging of Jeff Davis on a sour-apple tree, its hosannas to factories and mines and the growth of populations as the only criterion of progress, and the crying down and discrediting of anything agrarian as old-fashioned and backward. As time rolled on, the chorus of "John Brown's Body" swelled ever louder and louder until the lusty voices of grandchildren and great-grandchildren of rebels joined in the singing. Lee, largely through the perverse generosity of Charles Francis Adams, Jr., was permitted to be worshiped in the Southern edition of the Northern tradition because Lee made a good showing abroad as a represent-

(65)

ative of American military genius. However, Lincoln was the real Southern hero because Lincoln had saved the Union. So they were told!

Thus the North defeated the South in war, crushed and humiliated it in peace, and waged against it a war of intellectual and spiritual conquest. In this conquest the North fixed upon the South the stigma of war guilt, of slave guilt, of treason, and thereby shook the faith of its people in their way of living and in their philosophy of life.

II

But a people cannot live under condemnation and upon the philosophy of their conquerors. Either they must ultimately come to scorn the condemnation and the philosophy of those who thrust these things upon them, or their soul should and will perish.

Not all the Southern minds, fortunately, were conquered by the Northern conquest. Even a few Northern intellectuals revolted against such an unnatural and vicious procedure. The most outstanding instance of this tough-mindedness is found in the Northerner, William Archibald Dunning of Columbia University, and the group of Southern students whom he gathered about him to study the history of the Civil War and Reconstruction. It was among this group that the Southern renascence began and the holiness of the Northern legend was first challenged. The history of the Civil War and Reconstruction was written carefully and ably and with detachment by this group of Southern scholars, in such works as Garner's *Reconstruction in Mississippi*; Fleming's *Civil War and Reconstruction in*

Alabama, his *Documentary History of Reconstruction*, and his *Sequel of Appomattox*; Hamilton's *Reconstruction of North Carolina*; Ramsdall's *Reconstruction of Texas*; Staples' *Reconstruction of Arkansas*; and Davis's *Reconstruction of Florida*. The smugness of victory was somewhat undermined. Later followed other writers on this period of history who have been less detached and more outspoken:— such writers as Bowers, Stryker, and Beale—Northerners; and Eckenrode, Tate, Robert Penn Warren and others— Southerners. These men have scorned the injustice and hypocrisy of the condemnation of the South. But after all, mass opinion, prejudice, and smugness have not been touched by the efforts of such as these. The North still sits in Pharisaical judgment upon the South, beating its chest and thanking-Thee-O-Lord-that-I-am-not-as-other-men and imposing its philosophy of living and life upon the South. The South, confused, ill informed because taught by an alien doctrine so long, unconsciously accepts portions of the Northern legend and philosophy; sullenly and without knowing why, it rejects other portions, and withal knows not where to turn.

The South needs orientation and direction in its thinking, and all things must begin at the point where it was thrown from its balance. It must know that the things for which it stood were reasonable and sound, that its condemnation at the hands of the North has been contemptible, and that for it, at least, the philosophy of the North is the religion of an alien God. It is the hope of the essayists in this book to aid the South in its reorientation and in a return to its true philosophy. It is the particular object of this essay to point out the untruth of the self-righteous Northern legend which makes the South the war criminal.

III

What lay behind the bitter sectional quarreling between 1830 and 1860? What made the war which followed this quarreling so deadly? Why the cruel peace that followed war? Why the intellectual conquest of the South? The old answer for these questions and the answer which is yet given by the average Northerner is that the whole struggle from beginning to end was a conflict between light and darkness, between truth and falsehood, between slavery and freedom, between liberty and despotism. This is the ready answer of the Babbitts, who, unfortunately, have obtained much of their information from historians such as James Ford Rhodes and John Bach MacMaster. The Southern historians of the Dunning school, all the third-generation "rebel historians," and many of the recent Northern historians reject such an explanation as naïve if nothing else. They have become convinced that slavery as a moral issue is too simple an explanation, and that as one of the many contributing causes of war it needs an explanation which the North has never grasped—in fact, never can grasp until the negro race covers the North as thickly as it does the lower South. They are more inclined to take seriously the Southern championship of state rights in the face of centralization as a cause of the struggle; they see that the protective tariff was as fundamental in the controversy at times as the slavery question, and that the constant expansion of the United States by the annexation of territories

and the constant admission of new states from these territories was a vital factor in producing the Civil War—in
short, that the sectional controversies which finally resulted in the Civil War and its aftermath were deep rooted
and complex in origin, and that slavery as a moral issue has
too long been the red herring dragged across the trail.

Complex though the factors were which finally caused
war, they all grew out of two fundamental differences which
existed between the two sections: the North was commercial and industrial, and the South was agrarian. The fundamental and passionate ideal for which the South stood and
fell was the ideal of an agrarian society. All else, good and
bad, revolved around this ideal—the old and accepted manner of life for which Egypt, Greece, Rome, England, and
France had stood. History and literature, profane and sacred,
twined their tendrils about the cottage and the villa, not
the factory.

When America was settled, the tradition of the soil found
hospitable root-bed in the Southern colonies, where climate
and land combined to multiply the richness of an agrarian
economy. All who came to Virginia, Maryland, the Carolinas and Georgia were not gentlemen; in fact, only a few
were of the gentry. Most of them were of the yeomanry,
and they were from rural England with centuries of country and farm lore and folk memory. Each word, name,
sound, had grown from the soil and had behind it sweet
memory, stirring adventure, and ofttimes stark tragedy.
Thoughts, words, ideas, concepts, life itself, grew from
the soil. The environment all pointed toward an endless
enjoyment of the fruits of the soil. Jefferson, not visualizing

the industrial revolution which whipped up the multiplication of populations and tore their roots from the soil,
dreamed of America, free from England, as a boundless
Utopia of farms taking a thousand generations to fill.

Men so loved their life upon the soil that they sought
out in literature and history peoples who had lived a similar
life, so that they might justify and further stimulate their
own concepts of life and perhaps set a high goal for themselves among the great nations which had sprung from the
land. The people whom they loved most in the ancient
world were the Greeks and the Romans of the early republic. The Greeks did not appeal to them as did the Romans,
for they were too inclined to neglect their farms and turn
to the sea and to handicraft. But the even-poised and
leisurely life of the Greeks, their oratory, their philosophy,
their art—especially their architecture—appealed to the
South. The Greek tradition became partly grafted upon the
Anglo-Saxon and Scotch tradition of life. However, it was
the Romans of the early republic, before land speculators
and corn laws had driven men from the soil to the city
slums, who appealed most powerfully to the South. These
Romans were brave, sometimes crude, but open and without guile—unlike the Greeks. They reeked of the soil, of
the plow and the spade; they had wrestled with virgin soil
and forests; they could build log houses and were closer
to many Southerners than even the English gentleman in
his moss-covered stone house. It was Cincinnatus, whose
hands were rough with guiding the plow, rather than Cato,
who wrote about Roman agriculture and lived in a villa,
whom Southerners admired the most, though they read and

admired Cato as a fine gentleman with liberal ideas about tenants and slaves and a thorough knowledge and love of the soil. The Gracchi appealed to Southerners because the Gracchi were lovers of the soil and died in the attempt to restore the yeomanry to the land.

With the environment of the New World and the traditions of the Old, the South thus became the seat of an agrarian civilization which had strength and promise for a future greatness second to none. The life of the South was leisurely and unhurried for the planter, the yeoman, or the landless tenant. It was a way of life, not a routine of planting and reaping merely for gain. Washington, who rode daily over his farms and counted his horses, cattle, plows, and bushels of corn as carefully as a merchant takes stock of his supplies, inhaled the smell of ripe corn after a rain, nursed his bluegrass sod and shade trees with his own hands, and, when in the field as a soldier or in the city as President of the United States, was homesick at the smell of fresh-plowed earth. He kept vigil with his sick horses and dogs, not as a capitalist who guards his investments, but as one who watches over his friends.

The system of society which developed in the South, then, was close to the soil. It might be organized about the plantation with its wide fields and its slaves and self-sufficiency, or it might center around a small farm, ranging from a fifty-acre to a five-hundred-acre tract, tilled by the owner, undriven by competition, supplied with corn by his own toil and with meat from his own pen or from the fields and forests. The amusements might be the fine balls and house parties of the planter or the three-day break-down dances

(71)

which David Crockett loved, or horse races, foot races, cock and dog fights, boxing, wrestling, shooting, fighting, log-rolling, house raising, or corn-shucking. It might be crude or genteel, but it everywhere was fundamentally alike and natural. The houses were homes, where families lived sufficient and complete within themselves, working together and fighting together. And when death came, they were buried in their own lonely peaceful graveyards, to await dooms-day together.

IV

This agrarian society had its own interests, which in almost all respects diverged from the interests of the industrial system of the North. The two sections, North and South, had entered the revolution against the mother country with the full knowledge of the opposing interests of their societies; knowing this difference, they had combined in a loose union under the Articles of Confederation. Finally, they had joined together under the Constitution fully conscious that there were thus united two divergent economic and social systems, two civilizations, in fact. The two sections were evenly balanced in population and in the number of states, so that at the time there was no danger of either section's encroaching upon the interests of the other. This balance was clearly understood. Without it a union would not have been possible. Even with the understanding that the two sections would continue to hold this even balance, the sections were very careful to define and limit the powers of the federal government lest one section with its peculiar interests should get control of the national government and use the powers of that government to exploit the other section. Specific powers were granted the federal government, and all not specifically granted were retained by the states.

But equilibrium was impossible under expansion and growth. One section with its peculiar system of society would at one time or another become dominant and control the national government and either exploit the other section or else fail to exercise the functions of government for its positive benefit. Herein lies the irrepressible conflict, the eternal struggle between the agrarian South and the commercial and industrial North to control the government either in its own interest or, negatively, to prevent the other section from controlling it in its interests. Lincoln and Seward and the radical Republicans clothed the conflict later in robes of morality by making it appear that the "house divided against itself" and the irrepressible conflict which resulted from this division marked a division between slavery and freedom.

Slavery, as we shall see, was part of the agrarian system, but only one element and not an essential one. To say that the irrepressible conflict was between slavery and freedom is either to fail to grasp the nature and magnitude of the conflict, or else to make use of deliberate deception by employing a shibboleth to win the uninformed and unthinking to the support of a sinister undertaking. Rob Roy MacGregor, one of the chief corruptionists of the present-day power lobby, said that the way the power companies crush opposition and win popular support is to pin the word "bolshevik" upon the leaders of those who oppose the power-lobby program. The leaders of the Northern industrial system could win popular support by tagging their opponents as *"enemies of liberty"* and themselves as "champions of freedom." This they did. Lincoln was a politician and knew all the tricks of a politician. Seward was a politician and knew every *in* and *out*. This is true of other leaders of the "party of high ideals" which assumed the name of Republican party. Doubtless, Lincoln, Seward, and others were half sincere in their idea of an irrepressible conflict, but their fundamental purpose was to win elections and get their party into power—the party of the industrial North—with an industrial program for business and a sop of free lands for the Western farmer.

The irrepressible conflict, then, was not between slavery and freedom, but between the industrial and commercial civilization of the North and the agrarian civilization of the South. The industrial North demanded a high tariff so as to monopolize the domestic markets, especially the Southern market, for the South, being agrarian, must purchase all manufactured goods. It was an exploitative principle, originated at the expense of the South and for the benefit of the North. After the South realized that it would have little industry of its own, it fought the protective tariff to the point of nullification in South Carolina and almost to the point of dissolving the Union. In this as in other cases Southerners saw that what was good for the North was fatal to the South.

The industrial section demanded a national subsidy for the shipping business and merchant marine, but, as the merchant marine was alien to the Southern agrarian system, the two sections clashed. It was once more an exploitation of one section for the benefit of the other.

The industrial North demanded internal improvements—roads, railroads, canals—at national expense to furnish transportation for its goods to Southern and Western markets which were already hedged around for the benefit of the North by the tariff wall. The South objected to internal improvements at national expense because it had less need of transportation than the North and because the burden would be heavier on the South and the benefits greater for the North—another exploitation of the Southern system. The North favored a government-controlled bank; but as corporate wealth and the quick turnover of money were confined to that section, such an institution would be for the sole benefit, the South believed, of the North. There were many other things of a positive nature which the system of society in the North demanded of the federal government, but those mentioned will illustrate the conflict of interest between North and South.

It is interesting to observe that all the favors thus asked by the North were of doubtful constitutional right, for nowhere in the Constitution were these matters specifically mentioned; it is further significant that all the powers and favors thus far demanded by the North were merely negatived by the South; no substitute was offered. The North was demanding positive action on the part of the federal government, and the South was demanding that no action be taken at all. In fact, it may be stated as a general principle that the agrarian South asked practically nothing of the federal government in domestic legislation. It might be imperialistic in its foreign policy, but its domestic policy was almost entirely negative. Even in the matter of public lands the South favored turning over these lands to the state within which they lay, rather than have them controlled by the federal government.

Had these differences, inherent in agrarian and industrial civilizations, been the only ones, it is obvious that conflict would have been inevitable and that two different political philosophies would have been developed to justify and rationalize the conflict which was foreshadowed in the very nature of the demands of the sections: centralization in the North and state rights in the South. But there was another and deadlier difference. There was the slavery system in the South. Before examining the Southern doctrine of state rights, which was its defense mechanism for its entire system of society rather than, as has been claimed, for slavery alone, let us turn to the slavery problem as one of the elements of conflict between the two sections.

v

Slavery was no simple question of ethics; it cut across the categories of human thought like a giant question mark. It was a moral, an economic, a religious, a social, a philosophical, and above all a political question. It was no essential part of the agrarian civilization of the South—though the Southerners under attack assumed that it was. Without slavery the economic and social life of the South would have not been radically different. Perhaps the plantation life would not have been as pronounced without it, yet the South would long have remained agricultural—as it still is after sixty-five years of "freedom"! Certainly the South would have developed its political philosophy very much as it did. Yet the slavery question furnished more fuel to sectional conflict and created more bitterness than any or all the other elements of the two groups.

Slavery had been practically forced upon the country by England—over the protest of colonial assemblies. During the eighteenth century it had ceased to be profitable, and colonial moral indignation rose correspondingly. However, when the Revolution came and the Southern colonies gained their independence, they did not free the negroes. The eternal race question had reared itself. Negroes had come into the Southern Colonies in such numbers that people feared for the integrity of the white race. For the negroes were cannibals and barbarians, and therefore dangerous. No white man who had any contact with slavery was willing to free the slaves and allow them to dwell among the whites. Slaves were a peril, at least a risk, but free blacks were considered a menace too great to be hazarded. Even if no race wars occurred, there was dread of being submerged and absorbed by the black race. Accordingly, all slaveholders and non-slaveholders who objected to slavery, objected even more to the presence of the free negro. They argued that the slaves could never be freed unless they could be deported back to Africa or to the West Indies. This conviction became more fervent when the terrifying negro insurrections in Santo Domingo and Hayti destroyed the white population and civilizations almost completely and submerged the remainder under barbarian control. All early abolitionists—which meant most

(77)

of the Southern people up until around 1800—were abolitionists only on condition of colonization. As a result there
were organized many colonization societies, mostly in the
South during this period.

But colonization was futile. It was soon realized by all
practical slaveholders that the negroes could not be deported successfully. Deportation was cruel and expensive.
Few of the black people wished to leave the South. The
Southern whites shrugged their shoulders and deplored the
necessity of continuing the negroes in bondage as the only
alternative to chaos and destruction.

Then the invention of the cotton gin and the opening
of the cotton lands in the Southwest, 1810-36, made the
negro slave an economic instrument of great advantage.
With the aid of the fresh cheap lands and the negro slave
vast fortunes were made in a few years. Both North and
South having now conceded that emancipation was impossible, the Southern planters made the most of their new
cotton kingdom with a fairly easy conscience. They had
considered emancipation honestly and fairly and had found
it out of the question. Their skirts were clear. Let the blood
of slavery rest upon the heads of those who had forced it
upon the South.

But the opening of the "cotton kingdom" gave dynamic
power to the agrarian section, and new lands were desired
by the West and South. The now industrial East saw its
interest threatened if the South should colonize the territories to the West, including those gained and to be gained.
With the tremendous impetus given to the expansion of
the Southern system by the growth of the cotton industry

(78)

and culture, the North became uneasy and began to show opposition to the continued balance of power. This first became manifest in the struggle which resulted in the Missouri Compromise of 1822. Up to this point the objection to slavery was always tempered by the acknowledgment on the part of the North that the South was a victim of the system of slavery and ought to be sympathized with, rather than the instigator of the system, who ought to be condemned as a criminal.

But in 1831 a voice was raised which was drowned only in the roar of battle in 1861-5. It was the cry of William Lloyd Garrison that slavery was a crime and the slaveholders were criminals. He established the famous *Liberator*, which preached unremitting and ruthless war upon slavery and the slaveholder. He knew no moderation. He had no balance or sense of consequence. His was the typical "radical" mind which demands that things be done at once, which tries to force nature, which wants to tear up by the roots. Although he was completely ignorant of the South and of negro slavery, he dogmatically assumed an omniscient power of judgment over the section and the institution. In the *Liberator* or in the anti-slavery tracts fostered by the anti-slavery societies which he aided or instigated, he set no bounds of accusation and denunciation. The slave master, said Garrison, debauched his women slaves, had children by them, and in turn defiled his own children and sold them into the slave market; the slave plantation was primarily a gigantic harem for the master and his sons. The handsome octaroon coachmen shared the bed of the mistress when the master was away from home, and the daughters were frequently away in some secluded nook to rid themselves of undesirable negro offspring. Ministers of the gospel who owned or sanctioned slavery were included in his sweeping indictment of miscegenation and prostitution. In short, Garrison and the anti-slavery societies which he launched, followed soon by Northern churchmen, stigmatized the South as a black brothel. This was not all! The Southern slaveowners were not merely moral lepers; they were cruel and brooding tyrants, who drove their slaves till they dropped and died, who starved them to save food, let them go cold and almost naked to save clothing, let them dwell in filthy pole pens rather than build them comfortable cottages, beat them unmercifully with leather thongs filled with spikes, dragged cats over their bodies and faces, trailed them with bloodhounds which rent and chewed them,— then sprinkled their wounds with salt and red pepper. Infants were torn from their mothers' breasts and sold to Simon Legrees; families were separated and scattered to the four winds. This brutal treatment of the slaves reacted upon the masters and made them brutal and cruel in their dealings with their fellow whites. Such charges, printed in millions upon millions of pamphlets, were sent out all over the world. Sooner or later, much of it was accepted as true in the North.

In the South this abolition war begot Nat Turner's rebellion, in which negro slaves in Virginia under the leadership of Nat Turner, a freedman, massacred their masters, including women and children. The new situation, in turn, begot a revolution in Southern attitudes. Struck almost out of a clear sky by the Garrisonian blasts and the Nat Turner rebellion, Southern leaders were dazed. They discussed momentarily the expedient of freeing the slaves, then closed forever their minds upon the subject as too dangerous to undertake. Then came a counter-blast of fierce resentment, denying all accusations. The South threw up a defense mechanism. The ministers searched the Scriptures by day and night and found written, in language which could not be misunderstood, a biblical sanction of slavery. Abraham, Moses, the prophets, Jesus, and the disciples on many occasions had approved slavery. History from its dawn had seen slavery almost everywhere. A scriptural and historical justification was called in to meet the general indictment of the wrongfulness of slavery in the abstract. Partly as a result of this searching of the Scriptures there took place a religious revival in the South, which had tended heretofore to incline to Jeffersonian liberalism of the deistic type. The South became devoutly orthodox and literal in its theology. But the abolitionists were not willing to accept scriptural justification of slavery. There was an attempt to prove the wrongfulness of slavery by the same sacred book, but, finding this impossible, many abolitionists repudiated the Scriptures as of divine origin. Partly as a result, the North lost confidence in orthodoxy and tended to become deistic as the South had been. One could almost hear Puritan New England creaking upon its theological hinges as it swung away from its old position.

But there were philosophers and thinkers at work in the South who would meet the abolitionists upon their own grounds. Hammond, Fitzhugh, John C. Calhoun, Chancellor Harper, Thomas R. Dew, either because they felt that scriptural justification of slavery was inadequate or because they realized the necessity of getting away from the theological grounds in order that they might combat the abolitionists upon common ground, approached slavery from the social and economic standpoint. Their general conclusions were that two races of different culture and color cannot live together on terms of equality. One will dominate or destroy the other. There was no middle ground. It had ever been thus. They contended that the negro was of a backward, inferior race. Certainly his culture was inferior. He must either rule or be ruled. If he ruled, the white race would be destroyed or submerged and its civilization wiped out. For the Southern people there was no choice; the negro must be ruled, and the only way he could be controlled, they believed, was by some form of slavery. In other words, Calhoun, Fitzhugh, and the "philosophers of slavery" justified slavery upon the grounds of the "race question"—which U. B. Phillips has called the theme of Southern history, before and after the Civil War. Aside from the scriptural and social justification, these men defended slavery as an economic necessity. They contended that the culture of rice, tobacco, sugar cane, and especially cotton upon which the world depended could not be carried on without slaves. The South, including the up-country and the mountains, accepted the scriptural justification of slavery, to a great extent. The up-country did not accept the economics of slavery, but slavery, in its aspect as a race question, was universally approved in valleys, plains and mountains. It found, in fact, its strongest supporters among the poor whites and the non-slaveholding small landowners.

(82)

Their race prejudice and fears were the stronger because they knew nothing of the better side of the negro and regarded him as a vicious and dangerous animal whose freedom meant war to the knife and knife to the death. It was the old fear which we have spoken of, common to all in the days of the Revolution and in the days when Jefferson and Washington were advocating emancipation only on condition that the freedman be sent from the country. Outside of the common agrarianism of the multitudinous sections of the South which acted as a common tie, the race question which underlay slavery, magnified and aggravated by the abolition crusade, was the hoop of steel which held men together in the South in the great final argument of arms.

This abolition crusade on the part of the North and justification of slavery by the South were principally outside of the realm of politics in the beginning. The abolitionists, in fact, had a tendency to abjure politics and demand "direct action," as some of our recent radicals do. But the leaven soon spread, and slavery became a burning political issue. The political leaders of the North, especially the Whigs, after the dynamic growth of the South in the first quarter of the nineteenth century, became fixed in their determination that the agrarian section should have its metes and bounds definitely limited. Industrialism, which had undergone an even greater development than had cotton-growing, declared that the balance of power between agrarian and industrial sections must go. Because slaveholding was the acid test as to whether a state would remain agrarian or become eventually industrial, the Northern leaders wished that no more slave states should be carved from the Western territories. Between 1836, when the annexation of slaveholding Texas was advocated by the South, and 1860, when Lincoln was elected upon a platform which declared that no more territory was open to slavery, the major issues in national politics were the struggles between North and South over the admission or exclusion of slavery from the national territories. That is, it was a question whether the territories would be equally open to both sections or whether the North should have an exclusive right in these territories to found its own states and system and thereby destroy the balance of power and control the federal government in the interest of its own economic and social system. Unfortunately for the South, the leaders of the North were able to borrow the language of the abolitionists and clothed the struggle in a moral garb. It was good politics, it was noble and convenient, to speak of it as a struggle for freedom when it was essentially a struggle for the balance of power.

So to the bitter war of the abolitionists and the bitter resentment of the South was added the fight over the balance of power in the form of the extension of slavery into the common territories.

VI

As it has been suggested, had there not been slavery as an added difference between the agrarian South and industrial North, the two sections would have developed each its own political philosophy to explain and justify its institutions and its demands upon the federal government. The

(84)

North had interests which demanded positive legislation exploitative of the agrarian South; the South had interests which demanded that the federal government refrain entirely from legislation within its bounds—it demanded only to be let alone. While this conflict of interest was recognized as existing in the days of the Revolution when the first attempt at union was made, it was not until the first government under the Constitution was in power that it received a philosophical statement. In the beginning of Washington's administration two men defined the fundamental principles of the political philosophy of the two societies, Alexander Hamilton for the North and Jefferson for the South. The one was extreme centralization, the other was extreme decentralization; the one was nationalistic and the other provincial; the first was called Federalism, the other State Rights, but in truth the first should have been called Unitarianism and the second Federalism.

It has been often said that the doctrine of state rights was not sincere, but that it was a defense mechanism to protect slavery (implying that slavery was merely a moral question and the South entirely immoral). But Jefferson was an abolitionist, as nearly all the Southern people were at the time the doctrine was evolved and stated by Jefferson, and Calhoun's extreme doctrine of state sovereignty was fully evolved in South Carolina before the crusade had begun against slavery. However, there is no doubt that the bitter abolition crusade and the political controversies between the two sections between 1836 and 1861 over slavery in the territories gave added strength and exactness to the Southern doctrine. Another thrust has been made at the sincerity

(85)

of the doctrine of state rights: the principle has been laid down that state rights is a cowardly defense used by the industrial interests to shield themselves against the unfriendly action of a more powerful government. Such examples are noted as the extreme sensitiveness of big business to state rights in the matter of federal child-labor laws, federal control of water power, and prohibition. It is not to be denied that it should be easier for the water-power companies to purchase a state than a national legislature—as the market price of a Congressman is supposed to be somewhat higher than a mere state legislator (though there are certain well-known purchases of Congressmen which seem to contradict this impression). But observe the other side of the question. Big business has more often taken refuge behind the national government than behind the state. I have only to call attention to the way in which corporations take refuge behind the Fourteenth Amendment to avoid state legislation, to the numberless cases brought before the Supreme Court of the United States by corporations whose charters have been vitiated or nullified by state action, to the refuge sought by the railroads in national protection against the state granger legislation, and to the eternal whine of big business for paternalistic and exploitative legislation such as the tariff, the ship and railroad subsidies. Historically, then, the vested interests of industrialism have not had any great use for state rights. They are the founders of the doctrine of centralization, of the Hamiltonian and Republican principles; they have controlled the Republican party; why should they be unfriendly to their own principles and their own political instrument? They have not been! It may be suggested as a principle that for positive exploitation big business has desired large and sweeping powers for the national government, and that for negative business of defense it will hide behind any cover convenient, whether it be a state or the Fourteenth Amendment. The assertion that state rights was a defense mechanism evolved by slaveowners, for corporations later to hide behind, is inadequate if nothing else.

But state rights was a defense mechanism, and its defensive ramparts were meant by its disciples to protect things far more fundamental and larger than slave property. It was the doctrine of an agrarian society meant in the first place to protect the South as a whole against the encroachments of the industrial and commercial North. By upholding the doctrine of a rigid division of powers between state and nation and the literal interpretation of the Constitution such legislation as protective tariffs, ship subsidies, national banks, internal improvements at federal expense, would be avoided. It would also protect one part of the South against another. While there were infinite diverging interests between the industrial North and agrarian South which made a doctrine of state rights the only safe bulwark against Northern exploitation and encroachment, there were great regional differences within the South itself which made legislation that was beneficial to one section, harmful to another. One section grew cotton and cane, another tobacco and rice, another produced naval stores and lumber; one had slaves, another had none. To throw all these interests into a hodge-podge under one government would be to sacrifice all the minority interests to the one which was represented by the largest population and body of voters. Even among themselves the agrarians felt their local interests safer in the hands of the state than in the hands of a national government. But this was not the end of the logic of local self-government and regional autonomy. The states in turn, because of diverging interests between the Tidewater and Piedmont areas, allowed a large sweep to county government, and built up a system of representation for both state and federal government which would tend to place legislative power in the hands of economic groups and regions rather than in the hands of the people according to their numbers.

The whole idea then was local self-government, decentralization, so that each region should be able to defend itself against the encroachment of the other regions. It was not a positive doctrine; it did not contemplate a program of exploitative legislation at the expense of other regions. An unmixed agrarian society such as Jefferson and Calhoun had in mind called for no positive program. Such a society, as Jefferson visualized it, called for only enough government to prevent men from injuring one another. It was, by its very nature, a *laissez faire* society, an individualistic society where land, water, and timber were practically free. It only asked to be let alone. State rights, local and regional autonomy, did not make for a uniform, standardized society and government. It took cognizance of the fundamental difference between the agrarian South and West on the one hand and the commercial and growing industrial system of the East on the other; and it still further took note, as we have said, of the regional and local differences within

(88)

each of these systems. It might not make for a neat and orderly system of government, but this was the price of social and economic freedom, the price of bringing into one Union so many different groups and interests.

The interests pointed out have been largely economic and social. These were not the only interests which the state-rights doctrine was expected to protect from an overbearing and unsympathizing national government. Perhaps the greatest vested interest was "personal liberty," the old Anglo-Saxon principles expressed in the Magna Carta, bill of rights, habeas corpus act, supported in the American Revolution, and engrafted finally in every state constitution of the independent states, as "bills of rights." These bills of rights guaranteed freedom of religion, freedom of speech, of thought, of press, of assembly, right of petition, freedom from arbitrary arrest and imprisonment, right of trial by jury, and prohibited the taking of property without due process of law—guaranteed, in short, the fundamental rights which Jefferson had called the "inalienable rights of man" and Locke and Rousseau had called the "natural rights"—right of life, liberty, property, and the free pursuit of happiness as long as the free pursuit of this object did not encroach upon the pursuit of another's just rights. The famous Virginia and Kentucky Resolutions of 1798-9 had been directed at the violation of these liberties. The Alien and Sedition laws which had been pushed through Congress during the Adams administration had struck at many of these. Under the Sedition Act men had been prosecuted for criticizing the President or members of Congress or judges and had been sent to prison in violation of

(89)

the Constitutional guarantee of freedom of speech. Opinion had been suppressed, meetings broken up, arbitrary arrests made, men held without trial; in fact, the whole body of personal liberties had been brushed aside by the Federalist or centralizing party eight years after the founding of the present federal system under the Constitution. Jefferson and Madison, supported by the state-rights apostle of Virginia, John Taylor of Caroline, and the irascible old democrat, John Randolph, proclaimed that the federal government had thus shown itself to be an unsafe protector of liberty. So Jefferson announced in his inaugural, which was made possible by the excesses of the centralizing party of the East, that the states were the safest guardians of human liberty and called on all to support "the state governments in all their rights, as the most competent administrations for our domestic concerns and the surest bulwark against anti-republican tendencies." The founder of the party of the agrarian South and West upheld state rights as the safest guardian of the liberties and the domestic interests of the people.

VII

Thus the two sections clashed at every point. Their economic systems and interests conflicted. Their social systems were hostile; their political philosophies growing out of their economic and social systems were as impossible to reconcile as it is to cause two particles of matter to occupy the same space at the same time; and their philosophies of life, growing out of the whole situation in each section, were as two elements in deadly combat. What was food for the one was poison for the other.

When the balance of power was destroyed by the rapid growth of the North, and the destruction of this balance was signalized in the election of Lincoln by a frankly sectional, hostile political party, the South, after a futile effort at obtaining a concession from Lincoln which would partly restore the balance of power, dissolved its partnership with the industrial North.

This struggle between an agrarian and an industrial civilization, then, was the irrepressible conflict, the house divided against itself, which must become according to the doctrine of the industrial section all the one or all the other. It was the doctrine of intolerance, crusading, standardizing alike in industry and in life. The South had to be crushed out; it was in the way; it impeded the progress of the machine. So Juggernaut drove his car across the South.

JOHN GOULD FLETCHER

EDUCATION,
PAST AND PRESENT

"*The ordinance of heaven is termed the natural law; the principle which directs us to conform our actions to the natural law is called the rule of moral conduct, or the right path; the organized system of rules of moral conduct which puts us on this path is called the doctrine of duties or of institutions.*

"*The rule of moral conduct which should direct our actions is so obligatory that we cannot escape from it on a single point, or for a single instant. If we could escape it, it would no longer be an unchangeable rule of conduct. That is why the superior man, he who follows the right path, keeps watch in his heart over the principles which are not perceived by the many, and he meditates carefully on that which is not openly proclaimed or recognized as doctrine.*

"*Nothing is more evident for the sage than the things hidden in the secret conscience; nothing is more manifest to him than the most subtle causes of actions. That is why the superior man pays attention to the secret inspirations of his conscience.*

"*Before joy, satisfaction, anger, sorrow are produced in the soul, the state in which one finds oneself is known as balance. When they are produced in the soul, and have not attained beyond a certain limit, the state in which one finds oneself is called harmony. Balance is*

(92)

*the great fundamental basis of the world; harmony is
the universal and permanent law.*

*"When balance and harmony are carried to the point
of perfection, heaven and earth are in a state of complete tranquillity, and all beings receive their perfect
development."*—CONFUCIUS, *Chung-Yung,* chapter I.

I

THAT the human being is nothing without education
may be taken as an axiom; but what is education, or
rather what is the purpose of education? It is to bring out
something that is already potentially existent in the human
being. Thus we may be educated simply by using our own
natural faculties of observation, comparison, and application to the utmost; and many great men in the course of
the world's history have been thus educated. Or we may
go through school after school and college after college and
emerge more of a fool than the meanest farm labourer,
who knows, with precision, from the lore handed down
from his fathers, when it is likely to rain, when to sow and
reap, and what to give his cattle when they are ailing. All
that education can do in any case is to teach us to make good
use of what we are; if we are nothing to begin with, no
amount of education can do us any good.

It is necessary to state this at the outset, and to insist
upon it during the essay that follows, because the idea has
gotten abroad during recent years that we Americans are
destined to the leadership of the world precisely because of
our present-day system of education. The end of the Great
War witnessed in our country an outburst of enthusiasm

for education that has probably never been paralleled anywhere else in the world. It is safe to say that during the past ten years more sums of money have been spent on educational schemes in our country than had been spent from the time of the first permanent colony in Virginia down to the close of the Civil War—a period, be it remembered, of more than two hundred and fifty years. The last decade has witnessed everywhere in the United States an immense expansion of all the existing institutions of learning, and the establishment of dozens of others. So much has the educational scene changed that many an old graduate from some school that was well known before 1914, if he returns today to some anniversary reunion of his class, can recognize hardly a single building that was connected with the days when he mistranslated Virgil, or worked out algebraic equations on the blackboard. The very sites of a great many famous schools have been changed beyond recognition. As for lectureships, scholarships, endowments, it is simply impossible to enumerate them.

Yet all this bustle, all this fever and agony over the way we propose to produce first-class men and women, had its origin some seventy years ago. What we are witnessing today is merely the climax of a process that began about the time of the Civil War. The educational system of any community is very often the last thing that changes under the pressure of novel conditions; it follows the sound conservative principle which also exists in all other human affairs, that so long as a system is producing good results, it is useless to meddle or tinker further with it. Although the American States had achieved, in the political sphere, the essence of representative democracy long before George III and his ministers began to meddle with them, their system of education remained, after independence had been achieved, essentially what it was before; the system common in England and throughout European countries at the close of the eighteenth century. And this system in England still largely follows the lines laid down in the Middle Ages, established and fortified at the Renaissance.

The object of this essay is to try and show how and why this system became modified in America, first in the North and later in the South; what were the causes and results of the resultant overwhelming change; and lastly, to discuss what might be done to insure that our education be again put on a sound, historical, and conservative basis. For we shall not follow the custom of popular writers for the journalistic press, of assuming that because a man has been educated according to the principles of the eighteenth century, which taught him merely what might make him a reasonable being capable of reading the classics and understanding the value of a good conversation, he was thereby an uneducated man. We shall not even reproach our own mountaineer, poor white folk, for their little schooling and simpler manners, and for lacking those arts and graces that make the public-school product of New York City or Chicago a behaviorist, an experimental scientist in sex and firearms, a militant atheist, a reader of detective fiction, and a good salesman. For our knowledge of history teaches us this much: that the object of public education in the American Colonies and the later states up to 1865, was to produce good men. The system may have been imperfect in detail, but its aim was correct. Today the object of American education is to turn out graduates—whether good, bad, or indifferent we neither know nor care. Formerly, quantity had to give place to quality; today it is the reverse. Formerly we followed Goethe's maxim, to the effect that everything that frees man's soul, but does not give him command over himself, is evil. Today we are out to withdraw the command of men over themselves, and to free, to no purpose, their souls.

A brief glance at Southern educational history is necessary if we are to understand the revolution in educational theory and practice, that, set in motion after 1865, has worked as effectively to destroy the culture and leisure of our section as the present plague of factories and rash of cheap automobiles. Up to 1700, the population of the Southern Colonies was predominatingly English. The system of education introduced, therefore, was the system as evolved in England during the seventeenth century, resting upon the Latin grammar school, private tutorships in houses of the well-to-do, and the apprenticeship system, whereby poor orphans were bound to a trade and taught at least to read and write, at the public expense. Owing to the sparseness of population, the absence of urban settlements, and the poor means of communication, the grammar schools developed late in the South, and such institutions as Harvard and Yale (which began as grammar schools) took precedence in time of William and Mary in Virginia. Another difference needs be noted. What education there was in the Southern Colonies was in the hands of the Church of England, whereas in New England it was organized by rebellious dissenting sects.[1] For this reason, since the Established Church, in the persons of its churchwardens and min:_ters, was intrusted with the working of the English poor laws, which had come into operation with James I, there was probably actually more education of the poor in the South than in the North. For by the provisions of this law, which were later faithfully copied in Virginia and the other Southern Colonies, the overseers of the poor were obliged to expend the poor rate, paid by the parish, in binding orphans and other poor children as apprentices in certain trades, and were enjoined at the same time, "to educate and instruct them according to their best endeavours in the Christian religion and in the rudiments of learning" (quoted from the Virginia law of 1643). By later laws in Virginia, followed in all the other Southern Colonies, the master of every orphan bound to apprenticeship to service was legally obliged to teach him to read and write, and the elements of common arithmetic. This applied to all white indentured servants as well as to all apprentices to a trade, of whom there were in the South a great number. Later, by legislative enactment, it also applied to the negroes, in some states.

There was, be it noted, little of all this in New England. The New England Colonies also possessed the apprenticeship system, but in their case the number of apprentices was smaller, and less was done for them. It must be remembered that colonization in the North and the South

[1] It is interesting to note that the Society for the Propagation of the Gospel in Foreign Parts, an auxiliary of the Established Church, established missions, libraries, and schools, and supported teachers, in all the Southern Colonies except Virginia, by 1705.

came from two very different sources. In the North, the Colonists were dissenters from the Established Church, well-to-do members of the landowning or merchant class who had come to America precisely because of their quarrel with the Established Church, and who regarded education primarily as a means of training theological students in what they regarded as the correct doctrines. In the South, the Colonists were, on the other hand, dispossessed, poor, fleeing to Virginia or the Carolinas to better their fortunes, broken-down cavaliers after 1640, political refugees and adventurers of all sorts, and, after 1700, Germans and Scotch-Irish in increasing numbers. In the year of America's independence, it has been estimated that 225,000 Germans and 385,000 Scotch-Irish were in the Colonies, and of these a very great proportion, if not a majority, had settled in the South. The Scotch-Irish were in fact the first to establish classical schools in the South, and their influence on subsequent education was very great. Owing to the racial and religious diversity of the populations that settled in the South, compared to the uniformity of caste and observance which prevailed in New England, the pre-Revolutionary schools of the South were on the whole much more tolerant, more free and easy, more humanistic, and more open to all classes of the population than the corresponding schools of the North, which were tinged with the somber colours of Calvinistic, Congregational, or Unitarian orthodoxy.

With the coming of the Revolution, the Establishment of the English Church lapsed in all the Colonies, North as well as South. Along with it lapsed the system prevailing

(98)

in the South, of importing private tutors from England to the sons of well-to-do planters. This was in a sense a victory for the North, which had always resisted the too-worldly, secular, and conservative attitude of the Church. But the South found a means of transmitting to its own people the essentials of a good classical education, by the growth of an institution that never, to the same degree, affected the North. This institution was the academy. It was by its means and its operation that the older Southern life and culture became what it was, and remained until the catastrophe of 1861-5. But before we discuss the academy we must turn back to the larger question that has concerned us from the outset—the question of the object of all education.

II

We have a mental habit—not the least pernicious of all our habits—of regarding the savage races of mankind as rude and uncultivated, and of ourselves by contrast as "civilized" and even "progressive." But a few hours of reading at anthropology suffices to dissipate the illusion that there are any races on the earth's surface so primitive as to lack all the elements of culture. Apart, perhaps, from the extinct Tasmanians, the nearly extinct Bushmen, and a few other interesting survivals here and there, man shows at the very outset of his career the elements of tribal confederation. This, like the later social organizations of the clan, the family, the city-state, and the religious brotherhood, is essentially a band of individuals held together by certain practices which, it is assumed, will be of mutual benefit to its members. The tribe lives and acts in common, and its actions are motivated by a complete knowledge, embodied in totemism and taboo, of what is permitted and what is forbidden. These taboos—religious, social, moral—are the unwritten but infrangible laws of the tribal community. They represent the unconscious demands of that community embodied in definite practice—and all the actions of the tribe must respond to them. Culture without such a system of taboos is not culture, and we cannot understand the early Greeks, the American Indians, or any other race of antiquity without understanding first of all the system of taboos and of licit and illicit practices from which they sprang and took their being. The fact that these taboos were unconsciously assumed before all else gave to the tribes practicing them the quality above all of balance, embodied in the Confucian quotation that heads this essay.

When the Revolution came to the American Colonies, and succeeded in its aim of promoting political independence, the church-aided schemes of education under the guidance of church wardens and justices of the peace for the benefit of poor children, together with the system of importing private tutors to teach in well-to-do plantations, necessarily lapsed in the Southern States. Henceforward education was left, as the Revolution had been, to the enthusiasm and support of private individuals. It was felt, on the part of the chief leaders of the successful Revolution, that it was worth while to acquire the training of a gentleman. It was assumed that those who wanted to be thus educated would band together to get it and to pay for it. That a natural demand for schools would of itself create the supply, was the basis of this assumption; not, as at the present day, that all we have to do, in the matter of schools and of everything else, is to provide an unlimited supply in order to build up new and impossible demands.

Thus the private academy sprang up, stimulated by local endowments, governed by boards of trustees drawn from the most respectable members of the community, incorporated by the laws of the state, but not dependent on the state for support, situated frequently on a plot of waste ground of no particular value to the community, and consisting of anything from a single log building to a number of more or less well-built structures. Some were little better than the "old field schools" of the raw frontier, though they pretended to teach more; others, put up by especially public-spirited bodies of citizens, or by growing religious sects, were the equal, if not the superior, of the over-weighted preparatory schools of the North today. They were, above all, secondary schools in intention, if not always in accomplishment, and were a sound recognition of the fact stated by William H. Learned in his admirable Carnegie Foundation Report ("The Quality of the Educational Process in the United States and in Europe, 1927")[1] that "the years between twelve and eighteen or thereabouts, constitute the period during which proper education, combined with the development of sound health and normal habits, are of the utmost importance for the subsequent happiness of the individual and the welfare of the nation."

Above all, the academy was a popular institution—so popular that by the middle of the nineteenth century more

[1] I cordially recommend the reading of this report to all readers of this essay.

than two hundred had been incorporated in Virginia, while in Georgia, where the academies were supported by state funds, more than one hundred existed as early as 1831. Even in backward Arkansas, one of the latest Southern States to be admitted to the Union (in 1836), by 1850 ninety academies existed.[1] Nor is the reason for their popularity hard to find. They provided, for fees ridiculously low in comparison with our present-day preparatory schools and colleges, the essentials of a good secondary education. They educated only the class that had time and leisure, as well as an innate capacity and desire to learn something. As their numbers were large, so were their classes correspondingly low. Thus they responded to the profound philosophy inherent in all European schemes of learning, a philosophy which may be stated in these terms, quoted from the Official Outline of Teaching in the Prussian High Schools:[2]

"All instruction is *activity-instruction*. It requires that in choice of materials the teacher shall always consider, not the learning merely, but rather what powers in the pupil—particularly independence of judgment, of feeling, of imagination, and of will—can be developed and heightened. The necessary principle of such instruction is that the class exercises consist in co-operative give-and-take under the leadership of the teacher. The important thing is to give this activity a character that befits both the nature of the pupils and the educative purpose of the school. Its great and serious aim is to

[1] These facts, as well as others during the course of this essay, are taken from the summary of Southern Education prepared by Edgar W. Knight (*Public Education in the South*. Ginn & Co. 1922).

[2] Quoted by W. H. Learned in the Carnegie Report mentioned above.

bridge the natural gap between the certain acquisition of knowledge, without which higher mental activity is impossible, and the acquisition of the power for independent work, without which mere knowledge is unfruitful."

The academies solved the problem of this gap between the acquisition of mere knowledge and the "acquisition of power for independent work" by putting their pupils into direct contact, not with undisputed masses of information and up-to-date apparatus, but with such teachers as could be found. Their object was to teach nothing that the teacher himself had not mastered, and could not convey to his pupils. Their training was therefore classical and humanistic, rather than scientific and technical—as most of the available teachers were products of the older European and American schools. They had a prevailingly religious tone, but as the inhabitants of the Southern States represented many different religious creeds, they steered clear of the narrow sectarianism that early became an incubus upon the Northern schools. And though the teachers were not in many cases up to their task, yet enough teaching talent was available to give to us a Calhoun,[1] as well as many minor lights.

The chief fault of the older academies was that by concentrating solely on the type of individual known as the "good citizen" they tended to ignore other fields of intellectual activity. The graduation exercises of these old Southern academies (some of them survived down to the

[1] Taught privately by the Rev. Moses Waddell, founder of a famous academy that bore his name.

(103)

twentieth century) provided an almost undisciplined orgy of political oratory and of civic patriotism—with very little top-dressing of literature, æsthetics, and philosophic criticism. For this defect the peculiar social structure of the older South was largely responsible. Law and politics were then about the only careers open to gentlemen. And most, after a brief acquaintance with the inconsistencies of law, preferred to abandon it and devote themselves to politics. But it would have been better, no doubt, if the older Southern academies could have frankly encouraged literature, drama, the essay and the liberal arts from the beginning. We might then have easily challenged the North's beginning in these fields, and given America a very different History of Letters.

This, however, was not the defect upon which the opponents of the academy system rested their objections in the older South. On the contrary, the opposition to the academies, which arose in the South comparatively early, took a great step forward after 1836, and finally practically triumphed on the eve of the Civil War itself, was motivated solely by the fact that the academy did not draw into its net the children of the poorer settlers, who could not afford to pay the fees. The agitation for free public schools began as early as the Revolution, and its progress, though halted by the common feeling of the people themselves, was rapid and in the end disastrously complete.

It is generally supposed that the parent of this agitation was no less a person than Thomas Jefferson. A careful examination, however, of the famous "bill for a more general diffusion of knowledge" which he introduced into the

Virginia Legislature as early as 1779, will suffice to dispel the illusion that Jefferson was aiming at education for all members of the community. The object of the bill was to see to it "that those persons whom nature has endowed with genius and virtue should be rendered worthy to receive and guard the sacred deposit of the rights and liberties of their fellow-citizens, and that they should be called to that charge without regard to wealth, birth, or other accidental condition or circumstance: but the indigence of the greater number disabling them from so educating at their own expense, those of their children whom nature hath fitly formed and disposed to become useful instruments for the public, it is better that such should be sought for and educated at the common expense." In other words, Jefferson asked that the poor but brilliant pupil should have an equal opportunity with the well-to-do but lazy one. He did not demand, nor did he ever demand, that *all* should receive the same type of education in the *same way*, at the public expense, as is now done; he favored instead a rigorous selection of talent. The words, "those persons whom nature has endowed with genius and virtue" are significant. What Jefferson wanted was practically such a system of competitive scholarships for the poorer classes as prevails today in England and other European countries. Nor was such a demand out of the way in a Virginia harried by the Revolution and suffering from severe economic losses.

In 1797, Jefferson returned to the subject again, and his proposals then laid before the Virginia Legislature showed how far he was from the present-day conception of a public school as a receptacle for dullards as well as geniuses.

Briefly he proposed that each county of his native state should be divided into "hundreds" and that each hundred should erect a school of such convenient size that all the children might daily attend it. There they were to be taught, free of charge for three years, to cover the ground of primary education. Each county was in addition to this to possess a secondary school in which were to be taught "Latin and Greek, English grammar, geography and the higher parts of numerical arithmetic." These schools were open only to those who would pay the fees, but apart from this, each year a certain number of boys whose parents were too poor to educate them, and who had shown exceptional ability in the primary schools, were to be chosen by the overseers of the elementary schools, to be educated in the secondary grammar schools free of charge. Furthermore, the most promising of those who had advanced through the grammar schools were to be still further educated at the public expense, by three years at William and Mary College.

A brief examination of these proposals should suffice to dispel the illusion that the modern advocates of free education for all can claim an ally in Thomas Jefferson. It is true that he wished elementary education to be free to all that would take it (a measure already partially provided for under the old apprenticeship and poor laws). But his remaining proposals simply were an attempt to mitigate the sting of economic inequality, that to this day prevails in America as much as it does in most countries of Europe, and to give the poor student his chance to shine with the others. In other words, Jefferson was a democrat only in so far as he sought to make it possible to educate the poor on equal terms with the rich; in so far as he deliberately discouraged the dull, whether rich or poor, from proceeding beyond the elementary schools, he was in line with present-day European educational practice.

Nevertheless, Jefferson's example encouraged most of the Southern States to form what were known as "literary funds," derived from the interest on the sale of public lands, and which were usually applied to the education of indigent children in the so-called "pauper schools," or to the expansion of the existing academies. The Southern States admitted to the Union after the Revolution had, in addition, lands granted to them by Congress, consisting of the sixteenth section in every township, the revenue of which they were supposed to apply to free public education. In most cases these funds were either mismanaged or little used—for the reason that there were so few applicants for them, on the principle that taking charity implied some form of disgrace. So matters largely stood till the years 1836-7.

III

On the 1st of January of the latter year, Congress voted that the surplus revenue in the Treasury, arising from the sales of the public lands, and from the tariff, should be distributed among the several states on the basis of their representation in Congress. Whether this was done in order to placate the advocates of Jacksonian democracy (then in the saddle) or whether it was done in an attempt to stave off the financial panic of that year, I do not know; but in this way more than twenty-eight millions of dollars were distributed. Of this amount the then existing Southern States took some eight and a half millions, which in a great many cases were applied to increasing their public-school funds.

Had this sum come under the purview of such a man as Jefferson, one feels that he would have insisted upon Congress using it for the establishment of a national university. Such a university he had indeed recommended in his sixth annual message to Congress, but the suggestion had not been acted upon. Had Jefferson's plan borne fruit in the shape of a university at the national capital, the South might have taken the lead of New England, not only in education, but in letters. The general share-out among the various states of the loot of the federal treasury now not only considerably aided the movement already under way for the establishment of free public schools, but also had the effect of adding new elements of corruption to the already torturous course of local politics.

The case of Tennessee is instructive in this respect. As early as 1835, after long public agitation, a perpetual common-school fund was established. It is worth noting that, in Tennessee's case, the agitation for free public schools naturally came from the poor mountaineer population of the eastern half of the state and was opposed by the planter class of the western lowlands, who were able to support private academies. Yet it was not until 1838, after Tennessee had received her share of the federal surplus, amounting to more than $1,400,000, that an act was passed making use of the permanent school fund, to which was now assimilated the state's share of the surplus revenue, voted by Congress.

This act created the Bank of Tennessee, which was the third bank in the state to bear that name, and capitalized it at $5,000,000. The capital was to consist of the permanent school fund, the share of the surplus revenue to which the state was entitled, any unexpended interest thereon, the further proceeds of the sale of certain lands, and loans to bring up the amount to the sum stated. Of this sum $100,000 was to be paid annually to the board for common-school support, and $18,000 from the same source, for the support of academies. In 1837-8, it was discovered, however, that the State Treasurer, McEwen, had, by mismanagement and the support of various questionable schemes, succeeded in robbing this school fund of more than $120,000 and applying these sums to his own private use. A suit was brought to recover the deficit, but only $10,000 was actually recovered. Small wonder that the cause of free public school education languished in Tennessee thenceforward.[1]

The same story, with varying details, might be told of almost every Southern state that established, before the Civil War, public school funds. The fact has to be faced that there was no general demand for free public schools, and indeed, on the part of the wealthier planter class, there was strong opposition to them. There was, therefore, nothing to prevent waste and mismanagement of the funds arising from the sale of the public lands in every Southern state. The system of the academies for the well-to-do, and

[1]It is worth noting, in connection with these facts, that Tennessee can still boast of the most thorough of the old academies, in the Webb School, which was entirely a private enterprise.

of the "pauper schools" for those unable to pay for learning, sufficed in most cases up to the time of the Civil War. In fact, when one learns of the stubborn popular opposition to free public schools in the South, one is forced to the conclusion that the wisest Southern states were those which, like Virginia, used their literary funds for the education of poor children only, or, which, like South Carolina, established no school funds, or, which, like Georgia, employed one-half of their funds to support the local academies, and the other half on pauper schools.[1]

The American craze for simplifying, standardizing, and equalizing the educational opportunities of all, however, persisted and received a new great impetus in the South after the successful revolution promoted by Horace Mann during the years 1836-48 in the public schools of Massachusetts. It must be remembered that the reason why the system promoted by Mann succeeded first in the North was precisely because the North during those years was becoming industrial, with large urban populations, composed of European immigrants, while in the South the population remained homogeneous and still predominantly rural (80 per cent rural down to 1920). The South was not, as was charged by the North before and after the Civil War, indifferent to education. She simply preferred the older schemes of education which were best suited to her own rural populations, to such novel methods as Mann's, which were non-sectarian, non-religious, urban and egalitarian in

[1] Further details of the rise, use, and abuse of public-school funds in the Southern states will be found in Knight's book already cited. See also, for Tennessee, *Development of the Tennessee State Educational Organisation*, by Robert H. White, 1929.

scope. It would, no doubt, have been better for the old South if the remarkable scheme mooted by Governor Wise of Virginia on the eve of the Civil War, which provided for no less than twelve new colleges and three agricultural schools in the state, could have been earlier adopted. It would also have been better for the South if the scheme for establishing manual-labour academies, which combined agricultural and other craft activities along with literary instruction, and which had a brief vogue in several states around 1830-40, could have been persisted in, and not allowed to lapse. Either Jefferson's idea of only training the best and most promising, or the idea of combining precise agricultural knowledge along with some amount of general culture, would have been better for the South than what was actually adopted. For the purpose of education is to produce the balanced character—the man of the world in the true sense, who is also the man with spiritual roots in his own community in the local sense. The public-school system inaugurated by Mann and copied later in the North, ignored local and functional differences and resulted in producing a being without roots, except in the factory.

Nevertheless, it was naïvely supposed in the South that all that was needed to create a better educational system was to adopt the plan that had been so successful in the North. In 1845 Tennessee and Alabama adopted state-controlled systems of free public education, practically on the Northern model. North Carolina had already had such a system as early as 1839, and Louisiana in 1847. In Mississippi, Florida, Arkansas, and Texas the state funds existed to set the scheme in motion, but they were still not applied;

superintendents were not appointed, nor graded schools set up. Only in Virginia, Georgia, and South Carolina did the old system, tested from the birth of the republic, remain intact.

Then came the war and, with it, ruin to the South. Most of the existing academies were used as hospitals, barracks for troops, were occupied by the invading Federals, and emerged only as rotting shells of what they had been. Private endowment ceased. Some of the Southern states, such as Florida, had used their public-school funds for military purposes. All were practically bankrupt, as well as defeated. Under the circumstances, there was no chance that the old academy system could revive over large sections of the country. It was either the public-school system or nothing. Hence the South, under the provisional governments recommended and in some cases set up by Lincoln, and agreed upon by his successor, began to build up independently state-controlled systems of free schools, for both white and colored races. Movements in this direction were made in Alabama, Arkansas (where the election of a state superintendent of public schools was denied validity by the federal military officer in command of the district!), Georgia, Mississippi, North Carolina, and Tennessee. Despite the utterly depleted condition of all the state treasuries, some sums were raised for public education. Meantime, in the victorious North, a national convention of teachers, meeting in Harrisburg, Pennsylvania, in August, 1865, declared that the lately closed rebellion had been "a war of education and patriotism against ignorance and barbarism" and the president of the convention emitted the following colossal falsehood:

"How was it in the states where the institution of slavery prevailed? There was no common-school system. Exceptions there were in some of the cities—but as a general fact the statement is correct. The children of a large portion of the population were, *by law, prohibited*[1] the advantages of an education, and a large portion of the free population were virtually shut out from the means of an early culture."

What is one to think of these remarks, in view of the fact that over at least half the South the free public-school system had already spread by the time of the Civil War? However, the Northern Congress was soon to see to it that the "prohibition" of education to the free whites of the South was soon to become an accomplished fact. By the first Reconstruction Act, passed over President Johnson's veto on March 2, 1867, the provisional governments were destroyed, all the whites who had taken part in the rebellion were disfranchised, and the South was divided into five military districts under military commanders, who promptly put up state governments controlled by carpetbaggers and their misled dupes, the freedmen. These, during the eight years anarchy that followed, robbed the state treasuries of more than three hundred millions and did nothing for education, either state or private, beyond repeated discussions of the advisability of mixing white and negro children in the public schools.

From this quagmire the South lifted itself, and the fact that it did survive the horrors of the Reconstruction period

[1] Italics mine.

is perhaps the most heroic fact in all American history. Thanks to local patriotism (particularly in Virginia, where Lee performed feats of heroic patriotism greater than his acts on the battlefield) public-school laws were passed, superintendents appointed, some attempts were made to give agricultural training, and white and negro schools were kept separate. The dire poverty of the South prevented these attempts from coming to full fruition, but the coming of the Peabody Fund in 1867 gradually overcame that difficulty. Though little that resembled the old academy system was allowed to survive, yet at least we were granted permission by our Northern conquerors to be "educated" even as they. Perhaps for that we ought to feel grateful.

IV

Without questioning the necessity of schools of some sort for the South—public schools, if not private schools, on the principle that something is better than nothing—and without ignoring the honest intentions of George Peabody, who by bestowing three and a half millions to the cause of public education in the South gave back to the Southern people some of the sums that his Northern compatriots, aided by their freed negroes, had robbed us of—without questioning or denying all this, one may still ask whether the present-day public-school system in the South is an ally to culture and to civilization? This question is important, first, because the South is still predominantly rural and agricultural in population; second, because our experience of Reconstruction and other governments and of "the never-ending insolence of elected persons" generally, has made us suspicious of all schemes that propose to coerce our people to their alleged benefit; and third, because no one in his senses would, I hope, care to see the South attain to such summits of "public-spirited" progress as are aptly symbolized by places like Lowell (Massachusetts), Pittsburgh (Pennsylvania), and Paterson (New Jersey). There is reason to believe that the public-school system has had not a little to do with the industrial degradation of such places; and if the public-school system has not taken such a strangle hold on the South, that may be, after all, matter for congratulation.

Evidence has accumulated of recent years that our present-day system of free elementary schools, leading to the public high schools, and from there to the college, somehow fails to give us an intellectually mature body of citizens, capable of controlling the complexities of our social, economic, political, cultural, and religious life. As far as the primary schools go, there may be some benefit in the present system. Primary instruction in the English language, in the elements of grammar and mathematics, in geography, in elementary history, is, after all, largely a question of being able to remember certain facts. It depends on memory —on being able to repeat a lesson correctly once it is given. But once beyond that point, which in most cases is reached from ten to twelve years of age, the sole abiding object of education is not to convey information at all. It is to train the pupil's mind in such a manner that he can master for himself whatever subject he wishes to take up, and to enlarge his mental horizon by showing the relationship of this subject to the whole of human life. And in this respect our high schools completely fail.

A greater proportion of pupils from the primary schools enter our high schools than in any other of the European countries.[1] This fact has been seized on by partisans of our present state of standardized mass production, as a fresh proof that "democratic" America is culturally superior to "feudal" Europe. One might as well say that because we manufacture more automobiles than any other country, our automobiles are of superior design and are employed to better purpose than those made in Europe. As a matter of fact, the reason why so many Americans go from the primary schools to the high schools is because there is nothing to prevent them from doing so. The system under which the high schools run is exactly the same as that of the primary schools. There are the same recitations of memorized parroted facts; the same frequent tests (to insure that the memory does not waver), the same top-heavy classes, in which the pupil of exceptional quickness and ability has to keep mental pace with the most stupid, the same unlimited range of disconnected subjects, all open as possible "credits," and the same lack of an organic curriculum and of close contact between the minds of the pupils and that of the teacher. The result is that, after four years, the pupil of the high school emerges with a sufficient smattering of subjects to enable him to fill up a college-entrance examination paper (that is if his memory does not

[1] Pupils registered in first-year American secondary schools (fifteen-year age group): boys, 53 per cent; girls, 57 per cent. In the same year in Prussia: boys, 8.1 per cent; girls, 4.9 per cent. England: boys, 6.9 per cent; girls, 7.5.

(116)

collapse) but no knowledge of what all this is about, and no ability to apply it to his own life, or to planning his future career. Physically, he is mature; mentally, he is a stunted child.

It may be argued that this picture is far too gloomy to be exactly the truth. But why, it may be asked, have the best and most scholarly colleges of our country recently demanded from their freshmen one year's obligatory work in English composition if the present-day high-school product has really learned to read and write? And what, it may also be asked, is the chief interest of the present-day American high-school product? He (or she) is chiefly interested, not in learning, but in athletics.[1] And rightly, because athletics offers the only opportunity for the spirit of healthy competition; it definitely gives the growing youth a chance to show that he is actually good at something. At least it ought to do so; and it did, until recently, when the commercialization of athletics removed even that form of competition. The present-day high school, with its enormous classes, its curriculum of disconnected subjects, its staff of teachers that vary from year to year throughout the course, its utter inability to select out of the mass the saving remnant who might under proper encouragement become masters in their several fields, gives no opportunity to the youth who has in him the spark of desire to rise intellectually. In fact, if it did, it would have to limit itself to youths of that type, and become thereby not standardized, but selective, not industrial but cultural, and thereby "un-

[1] It is worth noting that what took the place of athletics in the older schools of the South were literary and debating societies. See, for example, *College Life in the Old South*, by E. M. Coulter, 1928.

democratic" in the eyes of the taxpayers. Nobody, incidentally, among those same taxpayers asserts that high-school and college athletics are, because they aim at the best that can be done, thereby "undemocratic." But such is the logic of our industrialized America.

The high school is, in its essence, nothing more than a mass-production factory, with the essential aim of making as many graduates as possible with as little trouble to either teacher or pupil as possible. The product, the high-school pupil, is at every stage of the process shepherded along, dragged through the machinery of classes, tests, recitations. What American parent does not receive monthly reports of the progress of his boy or girl? And there are written examinations, frequent and exhaustive, to face—just as there is of the malleability of steel in a present-day steel works! One need only compare this with the system employed in the secondary schools of France or Germany today or the great public schools of England. There examinations come at the end of a three or four years' course—not before—and are tests, oral as well as written, of the pupil's ability to discuss his own subject in all its bearings, rather than to display how much knowledge he has been able to amass about it, by diligent cramming and memorizing.

That this system of high-school instruction should have spread to the South from the North, in the wake of Reconstruction, was a disaster of the first magnitude. It was not and is not adapted to Southern life, for three reasons. First, our population is still predominantly agricultural and rural. The difficulty of finding capable teachers for rural high schools is admitted by such authorities and advocates of the present system as Edgar A. Knight; and what is the good of sending an unspoiled country boy or girl to a city high school and still later to a college, if after some seven years' sophisticated flirting with knowledge he or she has to return and unwillingly take up ploughing and washing dishes again? Second, a considerable proportion of our population are negroes. Although there is no doubt that the negro could, if he wished, pass easily through the high school and college mill (such a task does not require any profound knowledge of self or determination of mind), yet under the present social and economic conditions under which he has to live it is simply a waste of money and effort to send him there. Third, our present system of "putting through" every type of mind that can somehow rake up enough credits to "make the grade," year after year, in high school and college, represents nothing organic; it does not lead anywhere, or help the pupil to fulfill any later task in life. Many of our most prominent colleges have recognized this fact by adding to their curricula courses in technical training, applied science, and business administration. But it is worthy of note that in most European countries, schools running such courses are equally open to the pupil from the moment he finishes the elementary school! If he goes into them, that is the end of his education. If he remains in the secondary school and college, it is to learn something else. Why do we, as a people, waste time and money and effort on teaching the young man or woman something that later he or she is to forget?

The inferior, whether in life or in education, should exist only for the sake of the superior. We feed and clothe and exercise our bodies, for example, in order to be able to do something with our minds. We employ our minds in order to achieve character, to become the balanced personalities, the "superior men" of Confucius' text, the "gentlemen" of the old South. We achieve character, personality, gentlemanliness in order to make our lives an art and to bring our souls into relation with the whole scheme of things, which is the divine nature. But the present-day system of American popular education exactly reverses this process. It puts that which is superior—learning, intelligence, scholarship—at the disposal of the inferior. It says in effect that if the pupil acquires an education, he will be better able to feed and clothe his body later. It destroys the intellectual self-reliance of character, and the charm of balanced personality, in order to stuff the mind with unrelated facts. Its goal is industry rather than harmonious living, and self-aggrandisement rather than peace with God. That is the indictment against it, and that is what we of the South now have to face.

What can we do about it? How can we preserve what little is now left to us of the traditions of leisure, of culture, of intellectual tolerance and sane kindliness, which are all that our fathers had to give us as a legacy from the past that was broken in the Civil War? We cannot, apparently, destroy the public-school system. That is now rooted, whether for good or evil, in our midst, just as the industrial system is. Neither can we afford to ignore or take for granted the public-school system. We can only agitate and discuss the possibility of making the system more selective of excellence in something. We can pick out the most

(120)

promising and enterprising pupils who appear in our high schools annually and set them apart, as actual students taught by real teachers, to form an intellectual *élite*—a thing we had from the Revolution down to the Civil War, and do not possess today. We can insist that all pupils, from the age of at least fourteen, should be required to take groups of related courses, instead of elective credits. We can spend less money on equipment and buildings and more on scholarship and intellectual achievement. We can within the proper limits support other institutions; for example, the state agricultural colleges, which, so far as they encourage and help people to remain on the land, may be considered a benefit. We can also support, and should have supported for years past, such institutions for training the negro as Tuskegee and the Hampton Institute, which are adapted to the capacity of that race and produce far healthier and happier specimens of it than all the institutions for "higher learning" that we can ever give them. We can cease being sectarian, and stop fanning the fires of narrow-minded religious intolerance, by realizing that, after all, religion is a matter of personal choice, but intelligence is a matter of communal responsibility. We can stop putting our eggs into one basket, and create flourishing schools for manual training, arts and crafts, and give them a place of equal honor along with our high schools. Unless we do something toward all these goals, and if the present system persists, in another generation nothing will remain of the local color, the diversity, the humanity, the charm of our South, and we will become assimilated outwardly and inwardly to the street gangs of New York and Chicago.

(121)

LYLE H. LANIER

A CRITIQUE OF THE
PHILOSOPHY OF PROGRESS

I

PROGRESS is both a slogan and a philosophy, a device for social control and a belief in the reality of a
process of cosmic development toward "some far-off divine
event." The idea has been vigorously assailed as a superstition or a myth, and has been defended with equal energy
as an aspect of the natural necessity of the world. Material-
ists and idealists alike have adopted it as a *Weltanschauung*;
both skeptics and theologians have denounced it as an
aberrant delusion. John Dewey believes that modern industrial technology provides us with a method for securing
progress and for preserving our culture against decline;
Oswald Spengler looks on industrialism and its concomitant
manifestations as evidence of decay in the spirit of Western
life. Sociologists have struggled with the notion of progress
for a long time, and for the most part have adopted an
agnostic attitude. They have failed to find either a satisfactory definition of progress, or any criterion to determine
whether or not a specific social change is really "progressive" in any final sense.

The agnostic attitude would seem to be the only sensible
one, in view of such conflicting views, were it not for the
fact that in contemporary America the doctrine of progress

is of immense social consequence. Modern industrialism has found the use of "progress," as a super-slogan, very efficacious as a public anæsthetic. The magic word is even imprinted on the automobile license plates of one of our "advancing" states, thus recalling the charms used in primitive cultures. Progress is perhaps the most widely advertised commodity offered for general consumption in our high-powered century, a sort of universal social enzyme whose presence is essential to the ready assimilation of other commodities, material and intellectual, generated by the machine age. A steady barrage of propaganda issues through newspapers, magazines, radios, billboards, and other agencies for controlling public opinion, to the effect that progress must be maintained. It requires little sagacity to discover that progress usually turns out to mean business, or else refers to some activity which serves to allay the qualms of the business conscience. General sanction of industrial exploitation of the individual is grounded in the firm belief on the part of the generality of people that the endless production and consumption of material goods means "prosperity," "a high standard of living," "progress," or any one among several other catchwords. The conviction that our noisy social ferment portends progressive development toward some highly desired, but always undesignated, goal is perhaps the central psychological factor in the maintenance of our top-heavy industrial superstructure. This belief is strengthened by certain popular "interpretations" of the spirit of America which proclaim a mystic faith in the industrial destiny. With a rather complete disregard of specific economic and social trends, authors of this "inspirational" criticism conjure up a magic venturesomeness of spirit which they expect to well up momently in sturdy breasts and automatically bend economic forces to its will. They derive a vicarious feeling of power and importance from acquiescence in what they feel to be the mighty trend of progress, encouraged in many instances by the designing notice conferred upon them by dominant business leaders. Such acquiescence, curiously enough, is experienced as real casual efficiency, being transformed into an illusion of leadership or a sense of "prophecy." This romanticized type of rationalization of industrialism might be ignored were it not for the fact that it tends to confirm the confused business mind in its false sense of security, and thus impedes the development of a sound program of economic and social adjustment.

Such considerations as these suggest that neither social science nor social philosophy can afford to ignore the problems presented by the hypostatization and misuse of the questionable concept of progress. The measure of social control secured through the use of that modern magic, advertising, necessitates an evaluation of the ends which such mass suggestion aims to secure. As Dewey has pointed out, the instability in a social order which renders its members susceptible to control in this facile manner is dangerous, since sooner or later exploitation will run its course, with the probable result that the masses will be activated with equal ease against their present dominators. Hence the analysis of the notion of progress and the study of the uses to which it is put are not mere academic or abstract problems. They are immediate concrete issues for a social philosophy which would relate its thought to the evaluation of the social and moral ideas of its time, and for a comprehensive social science which would deal intelligently with the effects of such ideas on human economy. The problem of progress really coincides with what Windelband has called the problem of Civilization, which asks the question "whether and how far . . . the change in human impulses and in the relations of human life . . . has served to further the modern order and man's true happiness." The fact of change is unquestioned, but has there been *progress*? Even if there is little chance of arriving at any conclusive factual determination as to the reality of the phenomenon, the issue should be clarified by an attempt to evaluate the idea in terms of its historical development, its normative implications, and the relationship between the latter and such social phenomena as are relevant to them.

II

Progress is a comparatively modern idea. The chronological succession of events meant little or nothing to the Greeks, as far as having any cumulative significance in terms of "progress" toward some end was concerned. Man and the human race were but episodes in the world-process, which repeated itself forever according to like laws. Greek thinkers attempted to discover the nature of the abiding essence which manifested itself in these eternal cycles. They had no philosophy of history, saw no meaning in history as such. It was not until the Hellenistic-Roman period that a definite philosophy of history appeared, based upon the doctrines of Christianity. Man was regarded as a personality endowed with freedom and convicted of sin; his earthly sojourn was a period in which he should purge himself of sin through faith, in order to return to heaven at the end of it. The doctrine of the temporal finitude of the earth, with corporeal resurrection, as a culmination, marks probably the first attempt on the part of man to conceive the flux of events historically or teleologically. But this teleology has no affinity with our modern "progress," for it was based upon a belief in the innate depravity of man's nature and upon a denial of all value to earthly life.

The Church, which alone survived the downfall of the Roman Empire, dominated the intellectual, political, and religious life of western Europe for about a thousand years. There was little evidence during this period of a shift in interest from other worldliness to progress of the human race in this world. Scholastic philosophy identified the search for truth with the attempt to rationalize Church dogma, and as a consequence the teleology of history remained largely a matter of Christian theology. There was little knowledge of Greek science, and the schooling of the Middle Ages was largely formal and dialectical. Interest in nature was necessarily stifled by a philosophy which renounced the world.

The barrenness of scholastic learning could not fail to irk men of an empirical turn of mind, as well as those inclined toward speculative philosophy and mysticism. Roger Bacon was in a sense a concretion of the spirit of dissatisfaction with scholasticism, and his scientific studies presaged its downfall. Although some three centuries were to elapse between Bacon's work and the true scientific revival of the sixteenth century, there was nevertheless during this period a growing interest in nature and science, encouraged by the study of Aristotle's works on physics and by the Arabian schools of Spain. This interest is reflected in the great development of magical means of "controlling" or "forecasting" natural events, as manifested especially in the pseudosciences of astrology and alchemy.

The "revival of letters" in the fifteenth century accelerated the process whereby the Church lost control of Western thought, and prepared the way for a philosophy favorable to views of terrestrial progress. According to Windelband, "the philosophy of the Renaissance is in the main the history of the process in which the natural science mode of regarding the world is gradually worked out from the humanistic renewal of Greek philosophy." Renaissance philosophy reflects the discovery of Greek civilization on the one hand, and the excitement generated by scientific and geographical discoveries on the other. Columbus's voyage to America, Magellan's tour around the world, proving the hypothesis that the world is a globe, the astronomical works of Copernicus, Kepler, and Galileo, and numerous studies in mathematics, physics, and biology fired Renaissance thinkers with an intense zeal for knowledge about nature. Furthermore, and what is equally important for our purpose, these events were productive of a metaphysical view of the world which in a sense would seem to underlie all doctrines of progress, namely, the principle of *immanence*, which Hegel considered the ruling philosophical thought of the modern world. The notion of a transcendent God, apart from and perhaps indifferent to nature, was replaced by a view which in some sense identified the two. Weber believes that the Copernican astronomy which placed the sun at the center of the universe and located the earth among the planets was the primary source of this notion, inasmuch as the conception of an infinite universe destroyed the traditional distinction between heaven and earth. This introduced grave incompatibilities between Church doctrine and the theories of Renaissance scientists and philosophers. The fate of Bruno illustrates how serious the conflict was.

The essential result of these momentous changes, for our purpose, is embodied in the philosophy of Francis Bacon. Bacon is the precursor of the spirit of modern life. It is from him that we may, in a sense, date the pragmatic, "progressive" temper. He regarded the philosophy of the Greeks as puerile, talkative rather than generative, fruitful in controversies and barren in effects. He believed that "contemplative" or theoretical knowledge was largely responsible for what he considered the intellectual sterility of the Middle Ages. In opposition to the Aristotelian logic of demonstration which implied that knowledge consisted simply in bringing together a universal truth and a particular fact of observation, Bacon insisted that effective knowledge could be gained only by a careful study of the processes of nature. Such knowledge would be instrumental; it would be a means by which man could secure dominion over the world. Its validity would be judged by its effectiveness in producing progress, meaning by the latter the improvement of man's material and social welfare. This is indeed a new teleology as compared with that of the Middle Ages. Man henceforth would be concerned not so much with saving his soul as with making himself comfortable, and with improvement of the world through coöperative soci.. effort. Pragmatism, instrumentalism, positivism find a hearty progenitor in Bacon.

The latter part of the seventeenth century and the entire eighteenth century were marked by an intense interest in man, in social institutions, in morals, all of which served to prepare the way for more explicitly formulated notions of human progress. Institutions and customs were no longer regarded as self-justifying; they were subjected to critical rational analysis with a view to determining their efficiency in promoting the happiness of individuals .There was a decided interest in psychology, beginning with Descartes and Hobbes, and in the psychological bases of society and morals. The general result of the social philosophy of this period is best represented in the utilitarian theory of moral action. This view holds that an action is ethically pleasing in proportion as it secures or aims to secure the greatest happiness for the greatest number of individuals; virtue is measured by social utility. Although the general "enlightenment" of the period was restricted primarily to the upper classes, nevertheless there was a development of self-consciousness, so to speak, on the part of the masses, a movement which received articulate expression in the French Revolution. In general there was a tendency toward emancipation from the past, an attempt to settle the problems of man's nature and destiny in a purely abstract fashion and apart from the "vital force of historical reality" (Windelband). This break with history was not restricted to social philosophy; in metaphysics and theology we find Deism, a doctrine of an impersonal nature, substituted by many thinkers for the usual positive religions based upon belief in a personal God.

The positivistic spirit of British and French thought in the eighteenth century was met toward its close by German idealism. Kant's critical philosophy rejected the purely empirical doctrine of knowledge advocated by the sensationalistic school and emphasized the organizing power of the mind itself as a determiner of the phenomenal world and of values, both moral and æsthetic. This work paved the way for the metaphysical systems of Fichte, Schelling, and Hegel. It is in Hegel that we find the most systematic expression of what we have held to be the logical basis of all doctrines of progress, namely the idea of immanence. Reality for Hegel is world-process, the evolution of which proceeds from indeterminate being (primitive formless matter) to the human organism, which in its realization of the ideals of art, religion, and philosophy becomes absolute mind. He is the first thinker to formulate a complete philosophy of history; his system is a synthesis of all manifestations of reality, past, present, and future. This rationalization of all historical phenomena as the realization of the dialectic of logical development is in a way a doctrine of progress, a theory of evolution, although it has nothing in common with later positivistic and evolutionary theories. Hegel deduced the course of events from *a priori* principles, and although his philosophy of history played an important rôle in the development of German nationalism, his abstract theory was to be replaced by another doctrine of evolution which would appeal to the imagination of men inclined to think materialistically, and which for a long time seemed to provide intellectual sanction for the belief in progress.

German metaphysics did not alter very materially the course of development of the natural sciences throughout the nineteenth century, nor did the interest in social philosophy abate. To some extent, indeed, the influence of German idealism was added to that of utilitarianism in the production of social reform, especially in England. But developments in the natural sciences, mechanical inventions which made possible the utilization of physical energy on a large scale, a conception of social progress defined in terms of improvement in the material conditions of living for the masses, and the doctrine of the natural rights of mankind, all these were the essential factors which combined to change the social, economic, and political organization of the Western World from the close of the eighteenth century onward. Curiously enough, the trend toward democracy, which really began with the Renaissance and culminated in a sense at the close of the eighteenth century in the formation of the American and French republics, was now complicated by a counter influence in the form of the industrial revolution. We say "counter" influence because the political democracy of these republics was based upon an agrarian economy, upon an individualism which permitted great personal autonomy in the conduct of all phases of living, and which at the same time promoted social stability through attachment, in one form or another, to land. This agrarian economy which lay at the base of European and American social structure down to the close of the eighteenth century was disrupted by industrialism with its urbanization, shifting population, abnormal concentration of wealth, panics, unemployment, labor unions, and a train of attendant phenomena. The stream of goods from the machines, the drive for ever-increasing production and consumption, and the generally accelerated tempo of social change served to popularize the doctrine of progress. Visions of an endless upward sweep of democracy in which every individual would share increasingly in profits from glamorous industries, and have more and more mechanical luxuries to "enjoy," intoxicated the pliant imaginations of people loosened from traditional social moorings.

The dominant note of nineteenth-century thought was naturalism, in the form either of positivism or of materialism. There was, to be sure, a strong idealistic "opposition" in Germany, the aftermath of Kant and the great metaphysical systems, and to a lesser extent in England and America, but philosophies based upon natural science conceptions of phenomena tended to predominate, at least numerically. Positivism may be considered a refinement of Bacon's philosophy. The view is best presented in the philosophy of Auguste Comte, who held that the history of human thought, as well as the history of each positive science, passed through three stages—the theological, the metaphysical, and the positive. The theological stage is characterized by the tendency to explain the world anthropomorphically; in the metaphysical stage, explanation takes the form of abstractions considered as "intelligent" realities; the positive stage dispenses with all necessity for finding "efficient" causes of phenomena and regards invariable laws

(132)

of recurrence as sufficient both for practical and for philosophical purposes. As applied historically and socially, Comte believed that positivism meant the ultimate triumph of industrialism with social control in the hands of the proletariat. Influenced, no doubt, by Hegel, Comte viewed historical and social phenomena as connected with the same necessity as physical and biological phenomena, and thought that their laws could be discovered by the application of the positive method of inquiry.

The influence of Hegel and Comte is shown in the social philosophy of Karl Marx, who formulated a system of economic determinism, construing the Hegelian dialectic in terms of class conflict. Paralleling the work of Marx, the writings of Feuerbach, Duehring, and Strauss reveal a realistic conception of progress as an aspect of the natural necessity of the material world. Their materialistic leanings led them to a fatalistic optimism; they regarded pessimism as a romantic vestige of Christianity which held the world to be evil. But this brings us to the theory of evolution, which generated or appeared to substantiate not only the doctrine of progress, but also most of the materialistic philosophy of the nineteenth century.

Although the notion of progress did not originate with the theory of cosmic evolution, as we have already shown, nevertheless this theory was thought for a long time to justify the belief in progress. Spencer explicitly affirmed its reality and conceived the process as the evolution of the simple into the complex. This law of evolutionary progress was believed to operate throughout the entire realm of nature, whether in the development of the earth, or life, or society, of government, manufacturing, commerce, language, art, or what not. The universe was held to be an Unknowable Force which manifested itself in this peculiar form of differentiation of the homogeneous into the heterogeneous. Evolution necessarily meant a change for the better, the fact of survival constituting sufficient reason for a phenomenon's existence and worth. Along with this view of progress, Spencer held to a hedonistic theory of action, claiming that if an animal consistently followed a painful course of action it would soon cease to exist. He recognized, however, that "pleasure" and "progress" do not always coincide, and his hedonism came to be considerably modified in his definition of the highest conduct as that which conduces to the "greatest breadth, length, and completeness of human life." The highest stage in evolution is that reached when conduct simultaneously achieves the greatest totality of life in self, in offspring, and in fellow man. It requires little penetration to see that this goal is one which the process of evolution has been somewhat deficient, for the most part, in realizing. Such a naïve ethical determinism as is implied in this theory of evolution is no longer seriously held by social philosophers, although something of its spirit prevails in contemporary popular thought.

The evolutionary hypothesis has undoubtedly exercised considerable influence upon the course of civilization since the middle of the nineteenth century, particularly in its conflict with religious beliefs. But this influence, although carrying with it expressed theories of progress, had no direct economic concomitant and consequently has probably played little rôle as an instrument of social control. It has contributed, of course, to the loosening of emotional ties which bound Western people to the past, but its rôle is a minor one when compared with the effects of industrialism. The conquest of the West by machine technology produced social consequences without parallel in history. And it is not perhaps a matter of coincidence that toward the end of the nineteenth century, when the positivistic spirit wrought out such victories over nature, these endeavors should receive philosophic expression in the form of "pragmatism." William James, with whom the latter movement is generally associated, was not a defender of the industrialism of his time; his attitude toward the social practices of his era, the so-called Gilded Age in America, was not that of acquiescence, as Mr. Mumford has tried to show. Indeed, he reacted strongly against it. But his pragmatic theory of truth and his metaphysical pluralism, with the further hypothesis of an "open" world, a universe not closed but indeterminate and in the making, were congenial both to the spirit of practicality of his time and to the popular notion of the upward sweep of human progress. Casual relationships are difficult to establish, but without doing violence to fact one can say that in an age without fixed standards, with a flux of changing institutions and beliefs, with a vision of endless "progress," James propounded a philosophy of relativism, practicality, and an indeterminate universe. Perhaps the best interpretation is to view both James and his age as resultants of three centuries of Baconianism, the one in theory and the other in fact. And as one finds a wide discrepancy between the personality and teachings of James and the concrete social processes of his time, so one may perhaps expect gen-

(135)

erally to find considerable divergence between the abstract relativism of a highly moral character and the practical social consequences of relativism for humanity at large.

James was not especially concerned with social philosophy. His interest, like that of Emerson, was in human experience. His rejection of traditionalism, formal logic, institutionalism in any form, was largely grounded in his romantic belief in the validity of the intuitive immediacy of volitional experience. It is to John Dewey that we must turn to find how the pragmatic spirit deals with concrete social problems. All philosophy according to Dewey is social philosophy, whose task should be "to clarify men's ideas as to the social and moral strifes of their own day." Philosophic rationalization should take the form of defining specific social ends. Thought should be utilized in the realization of purposes by which life is liberalized and expanded. Dewey's general philosophic viewpoint is known as "instrumentalism," a word which appears to have many meanings, but which in the most general sense seems to imply that all human institutions and activities are, or should be, instrumental in the realization of moral values. The highest aim of society is "to set free and develop the capacities of human individuals without respect to race, sex, class, or economic status."

III

Mr. Dewey's philosophy initiates a new era in the development of the notion of progress. He has no interest in the absolutistic metaphysical theories, in which progress is a corollary of the system of abstractions by which they seek

(136)

to comprehend the universe. Nor does the theory of evolution appear to lend positive support to the belief in progress; the vague analogies between biological and social development are suggestive but not convincing. There is another set of factors, however, which Mr. Dewey regards as of genuine importance. The changes in social organization and ideas, and the developments in scientific technology—traced very inadequately in the preceding pages—are at least pertinent to the issue. They represent a reaction against absolutism both in social institutions and in intellectual endeavor, and this is held to be a necessary condition of progress, even if it does not automatically insure its realization. Inasmuch as Mr. Dewey's general philosophic position centers about problems of democracy, education, scientific and industrial technology, and the significance of these for progress, it will be profitable to examine his views on these questions.

The historic formula of democracy—liberty, equality, fraternity—is rationalized by Dewey in terms of his pluralistic metaphysics and his theory of social values. Liberty means "a universe in which there is real uncertainty and contingency, a world in which all is not in, and never will be, a world which is in some respects incomplete and in the making, and which in these respects may be made this way or that, according as men judge, prize, love, and labor." Liberty is not freedom to act in accordance with an immutable law, for the latter implies a fixed, closed world, a world in which progress and human endeavor have no real meaning. Equality means, similarly, that the world is not a fixed, hierarchical order of grades of human excellence;

"it means that every existence deserving the name of existence has something unique and irreplaceable about it, that it does not exist to illustrate a principle, to realize a universal or to embody a kind or class . . . it embodies, so to speak, a metaphysical mathematics of the incommensurable in which each speaks for itself and demands consideration on its own behalf." Fraternity means the interaction and association of such "equal" individuals without limit. "To say that what is specific and unique can be exhibited and become forceful or actual only in relationship with other like beings is merely, I take it, to give a metaphysical version to the fact that democracy is concerned not with freaks or geniuses or heroes or divine leaders, but with associated individuals in which each by intercourse with others somehow makes the life of each more distinctive."

This is a metaphysical rendering of communism or socialism which, in some form, Mr. Dewey has advocated for years as the only political and social system in which real moral values could be secured. For such a system implies, he thinks, communion, shared goods, shared experiences, liberation of capacity through intercourse. The industrial technology is an important agency through which these *desiderata* could be realized, for it facilitates commerce and exchange of ideas; it breaks down feudal intellectual barriers, class distinctions, and traditions. Thus the industrial processes fulfill an educational function, inasmuch as Dewey conceives education to be a process in which the distinctive aptitudes in art, thought, and companionship are released to a maximum degree in each individual.

Let it be understood at once that Mr. Dewey has no

illusions about the extent to which these ideal conditions have been realized in our present era of industrialism. The tremendous social changes since the Renaissance have broken down the barriers which have kept human society static, he thinks; they have provided an opportunity for progress, but this opportunity has not been realized. The bewildering spectacle of the changes has unfortunately been confused with progress. It would be difficult, we read in his latest essays, to find an epoch in history as lacking in solid and assured objects of belief and approved ends of action as the present. It is indeed refreshing to note his strictures upon our "economic anarchy" after being deluged with the puerile mouthings of would-be-scholars about the "spiritualism" of modern business.

The cause of the present disorder Mr. Dewey locates in the fact that there is a fundamental dualism between the individual's motivation to action and the means by which his action is executed. That is to say, an individual's motives are "unmitigatedly private," whereas the means of his action are corporate and collective. This motivation is the counterpart of an earlier individualism which is out of place in a corporate age. This individualism was natural in an agrarian society where there was considerable isolation and personal autonomy in the conduct of life, but such a spirit has no place in a machine age where the conditions make for an aggregate mental and emotional life. Hence we need, according to Dewey, to inhibit the principles and standards that are merely traditional, opinions and ideals that have no living relationship to the situation in which we live, and attempt to achieve a new individualism. The

latter will be a function of the socialistic state in which
there is collective control over the processes and results of
corporate enterprise. This collective participation would
mean not only an equitable distribution of profits, but
would mean an attachment to the processes of industrialism of such a nature that the use of thought and emotion
would not be excluded from the individual's daily work.
This would produce an individual as much related and
unified as the present individual is divided and distracted.
When we begin thus to utilize the resources of technology
for purposes avowedly social we can talk about progress.

The picture drawn by Mr. Dewey of the fundamental
disorder of the contemporary mind is admirable. His
disgust with the "nauseating idealism" which ignores or
misrepresents the concrete cultural scene in America is
undoubtedly justified. Equally commendable is the criticism
of those individuals who attempt to insulate themselves
against contemporary vulgarity with an artificial and alien
"culture." There are, however, certain rather fundamental
propositions involved in Mr. Dewey's remedial measures
which, to the writer at least, are not at all self-evident. In
the first place, the assumption that socialism or communism
is a desirable or even possible basis of human society needs
considerably more evidence than the logical considerations
which impel Mr. Dewey to suggest it. Some form of socialism has often been advocated as a panacea for the evils
of current economic and political systems. It seems such
a plausible method for dealing with one of the major ethical issues of the human race, namely the tendency to exploit other individuals. Systems of slavery or domination in

some form constitute one of the outstanding facts of history. Our contemporary variety is perhaps as complete and vicious as any form of outright ownership, for there is no feeling of responsibility even for the physical welfare of individuals dependent for a living upon the caprice of modern industry. A logical method of abolishing this unethical system would seem to be the communistic state based upon a metaphysics of equality and upon patterns of economic, political, and social participation by all individuals in all forms of activity. Unfortunately, logical cogency is no criterion of empirical practicability in the realm of social reorganization. The Utopias of the seventeenth and eighteenth centuries illustrate the futility of trying to deal with social problems in an abstract fashion, apart from historical and psychological realities. And socialism is another Utopia, despite the superficial similarity between many of its proposed features and the forms of economic enterprise in our corporate age. It is this resemblance which suggests to Mr. Dewey that in the mechanisms of industry as they exist in America we have an economic framework which would be essential to the socialistic order. In fact, he asserts that we are in for some kind of socialism, whether or not we like it, and that our choice must be between a socialism that is public and one that is capitalistic. The latter, however, is not socialism at all, as Mr. Dewey would probably grant; his term "economic anarchy" is a better description. As a matter of fact, the corporate form of our economic system makes possible a scale of exploitation unheard of in history. The industrial technology which Mr. Dewey exalts so highly is a two-edged sword; theoretically it might appear to be the mechanism by which the ideal collective existence could be consummated; actually it is a form of legerdemain through which a stupendous concentration of wealth and power is achieved, along with a corresponding degree of exploitation of human effort. Centralization of political power and governmental regulation of industrial processes—far from being tendencies toward any real socialism—offer even greater possibilities of economic domination, because of the comparative ease with which control of government agencies is secured by industrial interests.

In spite of these adverse consequences of the corporate régime, Mr. Dewey believes that "public" socialism is possible, even though we should have to *remake human nature* to secure it. One is forced to ask if attempts to remake human nature are not largely responsible for our present disorganization? Is there not perhaps in man a grain against which the artificial constraint of social patterns cannot successfully go? Are not all systems of socialism likely to founder on just the complex of human tendencies which make for what Mr. Dewey calls the "old individualism"? Remaking human nature in any fundamental sense is a process of very dubious prospect, even if the desirability of it be granted. Man is not a *tabula rasa* on which arbitrary patterns of conduct may be inscribed without regard to his natural propensities. His bodily organization at birth prescribes the general limits within which not only his overt forms of action, but also the dependable motives through which he can be stimulated, will tend to lie. The latter factors are especially important and are perhaps less variable than the former. The neuro-muscular-glandular systems which underlie affective behavior and which operate to energize the individual cannot be excised or fundamentally modified by social patterns. Man is remarkably plastic in the sense that he possesses few if any complex instinctive pattern reactions at birth, but there are structural conditions determining his organic needs, as well as the energizing mechanisms important in affective and emotional reactions closely related to these needs, which are largely due to innate conditions and which are relatively stable. Such direction of man's overt habit formation as may be secured by education must conform rather than run counter to these conditions if we are to secure any integration of the individual's efforts and aspirations into a unitary personality. The old individualism was perhaps not at all an aberrant condition; it is more intelligible when regarded as a natural product, in its general features, of those tendencies in man which are most fundamental, most dynamic, and the inhibition of which can be expected to produce distortion of human development. Man's motivation to action will no doubt forever be "unmitigatedly private," in a basic sense, and any plan for social readjustment will do well to proceed on this basis. Such motivation is not necessarily unethical in nature, although antisocial tendencies may predominate in many individuals where the environment is such as to fail to provide conditions essential to a stable, well-rounded development.

A second important implication of Mr. Dewey's proposed collectivism relates to the means of securing social direction and action. In conformity with the metaphysics of equality and uniqueness of individuality, Mr. Dewey seems to rely upon a kind of collective generation and expression of group purposes and ideals, rather than upon "geniuses," "heroes," or "divine leaders" (*i.e.*, superior individuals). There is an implied hope that somehow the greater association among individuals (which does not, in fact, occur, as will be shown below) and the consequent release of capacities to a maximum degree will result in the articulation of ethically approved goals and in the discovery of practical means of realizing them. The facts of ethnology, history, and psychology do not appear to substantiate such a hope. Collective behavior such as Mr. Dewey has envisaged for the ideal democratic state is not characteristic of actual group thought and action, either past or present. Essertier, in a valuable study, has shown that only the rare, heroic individual rises above the level of what he terms "inferior forms of explanation." By the same token we may expect that if there is ever any development of really humane social institutions this will occur only when the impulses of a people are rendered articulate and given direction by superior, dominant individuals. We may expect further that a scheme of things in which geniuses are identified with freaks, which depends upon the expression of a magic collective intelligence for its ideals and ideas, which proposes as a standard of social worth an esoteric equality of individuals as opposed to a concrete criterion of social conduct, will undoubtedly find itself impotent to descend from the level of pure abstraction on which it now reposes. If one derives any personal satisfaction from the belief in the metaphysical and moral equality of individuals, there is perhaps no harm in harboring it. Americans, however, should find it difficult to expect that an effective moral order will originate in a recondite communism of spirit in a people without leaders. We have been operating on some such basis for a number of years, and if ever a nation needed "geniuses," "heroes," or "divine leaders" it is America now.

A third important point raised by Mr. Dewey in his discussions of the advantages of the communistic order is that concerning the extent to which association among individuals would be promoted by it. He holds that the industrial, corporate order tends to make for an aggregate mental and emotional life, to promote human association, and thus to enhance the "liberation of capacity" which is the all-important function of education. It seems to me that two entirely different and even opposed conditions are confused here. The only association or communication of any psychological import is that of face-to-face interaction among individuals, and it appears that instead of more association of this sort in the corporate age there is actually less of it. We do indeed have greater similarity in the behavior patterns of individuals, more people doing the same thing in the same way and perhaps at the same time, but this by no means insures real communion. The fact that along with ten million other persons a man eats potato chips made in Detroit is of about zero order of significance as far as the humanizing process of liberation of spirit in social interaction goes. The two thousand patrons of a modern movie palace engage in no real communication or interaction, and consequently could scarcely be said to participate in an aggregate emotional life or to be sharing experiences in a manner calculated to produce development of personality. The performance of a train of activities along the same external pattern as that followed by millions of other people means no corresponding psychological communism. This real association exists, for the generality of people, only in the agrarian community and in the villages and towns which are its adjuncts. It depends upon a stable population, upon long acquaintances, since human beings do not bear spigots by which "fraternity" can be drawn off for the asking. The city necessarily means a diminution of these associations; the casual, fleeting, formal contacts with great numbers of people only enhance a sense of isolation, and consequently inhibit the very process of "liberation of spirit" which Mr. Dewey rightly regards as of great importance in mental development.

Another phase of the same problem is the decline of the family. This is perhaps much more important than any other phase of contemporary disintegration, since the family is the natural biological group, the normal milieu of shared experiences, community of interests, integration of personality. The segmentation of both adult and child activities which has accompanied the corporate age leaves little to the family beyond the details of finance and the primary sexual functions. Allport has recently pointed out in an excellent article that the moral and educational functions of the family are more and more intrusted to depersonalized external agencies which simulate the form of familial function but which are entirely devoid of its content. The following quotation summarizes the psychological importance of the family very well: "In youth as in age, in work as in play, in physical care as in education and morals, there remains a vital function which only such a face-to-face relation as the biological family can fulfill. No artifice of the social scientist, no new marriage contract or community agency, can replace this relationship as a medium for the development and integration of human personality. Fresh expectancies of conduct may be defined, new organizations may spring up to take over old familial duties; but these devices only dissipate our energies the further and realign us among new factions and patterns. . . . The only reality which is ultimately worth considering is that of human beings which associate together; and the life of the family is the life which actual fathers, mothers, and children live in one another's company. Unless there are opportunities for individuals to grow and to realize their potentialities through free contact with one another, the most highly perfected pattern of the sociologist will be only an empty formula." We have of late been deluged with psychoanalytic literature on the abnormal influence of parents upon children. Dire pictures of sex attachments and conflicts within the family have driven some of these hardy souls to urge that the institution be scrapped. There is, of course, some basis for their claims, but the percentage of abnormalities resulting from familial association is negligible in comparison with the benefits for people generally. And these benefits we are fast surrendering to the industrial order, whose patterns of conduct are incompatible with the conditions necessary to the stability and integrity of family life.

The sequel of industrialism is, then, personal isolation, and a fractionation of life functions into an ever-expanding and differentiating system of formalized institutions. How can the individual "refind" himself, to use Mr. Dewey's term, when all of the dominant tendencies of the age are trying to lose him? Both in the economic and in the psychological sense we observe that the theory and the practice of the corporate industrial régime diverge widely. It should be productive, we are told, of greater sharing of goods and of experiences, of an economic and psychological communism which the "mighty upward trend toward democracy" presumably has had for its goal. Actually, the conditions of life since the industrial revolution have been favoring greater exploitation in the economic sense and less "psychological" association of the sort essential to personality development. In view of these considerations, one wonders if industrialism is the inevitable destiny of Western civilization? By "industrialism" is meant not the machine and industrial technology as such, but the domination of the economic, political, and social order by the notion that the greater part of a nation's energies should be directed toward an endless process of increasing the production and consumption of goods. There is nothing inherently evil about a machine, although the operation of one on a lifetime scale would necessarily be pretty monotonous. I have spent many months in a large tire factory operating a machine for which I could never form any emotional attachment, in spite of Mr. Dewey's suggestion that modifications might be introduced in the ownership of machines of such a nature that feeling and emotion might enter into the tasks of daily life. It is not the machine, however, but the theory of the use of the machine to which I object, and if this theory, which we may call industrialism, is a valid hypothesis of the course of Western civilization, all discussion of "progress" would do well to cease. The only intelligible meaning of progress implies social institutions for producing psychological effects just the reverse of those so outstanding in our Machine Age. The question asked above relative to industrialism and the future must then be answered before any decision as to the possibility of progress can be reached. We shall now consider briefly a few important aspects of the industrial situation by way of trying to answer this question.

One outstanding fact in industry at present is that with the great increase in production and in new commodities, and with consumption coerced to the limit, there is a steady decrease in employment. Improvements in technology, as Mr. Stuart Chase has recently pointed out, "can mean only one thing. An equivalent tonnage of goods can be produced by a declining number of workers, and men must lose their jobs by the thousands—presently by the millions." The so-called "blotting-paper trades" which hitherto have absorbed many of these workers (but not all) are very soggy, thinks Mr. Chase. This seems only logical; there must be a saturation point somewhere in the consumption process, and we would seem to be approaching it. Chronic unemployment of some 2,000,000 out of 30,000,000 workers in the country, with the figure rising to 4,000,000 or more in times of cyclical depression such as the present, cannot be wiped out by charity, slogans, Hoover conferences which recommend increased buying, or increases in the tariff. Hungry and maladjusted men, women, and children, in numbers that bid fair to increase, is one of the promises of industrialism for the future. With the curve of employment running steadily downward, industry will be increasingly unable to maintain the present army of workers permanently and continuously.

The logical outcome of these conditions is growing internal dissension and, eventually, revolution. This result will be greatly facilitated by the instability in a "floating" populace concentrated in large urban industrial centers, unattached to that tremendous social anchor, land, and lacking in "solid and assured objects of belief and approved ends of action." Mr. William Green recently warned a Senate committee that the labor forces under his direction could not be held in line much longer unless drastic measures were taken to relieve the unemployment situation. The latter is, of course, only an aspect of the general problem of industrialism, and it is possible to alleviate the condition temporarily without removing its cause. Another world war, which the international struggle for markets suggests as not an unlikely prospect, would afford temporary "relief." Mr. Owen Young is quoted in press dispatches as saying that over-production with the consequent competition for foreign markets is a real menace to international peace. There is nothing very strange in this idea, inasmuch as we are now far enough away from the last war to understand the economic translation of "making the world safe for democracy." Another salvation drama would relieve the labor market and take care of the surplus for a while, but this is neither a permanent nor a very intelligent solution. The institution of various palliative measures by industrialists themselves may also serve to postpone the hour of reckoning. Among these are unemployment insurance, state unemployment compensation, the shortening of working hours with the consequent employment of more men, regularization of production, increase in the age limit of child laborers, and so on. These measures would undoubtedly stabilize conditions for a time, but it requires considerable optimism to believe that they would insure the permanent retention in industrial employment of the large portion of our population now engaged in it. Technological improvements, efficiency experts, and mergers would necessarily add regularly to the burden of any unemployment insurance or compensation plan. Like the present Farm Board's attempt to handle the wheat surplus, such devices are unnatural and temporary. Furthermore, granting the possibility of tiding over for a few years, even for twenty-five or fifty, the most that is offered to the worker is the bleak assurance that no serious physiological want will overtake him. The men, women, and children will have no humanized living; caught in the throes of these convulsions of a predatory and decadent capitalism, their drab existences will bear mute testimony that our century of Progress lies below the cultural level of the Pyramids.

The alternative course to this blind temporization is to renounce the capitalistic industrial program. This does not mean that the industrial technology should be scrapped; on the contrary, further mechanization of industrial production should be encouraged, since this would mean that progressively fewer persons would be required for its processes. The production of commodities should be stabilized in each industry, and the large surplus of chronically unemployed should be induced by all possible means to return to agriculture. The objection may be made that already there is over-production of agricultural commodities; the answer is that agriculture is more than a process of "production." The millions of people who now hang on to the fringes of industry would find a place to live and food to eat; they would no longer fill the "flop" houses and the bread lines. They would not have to look forward to the demoralizing prospect of the dole, even when made under the guise of "insurance." They would have a base on which to knit together the fragments of lives now broken on the wheel of what we are pleased to call civilization.

This is a project which demands far-sighted "social engineering." Agriculture is in a discredited state; it has been deserted on a large scale for the false glamour of cities and the paltry luxuries which the money in'ermittently available in industry promised to secure. But an even more important factor has been the economic discrimination against agriculture in the form of government subsidization of industry. The tariff has all but gutted beyond repair the pursuit which lies at the base of every social organization. Farmers have been kept in poverty, their farms have been heavily mortgaged and eventually deserted, through the purchase of needless luxuries and expensive machinery for which the advertising of industrialists has created a sense of need. It is, of course, always possible to *live* on a farm despite the tariff and the idiosyncrasies of climate, but it is impossible to compete with the industrial population for possession of a thousand and one gadgets which issue from the machines at price levels held up by the national government. Even reasonable luxuries are difficult to secure under such conditions, for the majority of the agricultural population, and there is consequently little incentive to remain in what appears to the farmer to be a flat and profitless occupation.

The unsalutary psychological and social consequences of the diminution of the influence of agriculture upon the general patterns of American life have already been indicated. Unless steps are taken toward the restoration of the balance of economic forces in America, which was destroyed in 1865, we cannot hope to avoid the unsavory sequel of industrialism outlined above. Industrialism bears its own antidote, but it is a bitter one; the consequences of its course of self-destruction are scarcely justified, even by that foremost American contribution to world-culture, the billionaire. If there exists any effective social and political intelligence in the country it might profitably be mobilized for the conduction of a specific program of rehabilitation of the agrarian economy and the "old individualism" associated with it. This program is not conceived in a spirit of pathological regression to the past, stimulated by repugnance toward contemporary conditions; it is the definition of a concrete social aim. The instrumentalities of intelligent political leadership, informed social science, and a definitive social philosophy could have no more important problem than that of trying to effect a synthesis, in some sense, of the unified manner of living inherent in the agrarian family and community with the energy and inventiveness which have been diverted into industrialism.

ALLEN TATE

REMARKS ON THE
SOUTHERN RELIGION

AT ONE time not inconceivably long ago the ordinary layman, or even the extraordinary one who took up the mysteries as a gentlemanly pursuit, had an impressive respect for the professional man of religion, who for some reason not clear to 1930 had authority to speak of the Higher Things. We have none of that respect now. The present writer, who is a layman of the more ordinary kind, is deficient in it. There is a priest here and there, even a Protestant clergyman or two, who as individuals seem to speak from the tripod; but they hardly—from the viewpoint of some fine past—represent their class; they are only laymen of the more extraordinary kind. So I begin an essay on "religion" with almost no humility at all; that is to say, I begin it in a spirit of irreligion, and without apology to those who know better, for there seems to be none, as a class, who have that high qualification. And this is a matter of deep regret; for one will have to think for oneself, a responsibility intolerable to the religious mind, whose proper business is to prepare the mysteries for others. This I cannot pretend to do.

[1] The writer is constrained to point out (with the permission of the other contributors) that in his opinion the general title of this book is not quite true to its aims. It emphasizes the fact of exclusiveness rather than its benefits; it points to a particular house but omits to say that it was the home of a spirit that may also have lived elsewhere and that this mansion, in short, was incidentally made with hands.

Religion is not properly a discussion of anything; so any discussion of religion is a piece of violence, a betrayal of the religious essence undertaken for its own good, or for the good of those who live by it. This is the sole justification of an amateur treatment of religion: my betrayal of religion betrays only my own, and instead of a public scandal it is only an instance of personal indecorum which can injure no one but myself.

But there is also a certain pretension in this incivility, and it may as well out: It is to the effect that my private fable was once more public and general, and that our public have fallen away from it on to evil days. I must therefore proceed at once to dress my fable in First Principles—which are indeed the only dress it will receive in this essay. I can hardly make a pretension convincing by leaving it in the simple condition that it enjoys in my own mind—that is, the condition of fairy story and myth. For a myth should be in conviction immediate, direct, overwhelming, and I take it that the appreciation of this kind of imagery is an art lost to the modern mind. There will be a few metaphors, but no pretty stories in this essay.

I

The reader must here be entreated to follow some pages of abstraction conducted in the interest of my religion, but partaking of that religion not an ounce. For abstraction is the death of religion no less than the death of anything else. Religion, when it directs its attention to the horse cropping the blue-grass on the lawn, is concerned with the whole horse, and not with (1) that part of him which

(156)

he has in common with other horses, or that more general part which he shares with other quadrupeds or with the more general vertebrates; and not with (2) that power of the horse which he shares with horsepower in general, of pushing or pulling another object. Religion pretends to place before us the horse as he is.

Since this essay is not religion, but a discussion of it, it does not pretend to put before you the complete horse. It does pretend to do the following: to show that the complete horse may be there in spite of the fact that this discussion cannot bring him forth. In other words, there is a complete and self-contained horse in spite of the now prevailing faith that there is none simply because the abstract and scientific mind cannot see him.

This modern mind sees only half of the horse—that half which may become a dynamo, or an automobile, or any other horsepowered machine. If this mind had much respect for the full-dimensioned, grass-eating horse, it would never have invented the engine which represents only half of him. The religious mind, on the other hand, has this respect; it wants the whole horse, and it will be satisfied with nothing less.

I should say a religious mind that requires more than a half-religion. A religion of the half-horse is preëminently a religion of how things work, and this is the American religion. By leaving half of the horse out of account, it can easily show that abstract horsepower, ideally, everywhere, infallibly, under other abstract and *half* conditions, works. Now the half of the animal that this religion leaves out won't work at all; it isn't workable; it is a vast body of

(157)

concrete qualities constantly conflicting with the workable half; today the horse saddled admirably, but yesterday he ran away—he would not work.

From this it is clear that there is another possible half-religion. It is very common at present. It asserts that nothing works—a poor if desperate refutation of the other half-religion. It says that no horse is workable; the horse is just an infinite object, and the more you contemplate him the more you see how futile it is to pretend that there is anything regular about him. He is unique beyond cure, and you can't predict either his conduct from one day to another or the conduct of Man o' War from the performance of Jim Dandy. This is as bad as saying that you can predict it completely. It is another half-religion: it is the religion of the Symbolist poets, and of M. Henri Bergson.

But how do we know that the religion of the completely workable is a religion? It has no altars—that is, no altars that befit it entirely, for it has only usurped the altars traditionally surviving; it has no formal ritual, and no priesthood wearing anything like a cassock or telling anything like beads. We know that the cult of infallible working is a religion because it sets up an irrational value; it is irrational to believe in omnipotent human rationality. Nothing infallibly works, and the new half-religionists are simply worshiping a principle, and with true half-religious fanaticism they ignore what they do not want to see—which is the breakdown of the principle in numerous instances of practice. It is a bad religion, for that very reason; it can predict only success.

The religion, then, of the whole horse predicts both success and failure. It says that the horse will work within limits, but it is folly to tempt the horse providence too far. It takes account of the failures—that is, it is realistic, for it calls upon the traditional experience of evil which is the common lot of the race. It is thus a mature religion, and it is not likely to suffer disillusion and collapse. Here it is very unlike the half-religion of work which has a short memory of failure; it can ignore its failures to a certain saturation point, beyond which they will be overwhelming, and the society living under it is riding for a crushing fall. It will be totally unprepared for collapse; it will have gone too far. It will have forgotten the symbol of itself in the career of the vaunting Œdipus, who, blind at last, cautioned us not to pronounce a man happy till we saw the end of his life. The half-religion of work has accomplished the murder of Laius and (I do not mean this as a hit) married Jocasta; it has applied its formula for life-action with astonishing success *up to now*; but the end is yet to come. Tiresias is yet to come.

Probably Mr. T. S. Eliot meant to show this when he brought Tiresias into his poem "The Waste Land"; for the seer presents the bankruptcy of the modern formula as this is acted out in that most terrible scene in modern poetry— the brutally indifferent seduction of the typist by the "small house-agent's clerk." The seduction "works"; it works perfectly, too well; but the very working testifies to its failure. It can only be mechanically repeated over again and again.

It is apparent that the image of the horse will "work" only in a limited number of logical distinctions; so I propose to discard it.

II

Take the far more complex image of history, if indeed it may be called an image at all. For as an image its content is mixed and incoherent, and reduces to a vast clutter of particular images. We are able each of us to take our choice; we may reconstruct this scene or that period. We have those people who prefer the Renaissance, and those who like better the Periclean age, or perhaps they concentrate their loyalty to a special kind of life in a particular document of an age or a people: there are Platonists and Aristotelians, Stoics and Hedonists, and there are the Christians, or at least there were the Christians who stood by two Testaments, both of which we are now instructed to say are of very ancient and obscure origin and of muddled contents.

These more concrete minds may be said to look at their history in a definite and now quite unfashionable way. They look at it as a concrete series that has taken place in a very real time—by which I mean, without too much definition, a time as sensible, as full of sensation, and as replete with accident and uncertainty as the time they themselves are living in, moment by moment.

But if you take history not as an image or many images, you have to take it as an idea, an abstraction, a concept. You need not feel any great interest in the rival merits of the Greek and Roman cultures; they were both ideas comprehensible after some comparison under a single law. There is no accident or uncertainty, for the illusion of contingency that seemed to beset the ages of the past is dissolved by the Long View—and this means that the ancient versions of nature were so limited that the ancients were not able to see apparent contradiction in the true light of all-embracing law. For this Long View history becomes an abstract series, opposed to the concrete series of the Short View. There are several questions here that need to be asked of the Long View: Is not this the religion of the half-horse? Does the law of identity which joins up the Greek and Roman cultures make them identical in any other respect than Law? Is it, in short, the Greek and Roman cultures themselves? Is it these cultures in any other sense than the working horse is the actual horse?

I have said that this view makes the past an abstract series; let it be called a logical series, and there is nothing to do but to resort to the customary *A, B, C,* of the textbooks. These letters may follow one another at all places at all times, without sensation, accident, or contingency; but did Greek culture live and have its being without sensation? The Short View maintains that it did not, for the Short View holds that the proper series for history to be placed in is the temporal or concrete series.

At this point I must, for brevity, do some violence to the reaches of the argument, and say: for the Short View, history is the specific account of the doings of specific men, who acted their rôles in a vast and contemporaneous setting which somewhat bewildered them and which prompted them to make up stories with an obvious moral. But, for the moment, I must leave this moral, and close this part of my argument with one final difference between the Long and the Short View.

It is apparent that a solvent which reduces the Greek and the Roman cultures to identity takes from us the privilege of choosing between them; or assuming that we are the offshoot of one of them, there is no reason why we cannot take up the other. The Long View is, in brief, the cosmopolitan destroyer of Tradition. Or, put otherwise, since the Christian myth is a vegetation rite, varying only in some details from countless other vegetation myths, there is no reason to prefer Christ to Adonis. Varying only in some details: this assumes that there is no difference between a horse and a dog, both being vertebrates, mammals, quadrupeds, etc. The Short View holds that the whole Christ and the whole Adonis are sufficiently differentiated in their respective qualities (roughly details), and that our tradition compels us to choose more than that half of Christ which is Adonis and to take the whole, separate, and unique Christ.

There is a nice and somewhat slippery paradox here: Why should our tradition compel us to choose anything? Particularly in view of the all but accomplished fact that tradition is destroyed? If the agency is shut up, the business cannot be transacted. And we have to confess that merely living in a certain stream of civilized influence does not compel us to be loyal to it. Indeed, the act of loyalty, or the fact of loyalty, must be spontaneous to count at all; tradition must, in other words, be automatically operative before it can be called tradition. For in its true function it is powerfully selective, and the moment it admits that Adonis is able to compete with Christ, though it regret the rivalry, it has gone over to the Long View; its faith has weakened; and we are at the verge of committing ourselves to the half-religions that are no religions at all, but quite simply a decision passed on the utility, the workableness, of the religious objects with respect to the practical aims of society.

So this is the paradox: is it Tradition or the Long View itself which prompts the present defense of the religious attitude? It is probably a little of both; though the conception is wholly irrational. It is irrational to defend religion with the weapon that invariably discredits it, and yet this is what seems to be happening. I am trying to discover the place that religion holds with logical, abstract instruments, which of course tend to put religion in some logical system or series, where it vanishes.

III

But this is due to our nature, which is a very different nature from that of the Russian or eastern European mind, whose religion is quite simply supernaturalism or the naïve religion of the entire horse. It never suspects the existence of those halves that render our sanity so precarious and compel us to vacillate between a self-destroying naturalism and practicality, on the one hand, and a self-destroying mysticism, on the other. For it seems that we are not able to contemplate those qualities of the horse that are specifically religious without forgetting his merely spatial and practicable half: we cannot let the entire horse fill our minds all at once. And thus we have a special notion of tradition— a notion that tradition is not simply a fact, but a fact that must be constantly defended.

(163)

This defense is what we call Dogma. The strictly qualitative half of the horse, his special uniqueness as a sensible fact, in a word, his image, must be defended against pure practicality, or his abstraction. The only defense we know is rational and scientific, and it is evident that Dogma is not a personal property of religion, but a mere instrument. And it is an act of sheer generosity when it sets about the defense of its natural enemy, the qualitative view of experience. But, in the Middle Ages, it was so enamoured of this enemy that it could not be brought to defend even itself.

It was both a great discovery and a great calamity when the Europeans found that Reason could be used in another way than the defense of something alien to it. It has always seemed a scandal to us that Scholasticism should try to make rational all those unique qualities of the horse which are spirits and myths and symbols. The men of the Renaissance effectively hushed the scandal up; they said: *Entia non sunt multiplicanda praeter necessitatem.* Which meant, Throw over the spirits and symbols, which are irrational anyhow, not rationally necessary, and find those quantities in nature which will *work*, the quantities that are barely necessary for work.

This was always the peril of the European mind (a mind that is at its most typical at present in its American form) and the mediæval Church knew it. By making Reason, Science, or Nature, an instrument of defense for the protection of the other than reasonable, the other than natural, it performed a tremendous feat of spiritual unity, and the only kind of unity that the Western mind is capable of.

Its special feature is the implied belief, which of course became often explicit—I simply mean that the belief was logically necessary—its special feature is an ineradicable belief in the fundamental evil of nature. Western Reason has always played the ostrich by sticking its head in the Supernatural. Woe betide when it took its head out and got so used to the natural setting that it found it good. And this is what has happened. For the Church knew that the only way to restrain the practical impulses of her constituency was to put into the mouth of nature the words, *Noli tangere.* The Eastern Church never had to do this, nor did it ever have to construct a plausible rationality round the supernatural to make it acceptable; it has never had a philosophy, nor a Dogma in our sense; it never needed one.

The Western Church established a system of quantity for the protection of quality, but there was always the danger that quantity would revolt from servitude and suppress its master; the danger that it would apply its genius to a field more favorable to spectacular success. Once reason ceased to be the instrument through which its purely qualitative features could be contemplated and enjoyed, without being corrupted by too much use, it began to see the natural setting as so many instances of quantity; that is, nature began to see the practical possibilities of knowing herself. The symbol and the myth meant that nature was largely an inviolable whole; once the symbol and the myth were proved to be not natural facts, but unnatural fictions that fitted into no logical series tolerable to the rational mind, nature became simply a workable half. It now thinks that it is a Whole of limitless practicability.

IV

This being true, how can Tradition, which is always embarrassing to practicality on a large scale, be defended? Has it not disappeared? And was it not always on the brink of compromise in the fact that it needed the support of its enemy? The answer is doubtless: It can always be defended, but a recovery and restoration is a more difficult performance.

Moreover, where can an American take hold of Tradition? His country is supposed to have preserved none from Europe, and if we take the prototype of the European tradition to be mediæval society, we must confess that America has performed wonders, considering her youth, in breaking it down.

Yet the very idea "America" must give us pause, for it is almost anything that a determined apologist may wish to represent. In a brief three hundred years she has recapitulated practically every form of European polity, if these separate polities may be seen as devoid of their religious background. She has repeated all the chief economic and political forms. But she has not repeated the religious forms. The religious history of America is perfectly continuous with that of Europe.

This anomaly gave us that remarkable society of the old South, which was a feudal society without a feudal religion. The reason for this is by no means obscure. It is just possible to see the Jamestown project as the symbol of what later happened to this country: it was a capitalistic enterprise undertaken by Europeans who were already convinced adherents of large-scale exploitation of nature, not to support a stable religious order, but to advance the interests of trade as an end in itself. They stood thus for a certain stage in the disintegration of the European religion, and their descendants stuck to their guns, which theoretically at least were Protestant, aggressive, and materialistic guns.

At the same time certain conditions of economy created a society which was, again theoretically, Protestant, but which was not aggressive and materialistic. It was a case of atavism, a "throwback." A distinguished contributor to this symposium argues that the Southern population were originally much less rebellious against European stability than were the Northern. It is doubtful if history will support this, though I should personally like to do so, for it is the myth-making tendency of the mind in one of its most valuable forms. The enemy, abstraction, or the view of history as the logical series, gives us another story; it is that soil and climate made the agrarian life generally more attractive than a barrener soil and a colder climate could have ever done, and that the propitious soil and climate made it possible for a feudal system of labor to take root and thrive. A people will, in short, return to an older form of economy, under certain local conditions, but international conditions, certainly since the sixteenth century, have made it impossible for any community of European origin to remain spiritually isolated and to develop its genius, unless that genius is in harmony with the religious and economic drift of the civilization at large.

(167)

The South could blindly return to an older secular polity, but the world was too much with it, and it could not create its appropriate religion.

There were two results of this anomalous position, which may be stated without too much historical argument. The South, as a political atmosphere formed by the eighteenth century, did not realize its genius in time, but continued to defend itself on the political terms of the North; and thus, waiting too long, it let its powerful rival gain the ascendancy. Its religious impulse was inarticulate simply because it tried to encompass its destiny within the terms of Protestantism, in origin, a non-agrarian and trading religion; hardly a religion at all, but a result of secular ambition. The Southern politicians could merely quote Scripture to defend slavery, the while they defended their society as a whole with the catchwords of eighteenth-century politics. And this is why the South separated from the North too late, and so lost its cause.

The second result of the anomalous structure of the Southern mind is a close and contemporary one. Because the South never created a fitting religion, the social structure of the South began grievously to break down two generations after the Civil War; for the social structure depends on the economic structure, and economic conviction is the secular image of religion. No nation is ever simply and unequivocally beaten in war; nor was the South. But the South shows signs of defeat, and this is due to its lack of a religion which would make her special secular system the inevitable and permanently valuable one. We have been inferior to the Irish in this virtue, though much less than the Irish have we ever been beaten in war.

It appears that the question put at the beginning of this section, How can the American, or the Southern man, take hold of Tradition, is further from being answered than ever.

V

Let us return to the two ways of looking at horses and history. Which are we permitted to say was the way of the old South? The answer to this question is not necessarily disconcerting, for it is simply both. And it is bound to be both because the South was a Western community, and a Western community is one that does not live in sackcloth and ashes and erect all of its temples to the gods. The Southerners were capable of using their horses, as they did one day at Brandy Station, but they could also contemplate them as absolute and inviolable objects; they were virtually incapable of abstracting from the horse his horse-power, or from history its historicity. For the horse fact and the historical fact, by remaining concrete, retained a certain status as *images*, and images are only to be contemplated, and perhaps the act of contemplation after long exercise initiates a habit of imitation, and the setting up of absolute standards which are less formulas for action than an interior discipline of the mind. There is doubtless from the viewpoint of abstract history not much difference between a centaur (since we speak of horses) and a Christ (since we speak of historicity), because both are mythical figments answerable to the same "laws." But the Short

View, as we have seen, is incorrigibly selective, and has been known to prefer Christ to the man horse.

After about 1820 the Southern communities alone stood for that preference with a single mind. The heresy of New England is beautifully recorded in the correspondence of John Adams and Thomas Jefferson, where the two sages discuss the possibility of morals. Jefferson calls his judgment "taste"—reliance on custom, breeding, ingrained moral decision. But Adams needs a "process of moral reasoning," which forces the individual to think out from abstract principle his rôle at a critical moment of action. The view of John Adams tells us how far New England had gone from Europe, how deeply she had broken with the past.

While the South in the nineteenth century trafficked with Europe in cotton, she took in exchange very little of manners, literature, or the arts. The Southerners were another community on the complete European plan, and they had no need, being independent, of importing foreign art and noblemen, commodities that New England became frantic about after 1830. For New England was one of those abstract-minded, sharp-witted trading societies that must be parasites in two ways: They must live economically on some agrarian class or country, and they must live spiritually likewise. New England lived economically on the South, culturally on England. And this created doubtless a disguised and involved nostalgia for the land—the New England "land" being old England. The homes and the universities of New England became a European museum, stuffed with the dead symbols of what the New Englander could not create because provision for it had been left out of his original foundation. In the nineteenth century New England confessed her loss of the past by being too much interested in Europe. If you take the Adams family at its best, you find a token of the whole New England mind: there is the tragedy of the "Education of Henry Adams" who never quite understood what he was looking for. He spent much of his youth, like Henry James, learning the manners of the English agrarians, without being by right of soil entitled to them, and thus never suspecting that the best he might hope to do was to learn them by rote. More significantly he passed his last days in Washington despising the "ignorant" and "simple" minds south of the Potomac, again never suspecting that his efforts in behalf of defeating this simplicity and ignorance in a recent war did something towards undermining the base of the civilized values that he coveted most.

If New England's break with Europe made her excessively interested in the European surface, the ignorance and simplicity of the South's independence of Europe, in the cultural sense, witness a fact of great significance. The South could be ignorant of Europe because it *was* Europe; that is to say, the South had taken root in a native soil. And the South could remain simple-minded because it had no use for the intellectual agility required to define its position. Its position was self-sufficient and self-evident; it was European where the New England position was self-conscious and colonial. The Southern mind was simple, not top-heavy with learning it had no need of, unintellectual, and composed; it was personal and dramatic, rather than abstract and metaphysical; and it was sensuous because it lived close to a natural scene of great variety and interest.

Because it lived by images, not highly organized, it is true, as Dogma, but rather more loosely gathered from the past, the South was a profoundly traditional European community. The Southerners were incurable in their preference for Cato over the social conditions in which he historically lived. They looked at history as the concrete and temporal series—a series at all only because they required a straight line back into the past, for the series, such as it was, was very capricious, and could hardly boast of a natural logic. It could entertain the biblical mythology along with the Greek, and it could add to these a lively mediævalism from the novels of Sir Walter Scott. They saw themselves as human beings living by a humane principle, from which they were unwilling to subtract the human so as to set the principle free to operate on an unlimited program of practicality. For that is what a principle is—the way things will work. But the Southerner, or more generally the die-hard agrarian, was not willing to let the principle proceed alone, uncontrolled; for all that he values in the working of principle is the capacity that he retains of enjoying the work it does. The old Southerners were highly critical of the kinds of work to be done. They planted no corn that they could not enjoy; they grew no cotton that did not directly contribute to the upkeep of a rich private life; and they knew no history for the sake of knowing it, but simply for the sake of contemplating it and seeing in it an image of themselves. And aware of the treachery of nature, as all agrarians are, they tended to like stories, very simple stories with a moral.

We have already considered some of the possible reasons why they broke down.

VI

They had a religious life, but it was not enough organized with a right mythology. In fact, their rational life was not powerfully united to the religious experience, as it was in mediæval society, and they are a fine specimen of the tragic pitfall upon which the Western mind has always hovered. Lacking a rational system for the defense of their religious attitude and its base in a feudal society, they elaborated no rational system whatever, no full-grown philosophy; so that, when the post-bellum temptations of the devil, who is the exploiter of nature, confronted them, they had no defense. Since there is, in the Western mind, a radical division between the religious, the contemplative, the qualitative, on the one hand, and the scientific, the natural, the practical on the other, the scientific mind always plays havoc with the spiritual life when it is not powerfully enlisted in its cause; it cannot be permitted to operate alone.

It operated alone in Thomas Jefferson, and the form that it took in his mind may be reduced to a formula: The ends of man are sufficiently contained in his political destiny. Now the political destiny of men is the way they work, and the ends they hope to achieve collectively by the operation of mechanical laws. It is not necessary to belabor this point, or to draw out the enormous varieties that such a theory may exhibit. It is sufficient to point out that the ante-bellum

Southerners never profoundly believed it. It is highly illuminating to reflect that *they acted as if they did*. There was, of course, a good deal of dissent: the Virginia Constitutional Convention repudiated Jefferson in 1832. It was a first step; but the last step was so far off that it could not possibly have preceded 1861.

The modern Southerner inherits the Jeffersonian formula. This is only to say that he inherits a concrete and very unsatisfactory history. He can almost wish for his ease the Northern contempt for his kind of history; he would like to believe that history is not a vast body of concrete fact to which he must be loyal, but only a source of mechanical formulas; for then he might hope to do what the Northern industrialist has just about succeeded in doing—making a society out of abstractions. The Southerner would conjure up some magic abstraction to spirit back to him his very concrete way of life. He would, in short, in his plight, apply the formula by his inheritance—that the ends of man may be established by political means.

The South would not have been defeated had it possessed a sufficient faith in its own kind of God. It would not have been defeated, in other words, had it been able to bring out a body of doctrine setting forth its true conviction that the ends of man require more for their realization than politics. The setback of the war was of itself a very trivial one.

We are very near an answer to our question—How may the Southerner take hold of his Tradition?

The answer is, by violence.

For this answer is inevitable. He cannot fall back upon

his religion, simply because it was never articulated and organized for him; if he could do this, he would constitute himself a "borer from within," and might hope to effect a secular revolution in his favor. As we have said, economy is the secular image of religious conviction. His religious conviction is inchoate and unorganized; it never had the opportunity to be anything else.

Since he cannot bore from within, he has left the sole alternative of boring from without. This method is political, active, and, in the nature of the case, violent and revolutionary. Reaction is the most radical of programs; it aims at cutting away the overgrowth and getting back to the roots. A forward-looking radicalism is a contradiction; it aims at rearranging the foliage.

The Southerner is faced with the paradox: He must use an instrument, which is political, and so unrealistic and pretentious that he cannot believe in it, to re-establish a private, self-contained, and essentially spiritual life. I say that he must do this; but that remains to be seen.

HERMAN CLARENCE NIXON

WHITHER
SOUTHERN ECONOMY?

SOUTHERN economic life is at the crossroads. Its agrarian predominance in fact and spirit is seriously threatened by the rising tide of industrial growth and aspiration, if not exploitation. The threat is greater because the figures and values of Southern industrialization are distorted somewhat in a sense suggestive of Sidney Lanier's remark "that small minds love to bring large news, and failing a load, will make one." This large news, or noise, of which I shall try to give a statistical view, is in contrast with the fact, as phrased by D. R. Hundley in 1860, "that cotton, sugar, rice, wheat, corn, tobacco and all other agricultural products grow in the country, and very *quietly* too at that." This distorted picture of industrial "progress" or "prosperity" is about to become part of the Southern state of mind. I have no intention to oppose Southern industrialization as a moderate fact, considered without exaggeration and without privilege. There is no point in a war with destiny or the census returns. But there seems strong ground for apprehension over the inner and articulate spirit of industrialism that is claiming so much for itself in the South today.

It is deplorable that the South's agricultural philosophy is imperiled by a non-philosophical pattern of society in which the highest aim of life is success in industry. It is deplorable

(176)

that this spread of the Southern worship of industrial gods after the World War, comparable to the Northern tide after the Civil War, is taking place at the time when dollar-chasing industrialism is being weighed in the balance and found wanting in America and Europe by such strong critics as John Dewey, Stuart Chase, John A. Hobson, R. H. Tawney, André Siegfried, and Mueller-Freienfels. L. C. Marshall, of Johns Hopkins University, even sees possible "foreshadowings of a tremendous cataclysm." The trend is deplorable in view of the South's opportunity, as noted by Count Keyserling and Glenn Frank, to offer a hope of cultural escape from the evils of industrialism. There are those who would throw the South physically and socially into an all-absorbing industrial system, at the expense of agriculture, although such an economic geographer as J. Russell Smith recognizes predictions of agricultural serfdom and suggests regional planning to prevent it. There are those who would standardize Southern economy after the manner of the industrial North, although Frederick J. Turner, the great interpreter of the American frontier, has lately emphasized the constructive significance of permanent sectionalism in American life; and Conrad Roser, a Connecticut Yankee, can discover, after four years in Dixie, that the "material growth of the South has been evolutionary and healthy," that this section "does not need to go elsewhere for its standards," and that it may exemplify "that balanced civilization the world so sorely needs." It is questionable policy to consider scrapping old-fashioned economic ways for new-fashioned ways that are already in

(177)

disrepute. If there is any law of progress, it involves in part a carry-over of the gains of the past.

Whatever be the future, it can yet be said that the South is like France in offering a fairly even balance between rural and urban populations, between agriculture and industry, with agrarian-mindedness predominating in the face of a long exposure to the industrial revolution. The percentage of farm population in the eleven ex-Confederate states in 1925 ranged upward from 20.7 for Florida and 36.6 for Louisiana to 53.2 for Arkansas and 63.1 for Mississippi. The estimated value of all farm crops in these states for 1927 as given by the *Statistical Abstract of the United States* (1929) was $2,770,500,000. This was less than half the gross value of Southern manufactures for the same year, which amounted to $6,401,782,000. But this latter large estimate must not be compared with the crop estimate, for agricultural values are virtually primary, while manufacturing values are secondary and fractional. It does not require a physiocrat to appreciate the significance of this point, regardless of the indirect dependence of both agriculture and manufacturing on other values like labor or power. Manufactured products directly derive important values from other processes, frequently from agriculture, that precede the manufacturing stage. A pound of tobacco or cotton yarn, for instance, leaves the factory as a manufactured product, but the material was first an agricultural product and part of the total final value is agricultural. Machine processing converts a farm hog into manufactured goods, but about four-fifths of the final value is derived from agriculture. This point is properly considered in the federal

(178)

statistics, but the figures as a rule are conveniently over-looked by the chirpers of industrial progress. A glimpse at this neglected column in the volume just cited shows that, while the manufactured products of Texas in 1927 had a value of $1,206,580,000, the value added to these products by Texas manufacturing was only $363,653,000, and that North Carolina manufacturing added approximately only half the final value of that state's manufactured products. The value added by Southern manufacturing to manufactured products in 1927 was estimated at $2,686,821,000, or $83,000,000 less than the estimated value of all Southern crops in that year. In other words, Southern crop values and manufacturing values are approximately equal in dollar terms, even with a tariff spread distinctly favorable to the latter. The comparison might be continued into the statistics of non-crop agriculture and the other industries assimilable by nature to manufacturing, with Texas petroleum required for the total of Southern mineral products to surpass in value the section's production of milk, chickens, and eggs.

The South's greatest activity is that of cotton-growing, and this agricultural pursuit is the basis for cotton-milling, the South's greatest manufacturing enterprise. One of the greatest agricultural productions, after cotton, is tobacco, and tobacco-manufacturing is, after cotton-manufacturing, one of the section's greatest industries. Even cottonseed constitutes the raw material for Southern mill products that are comparable in value to the lumber or the iron and steel manufactured below the Ohio and the Potomac. The South is the leading section of the country in the manufacture and use of fertilizer on account of agricultural needs, and this industry is partly based on cottonseed. Southern manufacturing may be considered as largely agrarian manufacturing, physically decentralized and not necessitating an excessive urbanization. The most highly industrialized Southern state of North Carolina contains only small-sized cities. Agriculture, directly and indirectly, furnishes the major share of Southern income, and it is significantly true that in 1927 the South's relative stage of industrialization as compared with the nation as a whole was about the same as in 1880, with little change from the relative status of 1860. The comparative and continued slowness of this industrialization is brought out by R. P. Brooks, of the University of Georgia, in a pamphlet study, *The Industrialization of the South,* which is a good antidote to the astronomical claims of certain boosters of change. Business throughout this agrarian region, according to data from *Bradstreet's,* was either "good" or "fair" at the end of 1929, with the exception of one "quiet" black spot in the district of Birmingham, the "Pittsburgh of the South."

Southern commerce and banking are largely built around agriculture. Memphis is an important city because it is the world's greatest inland cotton market; the Southern merchants who run afoul of a senatorial anti-trust inquisition are cotton dealers. It was largely agriculture that has given economic status to Southern public leaders, from the colonial Byrds to the latter-day John Sharp Williams and including Washington, Jefferson, and Jefferson Davis. From an agricultural background have come a majority of Southern college students with their comparatively large flair formerly for politics and later for literary productivity. More important in Southern thought and perspective than the mineral districts of the Appalachians or the oil wells of the Southwest are the blue-grass section of Kentucky, the tobacco lands of North Carolina, the "sugar bowl" of Louisiana, and the orange groves of Florida, not to mention the more important cotton-fields.

The Southern staple crops have long been established in the general regions where they are still to be found. Virginia produced tobacco three centuries ago and is today one of the big three tobacco states. Louisiana can be cited as a sugar country before and after the American cowboys rode the Western ranges. South Carolina was producing cotton abundantly before wheat invaded Iowa, and South Carolina is still a cotton state, while wheat has moved westward out of Iowa. Georgia, where the cotton gin was invented to meet a local need, is still a leading cotton state, though De Bow was proclaiming by 1850 that cotton-growing extended to the Rio Grande. Crops have not disappeared in the South; shifting frontiers have not chased frontiers so much as has been true in the East, the Middle West, and the West. Though great portions of Southern lands have remained uncultivated, there has been for a century a stretch of stabilized agriculture from the Potomac to the heart of Texas. The priority of the westward movement of the agricultural frontier in the South is indicated by a glance at William R. Shepherd's map of the "Westward Development of the United States" in his *Historical Atlas*. This map of the census lines of settlement shows that, while the American frontier in 1800 ran through Louisville, Kentucky, and Macon, Georgia, in 1830 it skirted the western border of Louisiana, made reverse curves through Arkansas and Missouri, and cut back to a point near Detroit. Alabama, Mississippi, Tennessee, and most of Louisiana are thus placed within the frontier line in 1830, while most of Michigan, part of Illinois, and all of Iowa and Wisconsin are placed beyond the frontier.

Southern agricultural expansion has long and generally been a matter of clearing and cultivating "new grounds" on the borders of farms, plantations, or communities, a steady series of little expansions here and there, not a great shifting along longitudinal lines. These "new grounds," with their frontier stumps, have generally been in fair proximity to lands of old settlement and frequently cultivated by old settlers, sometimes to permit the abandonment of older lands. The region has, therefore, never been free from frontier dots or spots, which become larger or more general in the mountainous sections. It might be said that a stable agricultural civilization penetrated the South early and swiftly, leaving many nooks and corners for later development. Hence the mixture of plantation and frontier, not only before the Civil War but in the twentieth century, with frontier economics never dominant.

This tendency of Southern agriculture to get its ground early and hold it appears natural in the light of economic geography. The distinctive Southern crops, as tobacco, rice, sugar, and cotton, have always furnished items of commerce with no appreciable consumption on the producing farm or plantation. The beginnings or introduction of these crops inevitably entailed mercantile contact, an influence which Julius Cæsar in his day observed to be destructive of frontier economy. These crops have had two transportation advantages over the grains of the Great Plains. One of these advantages results from the fact that the South is bounded on two sides by sea, with many ports and navigable rivers, making overland shipment shorter or less necessary. Another advantage, sometimes overlooked by the critics of the one-crop tendency, is the superior monetary value of these Southern agricultural staples in proportion to weight and bulk as compared with grains. A Southern team has always been able to move from the gin a load of cotton equal to several times the value of the grain a Western team could move from the field or the thrasher. The Southern crops also have transportation advantages over the rail shipment of hogs and cattle. The South has consequently been fairly conservative on the politico-economic issue of transportation, which has been the most enduring source of Western radicalism. If the rail penetration often took grain-growing into the West, cotton production often brought rail development into the South. It did not take a railroad to remove the Southern frontier. "Flush times in Alabama and Mississippi" denotes a plantation expansion before the railroads had reached the lower South. Before the railroads came or the Indians departed, there were cases of Indians in the lower South becoming planters of cotton and masters of slaves. Great was the contagion of cotton, and rapidly did it spread. It supplanted tobacco as the major crop for holding the South in an economic contact with Europe, especially with England, more definitely and continuously than was ever characteristic of any other

(183)

agricultural section of the United States. It was the chief factor in causing frontier economy to disappear more rapidly than frontier social life could be forgotten.

Cotton and the South distinguish each other. It is the case of an area, 3 per cent of the world's land, producing 60 per cent of the world's supply of an important commodity, though the Civil War and the World War have ardently stimulated the British Empire to develop other regions of supply. Cotton has been so important in and to the South that Southerners have often, to their detriment, overestimated its world importance. It is the chief basis of their grasp of regional and world economics. It is the leading item in their consciousness and in their phraseology. In the "Cotton Belt" or "Cotton Kingdom" or land of "King Cotton" one may hear of "cotton farms," "cotton plantations," "cotton gins," "cotton mills," "cotton oil mills," "cottolene," "cotton panics," "cotton exchanges," coöperative "cotton pools," a "Cotton Belt" railway route, and, at Greensboro, North Carolina, a "King Cotton Hotel." There is in "cotton planter" a term to refer both to a little red hopper on a wheel and to a human being who needs the executive ability of an army commander. "Cotton-picker" still implies ten active human fingers, notwithstanding many attempts to mechanize an important function. There are or have been "cotton merchants," "cotton factors," "cotton snobs," and "Cotton Whigs." The question Southerners most frequently ask and answer is the price query, "What's cotton?" It would be difficult to take issue with R. H. Vance's suggestion in his recent work, *Human Factors in Cotton Culture,* that much which is significant in South-

(184)

ern life "has developed as a kind of complex around the cotton plant," or to deny entirely the statement, "In the Belt—Black, Cotton, or Bible . . ." as he quotes a flippant journalist, "cotton is Religion, Politics, Law, Economics, and Art.'

The South's cotton production, which forms the basis of large commodity exchanges in the South, New York, and England, got a revolutionary start with the invention of the cotton gin in 1793, in the middle of the period of the British industrial revolution. This cotton-growing revolution of a decade or so has been followed by a century of evolution in the business of cotton farming. One of the greatest economic achievements in the world between 1800 and 1860 was the development in the South and largely by the South of a cotton business that played a large rôle in American finance and attained permanent primacy among the nation's exports. The value of the annual exports of American cotton increased from five and a quarter million dollars in 1800 to more than two hundred millions by 1860, while the tobacco exports rose in the same period from six and a quarter million dollars to twenty-one millions. The cotton crop was doubled every decade from 1800 to 1840 and trebled between 1840 and 1860, reaching two billion pounds in the census of the latter date. Much of this production was by slave labor, though one must heed the opinion of Alfred Holt Stone, planter-publicist of Mississippi, that white labor's share in Southern ante-bellum economic life "was far greater than was once supposed."

Grain and livestock production became subordinate and incidental to the commercial agriculture of cotton growing, especially in the lower South, which, prior to the Civil War, became a heavy purchaser of the products of the newly commercialized agriculture of the West. But the South has never been a completely one-crop section. In addition to the market staples of cotton, tobacco, rice, and sugar, the agricultural census of 1860 gave the eleven states that were to secede an annual corn production of nearly three hundred million bushels, which was an excess of 30 per cent increase over the preceding census and amounted to about thirty-one bushels per inhabitant. The wheat production was above thirty-one million bushels, an increase of nearly 80 per cent over that of the previous census. This grain production for 1860 was not an unfavorable showing for the cotton country to make in comparison with the grain country. And Southerners had more Southern sweet potatoes, proportionately to cotton or population, in the 'fifties than in the nineteen-twenties. The South had fifteen million hogs in 1860, not far from half the number for the entire country, though showing a considerable relative decline in this item of the census. There was a growing interest in the importance of an improved and diversified agriculture, partly stimulated by declines in cotton prices. Edmund Ruffin, of Virginia and South Carolina, was a practical preacher of agricultural reform, a subject that found much attention in the pages of *De Bow's Review*, the *Southern Cultivator*, the *Southern Planter*, and other ante-bellum magazines. In reality, the movement many years after the Civil War for the betterment of Southern agriculture was a sort of reëmergence of this earlier development that was cut short by the war.

(186)

Along with this broadening of agriculture, the seemingly dominant trinity of land, slavery, and cotton was in the 'fifties stimulating and releasing activity for non-agricultural purposes. Southern railway mileage was in these years trebled, and the total of nine thousand miles at the end of the decade was nearly one-third of the total for the country. Much of this mileage was constructed to serve cotton plantations and cotton centers, and cotton planters were not unknown on railway directorates. The small-scale manufacturing in the eleven Southern states met a rather rapid expansion in the 'fifties, showing at the end of the period 20,631 establishments, which employed 110,723 laborers and turned out products worth $155,531,281. These small establishments were largely dependent on home capital and local support, with hand manufacturing relatively important. Approximate figures for important classes of products included eight million dollars in cotton goods, one million in cotton gins, two and a third millions from blacksmithing, four millions in carriages, four millions in boots and shoes, and two and a half millions in men's clothing. Among the important ante-bellum industrialists of the South were William Gregg, South Carolina apostle of cotton mills, and Daniel Pratt, Alabama manufacturer of cotton gins. J. D. B. De Bow, with his *Review*, was the most abiding champion of Southern development of railroads and manufacturing to supplement agriculture and round out a system of economic diversification.

Southern industrialization had by 1860 assumed essentially the general direction and gradual pace, limited by agrarian interests, that have tended to mark its post-war growth. The Civil War was not necessary for Southern industrial development, and, if there is any meaning in a suggestion by W. L. Fleming or a definite interpretation by C. W. Ramsdell, this war was not necessary for the fairly early termination of slavery. The so-called old South, with its recruited aristocracy, was working toward a balanced industry, a reformed agriculture, and a free school system for the yeomen, when the war upset the orderly process of evolution. This fact is not subject to modification by any final verdict of war-guilt.

In disrupting and disorganizing the economic life of the South, the Civil War jolted from power and status the most articulate agrarian group known to American history, leaving no effective check to an industrial dominance in national public policy, particularly in tariff matters. It partially terminated and partially modified the distinctive plantation system, making Southern agricultural diversification and industrial recovery difficult for lack of physical goods and capital. It forced a dependence in the South on the one-crop system, temporarily reinforced by unusually high prices for cotton. It terminated slavery without removing negro labor. It brought to the South an appreciation of the common man and the dignity of labor with an accompanying loss in the appreciation of the uses of leisure. It created a Southern vacuum for an economic invasion, with the region becoming a suppliant for outside aid and yielding much control of its economic destiny. It destroyed real-estate values, not only with serious damage to pre-war owners, but with a consequential jungle of speculation, promotion, and "booms" as values moved upward again with many ups and downs. It tended to throw the Southern perspective toward a bourgeois materialism, to shift the embodiment of ideals from the country gentleman to the captain of industry or finance. With a mixture of justification and, perhaps, exaggeration, a spokesman of the *ancien régime* complained in *De Bow's Review*, November, 1866, that Southern railroads, factories, and debts were owned by interests in the North and East and that an elegant Southern aristocracy had been displaced by a new "Northeastern moneyed aristocracy." The world, he said, had never seen "an aristocracy half so powerful, half so corrupt, so unprincipled, and rapacious, nor one-tenth so vulgar and so ignorant, as the moneyed aristocracy of the Northeast." In more ways than one was there truth in the provincial epigram, "The bottom rail is on top now, mister."

As a result of the war, the Reconstruction mess, and the pressure of creditors, many of the former planters threw their lands on the market for what they would bring, and plantations that had brought $100,000 or more were sold for $10,000 or less. However, by 1876 Southern agricultural reconstruction was, in a sense, complete, with a cotton crop approximately the size and value of that of 1860. Through a fairly steady rate of increase for the next twenty-five years, the annual cotton production reached ten million bales, and the twentieth century has seen an increase but never to the extent of 100 per cent over this amount. The rate of increase since 1860 has been much less than before, with the crop showing some tendencies toward becoming stationary. The expansion since the Civil War has resulted partly from putting new lands in cultivation, especially in

the western and the up-country sections of the Cotton Kingdom, partly from the use of commercial fertilizer, and
partly from improved methods of cultivation. This period
has been marked by the rise of the tenant system and the
"crop lien" credit system together as a replacement for the
slave-labor system in the plantation regions, with the land-
lord, perhaps, living in town but nevertheless keeping in
closer touch with the soil than does the Iowa farmer who
leases his farm and moves to California. Cotton-growing
during this era has been accompanied by the development
of cotton-manufacturing and the rise of cottonseed oil mills
in the South, offering economic gains to the Southern
farmer.

The chief activity of the negro since slavery has been in
agriculture, and his chief place in agriculture has been in
cotton production. About one-fourth of the Southern farms
are worked by negro farmers, and about one-fourth of the
fourth are operated by negro owners, with this ownership
in number of farms increasing more rapidly than white
ownership. Negro tenantry and exploiters of negro tenantry
have been important factors in over-emphasizing a commercialized cotton production and delaying a wholesome
agricultural diversification. The writer can testify personally
to the difficulty of urging a negro "cropper" with a mule to
the successful production of anything but cotton. Southerners owe praise to Booker T. Washington for the persistency
with which he urged his people to get more land and keep
it and grow something besides cotton.

In the South since the Civil War there has been an increase in the number of small farms and farmers through

the break-up of plantations and the development of new or neglected lands. Sidney Lanier said in 1880, "The New South means small farming." Yet there has been since the post-war recovery a tendency for some of the best lands to aggregate into larger holdings, a tendency that is partly obscured by the statistics of the federal census, which treats every tenant unit as a "farm." Many of these large holdings are up-country estates, worked by tenants, and representing a modified reproduction of the ante-bellum plantation with a new agrarian gentry in the making. Account must also be taken of the large-scale farming in Texas, where agricultural machinery and white labor are more abundantly used and where the only *raison d'être* for a town may be that it is truly a "Farmersville." With its long furrows and "sedentary" farming, this state stands out in agricultural production per capita, but Texas cotton production per acre is often substantially below that of Georgia. Southern agriculture, even cotton production, though distinctive, is as varied as Southern geography, which is more varied than that of any other region of the United States with the possible exception of California.

The expansion of cotton production found a twentieth-century check in the spread of the boll weevil, a seeming misfortune that greatly stimulated a healthy diversification as well as a more scientific cultivation of cotton. Improvement in farming was also encouraged by a partial escape from the "crop lien" system and the popularization of agricultural education, notably the excellent demonstration work founded by S. A. Knapp. There still remains much room for such improvement. Grain production in the South today is relatively much less important in comparison with cotton than it was seventy years ago. The statistics of Southern corn, livestock, and poultry products look too much like the figures for the single state of Iowa to be highly creditable to a region of eleven states. Many a farmer whose market crop is cotton could with advantage make his farm more agriculturally self-sustaining and less dependent on the fluctuations of commerce and industry. Southern agriculture needs to balance itself, both in farm units and as a whole. It needs a prophetic warning against falling too much under the spell of industrialism with a lopsided development and an accompanying instability.

Southern industrial development since the Civil War has been most important in the Appalachian regions of coal, iron, and water power, with important lumbering taking place, particularly in the timber lands between the cotton-fields and the coast, while mention should be made of the lumber industry of Arkansas and of the petroleum development in Louisiana and the Southwest. Though largely based on agriculture, the post-war industrialization has sprung up chiefly in sections that were only slightly touched by the pre-war plantation economy. The geographical backbone of this later economic growth has thus been a newer, one might say a rawer, section than was that of the pre-war economic life, and it was not fortunate that this shift took place with revolutionary swiftness after the destruction of so much planter wealth and power. Without differing widely in external aspects from the industrial picture that was being formed in the 'fifties and would have continued had there been no war, the inner workings and influences of

(192)

this later industrialization owe much to the war and the subsequent coming of capital and capitalists from the North. This invasion served to emphasize the idea of industry and industrial progress to the neglect of agriculture, to obscure the ante-bellum industrial development, and to set up the false notion that but for the war the South would have had no industries. No longer were there to be "Northern men with Southern principles," for the influence was reversed to turn up-and-coming natives into "Southern Yankees."

With industry gaining on agriculture and the up-country gaining on the plantation country in economic power, the term "New South" came into vogue in the 'eighties as a *cliché* for the use of journalists and promoters. Henry Grady's Northern speeches come to mind, with his acceptance of the war outcome as best, though he said finer words about the old South than some of his imitators. Sidney Lanier used the label as an emphasis on small-scale diversified farming. An instance of a different use was *The Old South and the New*, which W. D. Kelley, a Northern man, published in 1888 to call attention to the industrial prosperity and possibilities of the "New South," or the "Emancipated South," as an "inviting field." Edward King had journeyed southward a little earlier and written more extensively on *The Great South*. The "New South" came to imply that there had been an "Old South" deserving of repudiation for its shortcomings, and that a Southern economic revolution, entirely beneficent, had occurred without any evolutionary background. It has often become the slogan of those who would exploit the agrarian interests, leaving them to depend too much on the narrow-minded

(193)

Tom Watsons or Ben Tillmans, with the Joseph Baileys and Oscar Underwoods becoming spokesmen for an industrial clientele. The agrarian protest in the South in the days of the Farmers' Alliance deserved a wider base and a wiser leadership than it had and also a more considerate treatment than it received at the hands of the "New South" element.

Industrialization in the South has become greater as a fact, and industrialism has become greater as a social force, since the World War, with many a booster seeking a revival of the industrial praises of the 'eighties and with the hopes of a Southern-Western agrarian protest much weaker than in the days of Jefferson or Bryan. The decline of the farmer seems to be taken as a matter of course as the South goes through "a remarkable industrial development," thanks in part to a newer and larger economic invasion from the North. Manufacturing corporations of the East are shifting their expansion southward for economies in labor, raw material, power, and taxation, and many Southern newspapers and legislators become timid in the face of this rising tide, showing less substantial friendship to farmers, for instance, than to manipulators of watered utility stocks. North Carolina has led in this expansion which has put Southern manufactures hundreds of millions ahead of Southern agricultural products in dollar estimates in the last few years, with the disparity intensified by the slump in agricultural prices and magnified by the repetition of many agricultural values in manufacturing values. Yet the recent textile strikes and strife in North Carolina indicate a limit to the extensive use of the cheap-labor argument by cham-

(194)

bers of commerce in the South for attracting industries southward.

This recent rapid industrial progress has given added impetus to the inroads into the South's traditional opposition to the national protective tariff policy, and this point is well stated by Jacob Viner, economist and tariff authority, who wrote in the *Century* for the winter number of 1930: ". . . the growing industrialization of the Southeast has brought with it the tariff attitudes of the older industrialized areas. Although the South as a whole is still clearly in the position of having more to lose than to gain from the tariff, the gains come in concentrated parcels to well-organized groups, while the losses are diffused thinly and widely and are not as visible as the gains, even though they are real and quantitatively more important." A similar tendency to burden the farmer is observable in the sphere of general taxation, which is becoming constantly heavier on agricultural lands and capital without regard to income. Readjustments are necessary to give the Southern farmers and other farmers a square deal in the fields of tariffs and taxation, or Seligman, Nourse, Yoder, and several other economists must be classed as morons. Perhaps something of a crusade is required to secure an equable public treatment as between industry and agriculture in the South, to preserve the agrarian group from industrial exploitation.

Southerners in strategic or public position should take warning against the evils of a discriminatory encouragement of rapid industrialization in their section. They can profit by recalling that the decline of the Roman Empire was accompanied by the neglect of agriculture and the

growth of an idle urban proletariat of unwieldy proportions. They can profit by comparing the depression of
England, now a country of big industries and big armies
of unemployed, with the economic soundness of France, a
country of moderate industries, much agriculture, and little
unemployment. They can profit by observing the happiness
and stability of Denmark, where the farmer's will prevails
in public policy. They can profit by noting that agriculture
in the United States has furnished the chief escape from
socialism, which in some form or degree inevitably follows
an excessive industrialization, as in England and Germany.
They should be reminded that Southern industrialization
is ardently championed by advertising minds at the very
time when there is serious alarm in America and Europe
because of over-industrialization, unregulated production,
disproportionate distribution, and serious unemployment,
mounting in the United States alone to estimates of three
to five million. Even the conservative National City Bank
of New York noted in its bulletin of March, 1930, that
"with increasing specialization and increasing mass production the evil results of heedless, disproportionate and unbal-
anced production are more apparent than ever before." With
industry facing a giant break-down, it is no disservice to be
different from the common trend and to consider the
superior power of a healthy agricultural civilization to en-
dure an economic crisis over a long period of time. It is
worth bearing in mind that a provincial economy can be
good for the South without necessarily being adequate for
the world, and there should be a hesitancy in pushing the

South into an aimless industrial system that knows only self-worship and expansion.

Any general policy of Southern industrial expansion should find discouragement through a consideration of the national and the world aspects of industrialism, which has furnished the dominant motives and tools of modern imperialism. The economic analysis of a Britisher like John M. Keynes or John A. Hobson and the fact-laden work of the American historian, Parker T. Moon, on *Imperialism and World Politics*, emphasize with cumulative effect the point that industrial imperialism was a fundamental condition of the major alignments and issues that caused the World War and made it a *world* war. The rivalry between industrial England and industrial Germany was about the greatest factor in bringing on this industrialized and industrializing war, with Germany the more immediately and amazingly geared to efficiency, applied science, and "progress." As Keynes, in *The Economic Consequences of the Peace*, pithily puts it, Germany was "a vast and complicated industrial machine, dependent for its working on the equipoise of many factors outside Germany as well as within. . . . The German machine was like a top which to maintain its equilibrium must spin ever faster and faster." If the industrialism of the former German Empire was a menace, American industrialism is potentially a much greater menace, for the American machine is a top with a higher speed and a larger orbit than was the pre-war German top. Already in control of many subject lands and the world's greatest creditor nation with more than twenty-five billion dollars in foreign loans and investments, the

United States as a *de facto* empire is getting into a scramble for oversea markets, raw materials, and investment arrangements to complement industrialization at home in a way which makes Europe's pre-war scramble look small and which rejects the teachings of history as those of an idle fable. The American industrial system is expanding faster than the nation and the world can absorb it, and American tariff encouragement to industry might well be supplanted by legislative checks in order to slow down a blind trend toward an inter-continental or an inter-class struggle that may usher in a socialistic receivership of metropolitan and cosmopolitan proportions. Speed in a dangerous direction or in a vicious circle is no virtue, and the South can well afford to be backward in a movement toward an internal collapse or an external collision. The section's historic agrarianism offers a check and contrast to America's rush from a continental frontierism to a world-penetrating industrialism under a maximum play of materialistic motive and a minimum restraint of traditional background.

Were it not for the more excessive gains in Southern manufacturing, the gains of the past twenty-five years in Southern agriculture would seem striking when passed in review, with crop values doubling if no allowance be made for decline in the purchasing power of the dollar. The recent physical changes in Southern agriculture are sufficient to make a young man feel old when viewing his rural birthplace, and they are almost too rapid for social adjustment, in instances showing too much progress for business success. But the gains and changes in Southern manufacturing in recent times have been about twice as great and rapid, with a still greater margin over agriculture expected to show up when the returns from the fifteenth census are analyzed. The South's passive indifference to industrialism is not adequate to withstand realtors' activities and campaigns to wake up the section and over-advertise it unless the traditional leanings toward agrarianism are reinforced by a critical sophistication that is native to Southern soil. It is time for Southerners to say affirmatively that the South must cultivate its provincial soul and not sell it for a mess of industrial pottage, that the section can and should work out its own economic salvation along evolutionary lines.

Having come slowly and largely as a balance to agriculture, Southern industries call for less social complexity and less technological tenuousness than do those of the Chicago and Pittsburgh districts. The South is not yet a land of "master builders" in the Ibsen sense, constructing to dizzy heights beyond their power to surmount and envisage. This limitation of industrial development demands no apology in the face of the industrial instability and depression as registered by the stock-market crash in the autumn of 1929. For the South agriculture is much more important than industry, in view of the contributions that it makes to industry and commerce and in view of its unrecorded contributions to rural subsistence. It may be confidently said that the physical operations of agriculture will continue in the South, just as certain processes of industry are expected to continue in the South. But the human civilization now based on Southern agriculture is in no little peril, and industrial civilization under the capitalistic system does not offer a satisfying substitute in human values. If Southern

(199)

farmers can be saved from exploitation and serfdom, it is possible for the South, which has had experience with slavery, to subordinate industrial processes to the status of slaves, not masters, and, thus escaping industrialism, to exemplify a cultural emergence from a too acquisitive society. The South is no longer conquered territory, not quite conquered, but a protest, articulate and constructive, is needed against another conquest, a conquest of the spirit. From a dull industrialism Southern civilization should be preserved with its supporting agrarian economy.

ANDREW NELSON LYTLE

THE HIND TIT

I

WHEN we remember the high expectations held
universally by the founders of the American Union
for a more perfect order of society, and then consider the
state of life in this country today, it is bound to appear to
reasonable people that somehow the experiment has proved
abortive, and that in some way a great commonwealth has
gone wrong.

There are those among us who defend and rejoice in this
miscarriage, saying we are more prosperous. They tell us—
and we are ready to believe—that collectively we are possessed of enormous wealth and that this in itself is compensation for whatever has been lost. But when we, as individuals, set out to find and enjoy this wealth, it becomes
elusive and its goods escape us. We then reflect, no matter
how great it may be collectively, if individually we do not
profit by it, we have lost by the exchange. This becomes
more apparent with the realization that, as its benefits elude
us, the labors and pains of its acquisition multiply.

To be caught unwittingly in this unhappy condition is
calamitous; but to make obeisance before it, after learning
how barren is its rule, is to be eunuched. For those who are
Southern farmers this is a particularly bitter fact to con-

sider. We have been taught by Jefferson's struggles with Hamilton, by Calhoun's with Webster, and in the woods at Shiloh or along the ravines of Fort Donelson where the long hunter's rifle spoke defiance to the more accelerated Springfields, that the triumph of industry, commerce, trade, brings misfortune to those who live on the land.

Since 1865 an agrarian Union has been changed into an industrial empire bent on conquest of the earth's goods and ports to sell them in. This means warfare, a struggle over markets, leading, in the end, to actual military conflict between nations. But, in the meantime, the terrific effort to manufacture ammunition—that is, wealth—so that imperialism may prevail, has brought upon the social body a more deadly conflict, one which promises to deprive it, not of life, but of living; take the concept of liberty from the political consciousness; and turn the pursuit of happiness into a nervous running-around which is without the logic, even, of a dog chasing its tail.

This conflict is between the unnatural progeny of inventive genius and men. It is a war to the death between technology and the ordinary human functions of living. The rights to these human functions are the natural rights of man, and they are threatened now, in the twentieth, not in the eighteenth, century for the first time. Unless man asserts and defends them he is doomed, to use a chemical analogy, to hop about like sodium on water, burning up in his own energy.

But since a power machine is ultimately dependent upon human control, the issue presents an awful spectacle: men, run mad by their inventions, supplanting themselves with inanimate objects. This is, to follow the matter to its conclusion, a moral and spiritual suicide, foretelling an actual physical destruction.

The escape is not in socialism, in communism, or in sovietism—the three final stages industrialism must take. These change merely the manner and speed of the suicide; they do not alter its nature. Indeed, even now the Republican government and the Russian Soviet Council pursue identical policies toward the farmer. The Council arbitrarily raises the value of its currency and forces the peasant to take it in exchange for his wheat. This is a slightly legalized confiscation, and the peasants have met it by refusing to grow surplus wheat. The Republicans take a more indirect way—they raise the tariff. Of the two policies, that of the Russian Soviet is the more admirable. It frankly proposes to make of its farmers a race of helots.

We have been slobbered upon by those who have chewed the mad root's poison, a poison which penetrates to the spirit and rots the soul. And the time is not far off when the citizens of this one-time Republic will be crying, "What can I do to be saved?" If the farmers have been completely enslaved by that time, the echo to their question will be their only answer. If they have managed to remain independent, the answer lies in a return to a society where agriculture is practiced by most of the people. It is in fact impossible for any culture to be sound and healthy without a proper respect and proper regard for the soil, no matter how many urban dwellers think that their victuals come from groceries and delicatessens and their milk from tin cans. This ignorance does not release them from a final

(203)

dependence upon the farm and that most incorrigible of beings, the farmer. Nor is this ignorance made any more secure by Mr. Haldane's prognostication that the farm's ancient life will become extinct as soon as science rubs the bottle a few more times. The trouble is that already science has rubbed the bottle too many times. Forgetting in its hasty greed to put the stopper in, it has let the genius out.

But the resumption by the farmer of his place of power in the present order is considered remote. Just what political pressure he will be able to bring upon the Republicans to better his lot is, at the moment, unknown. Accepting the most pessimistic view, the continued supremacy of this imperialism and his continued dependency upon it, his natural enemy, the wealth-warrior who stands upon the bridge of high tariff and demands tribute, he is left to decide upon immediate private tactics. How is the man who is still living on the land, and who lives there because he prefers its life to any other, going to defend himself against this industrial imperialism and its destructive technology?

One common answer is heard on every hand: Industrialize the farm; be progressive; drop old-fashioned ways and adopt scientific methods. These slogans are powerfully persuasive and should be, but are not, regarded with the most deliberate circumspection, for under the guise of strengthening the farmer in his way of life they are advising him to abandon it and become absorbed. Such admonition coming from the quarters of the enemy is encouraging to the land-owner in one sense only: it assures him he has something left to steal. Through its philosophy of Progress it is committing a mortal sin to persuade farmers that they can grow wealthy by adopting its methods. A farm is not a place to grow wealthy; it is a place to grow corn.

It is telling him that he can bring the city way of living to the country and that he will like it when it gets there. His sons and daughters, thoroughly indoctrinated with these ideas at state normals, return and further upset his equilibrium by demanding the things they grew to like in town. They urge him to make the experiment, with threats of an early departure from his hearth and board. Under such pressure it is no wonder that the distraught country-man, pulled at from all sides, contemplates a thing he by nature is loath to attempt . . . experimentation.

If it were an idle experiment, there would be no harm in such an indulgence; but it is not idle. It has a price and, like everything else in the industrial world, the price is too dear. In exchange for the bric-à-brac culture of progress he stands to lose his land, and losing that, his independence, for the vagaries of its idealism assume concrete form in urging him to over-produce his money crop, mortgage his land, and send his daughters to town to clerk in ten-cent stores, that he may buy the products of the Power Age and keep its machines turning. That is the nigger in the wood-pile . . . keep the machines turning!

How impossible it is for him to keep pace with the pro-cession is seen in the mounting mortgages taken by banks, insurance companies, and the hydra-headed loan companies which have sprung up since the World War. In spite of these acknowledged facts, the Bureau of Agriculture, the State Experimental Stations, farm papers, and county agents, all with the best possible intentions, advise him to get a little more progressive, that is, a little more productive. After advising this, they turn around and tell him he must curtail his planting. They also tell him that he (meaning his family) deserves motor-cars, picture shows, chain-store dresses for the women-folks, and all the articles in Sears-Roebuck catalogues. By telling him how great is his deserving, they prepare the way to deprive him of his natural deserts.

He must close his ears to these heresies that accumulate about his head, for they roll from the tongues of false prophets. He should know that prophets do not come from cities, promising riches and store clothes. They have always come from the wilderness, stinking of goats and running with lice and telling of a different sort of treasure, one a corporation head would not understand. Until such a one comes, it is best for him to keep to his ancient ways and leave the homilies of the tumble-bellied prophets to the city man who understands such things, for on the day when he attempts to follow the whitewash metaphysics of Progress, he will be worse off than the craftsman got to be when he threw his tools away. If that day ever comes, and there are strong indications that it may, the world will see a new Lazarus, but one so miserable that no dog will lend sympathy enough to lick the fly dung from his sores. Lazarus at least groveled at the foot of the rich man's table, but the new Lazarus will not have this distinction. One cannot sit at the board of an insurance company, nor hear the workings of its gargantuan appetite whetting itself on its own digestive processes.

He must close his ears because an agrarian culture and industrial warfare are sustained through the workings of two different economies. Nothing less than confusion can follow the attempt of one economy to react to the laws of another. The progressive-farmer ideal is a contradiction in terms. A stalk of cotton grows. It does not progress. In 50,000 years it may evolve into something different, but for us and our four score and ten, it grows.

This error is also seen in the works of those highly respectable historians who, pointing to the census returns and the mounting wealth of the industrial states during the early decades of the nineteenth century, declared that the Southern culture was then already doomed, and that the Civil War merely hastened its demise. This view holds that industrialism is *manifest destiny*, that it would have supplanted agriculture in the South even if the Confederacy had maintained its withdrawal from the already disrupted Union. It strangely argues that the victorious planter and the small yeoman farmer would have abandoned what they had waged a desperate war to preserve from others; and what, in spite of defeat, survived in its essential features until the second decade of the twentieth century; and what still possesses sufficient strength to make a desperate fight for its inherited way of life.

If an abundance of those things which a people considers the goods and the riches of the earth defines wealth, then it follows that that particular culture is wealthy in proportion to the production and distribution of just those things and no others; and it does not depend upon what another people may consider the goods and riches, no matter how

(207)

greatly those things have multiplied for them, nor how many individuals they have to possess them. What industrialism counts as the goods and riches of the earth the agrarian South does not, nor ever did.

It is true that the planting aristocracy bought freely from England and the North. It is also true that the Cotton Kingdom was hastened into being by the invention of the cotton gin, an apparatus of the Machine Age; but because of this, it did not assume the habits and conduct of a factory town. Stocks and bonds and cities did not constitute wealth to the planter. Broad acres and increasing slaves, all tangible evidence of possession, were the great desiderata of his labors; and regardless of their price fluctuation on the world market, if they were paid for, their value remained constant in the planting states.

But the farming South, the yeoman South, that great body of free men, had hardly anything to do with the capitalists and their merchandise. In the upland country, the pine barrens, in the hills and mountains, and interspersed between the large plantations or lying on their fringe, and in the bad-road districts wherever they lay, communication with the main arteries of trade was so difficult that the plain people were forced into a state of self-sufficiency. And those who could reach the main turnpikes or the rivers and those who owned a few slaves in the planting districts, when they sold their cotton in New Orleans, were even less dependent than the planters, for they kept their looms going and fed their stock home-grown feed. Even the planters were beginning to say in the middle 'fifties that horses do not fatten on bought corn.

By 1860 these broad, as yet somewhat flexible, outlines marked the structural formation of the Confederacy: belonging to the planting body, in round numbers, 3,000,000; slaves and free negroes, 4,000,000; townsmen, 1,000,000; plain people, including those who owned a few slaves, 4,000,000. By 1830 the lower South, leavened by Tennessee and Kentucky, became dominant in the agrarian stronghold below the line; and the lower South at this time was largely the plain people. From them the planter class was made.

After 1860 there would have been no fundamental economic rivalry between the yeoman farmer and the great landowner. The struggle before that time had been to determine who would rule, and the planters who emerged had done so because they were the more vigorous, the more intelligent, the more fortunate—the strong men of their particular culture. Jackson, demanding for the talented obscure the chance to grow rich and distinguished, expressed their demands politically. Jacksonian Democracy was, therefore, no Democracy; and although it claimed to be sired by Jefferson, his self-sufficient republic of freeholders did not contemplate any such leadership. "Down here, men like me and Gineral Jackson and Colonel Davy Crockett always demands our rights; and if we don't git 'em, somebody else is mighty liable to git Hell" is not the assertion of one contented to live easily and at peace on a fifty-acre steading. Cotton had changed the connotation of the demand.

In a society which recognizes the supremacy of nature and man's frailty each individual enjoys or subdues nature according to his capacity and desires, and those who accumulate great estates deserve whatever reward attends them, for they have striven mightily. This is the common way a ruling class establishes itself. The South, and particularly the plain people, has never recovered from the embarrassment it suffered when this class was destroyed before the cultural lines became hard and fast.

The Whig Party was evidence of the painful readjustment between the static East and the dynamic West, and it pointed to the metamorphosis of the two into Calhoun's Feudal Aristocracy. It is significant that when the Western states were changing their constitutions to deliver universal suffrage into the hands of the farmer and artisan, Dew from Virginia and Harper from South Carolina were publishing tracts defending the strictest sort of society.

The force of Jackson's character introduced tragedy into the drama. His fight with Calhoun divided the house with an internecine struggle and so confused the agrarian states that they were unable to stand united before the irrepressible conflict. Calhoun, a philosopher as well as a logician, could see beyond his times the conclusion to the premises; but Jackson and Clay, men of action, one a soldier, the other a politician, could only act the parts their periods gave them. It was impossible for them, living pleasantly on their country estates, to foresee the impending dominion of technology.

The story of these strong men and their negro slaves has been told and mistold; but the farming South has had few to tell of its virtues, and it has left fewer written records to tell its story. Oblivion has almost covered it in a generation.

The planters whom it looked to in the days of its strength to defend their common life have busied themselves after the migration to the towns with a defense of their own part in the story, ignoring or referring to the yeomanry as the pore white trash.

Travellers have remembered the bedbugs, greasy food, rough cribs found in some places, and all those disagreeable elements which in the midst of the fatigues and worries of travel over-emphasize the virtue of clean sheets and native food. Fresh linen has too often been mistaken for culture by people who scrub all the oil from their skins in the articles of the plumbing industry.

The most unique example of a garbled interpretation is found in the journals of one Olmstead, who traveled through the South in the early 'fifties. In the hill country he called to a young ploughman to inquire the way, and when not one, but several, ambled over and seemed willing to talk as long as he cared to linger, his time-ordered attitude was shocked at their lazy indifference to their work. Others who were mixed in their geography, who thought, for example, that New York lay to the south of Tennessee, amazed him. Although he could never know it, it was the tragedy of these people that they ever learned where New York lay, for such knowledge has taken them from a place where they knew little geography but knew it well, to places where they see much and know nothing.

This will be the most difficult task industrialism has undertaken, and on this rock its effort to urbanize the farm will probably split—to convince the farmer that it is time, not space, which has value. It will be difficult because the farmer knows that he cannot control time, whereas he can wrestle with space, or at least with that particular part which is his orbit. He can stop, set, chaw, and talk, for, unable to subdue nature, it is no great matter whether he gets a little more or a little less that year from her limitless store. He has the choice of pleasant conversation, the excitement of hunting, fishing, hearing the hounds run, or of the possibility of accumulating greater spoils. Olmstead's young ploughmen did well to stop and talk with the "quair strangy"; ask "whare he's bin"; "whare he's aimin' to go"; and "air he bin to see his kin in Texas?" for by so doing they exchanged an uncertain physical satisfaction for a certain mental pleasure.

But those records which have been left, some few in writing, some through the patronage of journalists like Olmstead, through folk-games, songs, and ballads, particularly in the bad-road districts, and scattered more generally than is supposed upon the farms of the South, make it clear just how Southern life, and that part of it which was the plain people, was crystallizing when the war came.

One of these records comes from C. C. Henderson's *Story of Murfreesboro*. Martin Van Buren, when he was Chief Executive, made a speech from the court-house balcony. Everybody who could travel was there, for no Southern man ever missed, or misunderstood, a speech. Among those who had come to town that day was one Abner L., a squatter living on a large farm near the town. The land-owner had promised Abner that he would introduce him to the President. After the speaking the planter moved through the crowd to keep his promise. This gentleman understood thoroughly the honor he was about to receive. In a becoming, if somewhat nervous, manner he received the hand of the New-Yorker, squeezed it damply, then turned and presented Abner. Unlike the planter, Abner stepped up with perfect composure, pressed His Excellency's hand deliberately down, and said in a calm, even tone:

"Mr. Buren, the next time you come down here I want you to come out my way and ra'r around some with us boys."

This man worked a little truck patch on somebody else's land; hunted at night for pelts; fished in Stone's River; and ra'red around when he was a mind to. He possessed nature as little as possible, but he enjoyed it a great deal, so well that he felt the President might be satisfied with what hospitality he had to offer. Whenever a society has at its base people so contented with their lot, it may not be perfect ideally, but it is the best politicians will ever effect and maintain.

When Confederate defeat destroyed the planter as a class, it upset the balance of the whole. The yeomanry, who had had little to do with the money crop before, moved down from the hills and bought for a song the planter's dismembered plantations. As this was done, it only prepared the way to undermine the Southern culture, for the destruction of the rulers did not mean its destruction. The plain man brought from his isolation his ways and habits, and the impoverished state which had fallen upon the country after war and reconstruction forced him to rely upon home manufactures. In the great exodus to Texas in 1873 all the emigrants wore homespun. It looked as if conditions were preparing to produce another set of rulers.

Unfortunately, the plain man did a thing which prevented this. When he took over the planter's land, he took over the worst of his habits, the furnishing system. Whereas with the planter it had been the factor of the great ports, with him it became the merchant of the county towns, the villages, and even the crossroads. The high price of cotton was responsible for this. When the prices broke in 1870, the small farmer was faced with a new experience: his reliance upon a money economy made him responsible to its laws. So long as they paid him well for his labors, it was profitable; but he learned that there was no assurance that this would continue. Something he could not understand was beginning to control his life. He could only hope for better days, and in the meantime mortgage next year's crop. Because it was the money crop, the merchant forced him to grow only cotton and buy the feed for his stock. This caused over-production, a drop in prices, more mortgages, and still greater over-production.

Such conditions broke many, and for the first time in the Cotton Kingdom, white tenantry developed. This was a definite social loss. With an entirely different race to serve the rich men as in slavery, the small white man could feel no very strong social inequality, and those who lived in isolation none at all. Now, economic dependence brought about social lines drawn, not upon a comparative use and enjoyment of nature, but upon a possession of cash.

This turned the plain man, for he had lost his independence, into something he had never been before, the pore

white, the hookwormed illiterate. Formerly, no matter how
wealthy or how powerful a neighbor might grow, or how
many slaves he might own, the small farmer who lived
next to his plantation was still a free man so long as he
paid his taxes and provided his family with food, clothes
and shelter. He was economically and politically independent.

The uses of fertilizers, making for a quicker maturity,
spread cotton culture northward and into Texas. Railroads
ended the isolation of those places which bad roads had
cut off from the markets, and the plain people who remained at home were brought into the money economy.
The Cotton Kingdom before 1860 was supported by black
backs. It now changed its nature. The small white farmer,
from raising 12 per cent gradually worked and picked the
greatest part of the crop. This spread of cotton meant the
spread of a false set of economics.

He had been misled, and he was to wander farther afield
under false doctrine. His former leaders, the generals and
colonels and lawyer-statesmen, moved into the towns and
cities and entered the industrial world. This move deprived
them of any right to lead or rule the farmer, for no longer
would his problems and theirs be the same. Nevertheless,
for a long time after the war, from habit and affection, and
because of the menace of the free negro, they still followed
the counsel of these men. The time came when they realized
their betrayal, for railroad and corporation presidents as
they spoke of chivalry and pure womanhood did not put
sow-belly in the pantry, nor meal in the barrel. This protest
expressed itself politically through Private John Allen from

(215)

Mississippi, Tom Watson in Georgia, and Bob Taylor in Tennessee, and farmer candidates everywhere.

But he had listened too long. He himself began to think more and more of money, and his inability to take much of it from the industrial scheme produced a feeling of moral defeat. His ambitious sons, instead of becoming the leaders of the farm communities, went North and West and to the growing Southern cities to make their fortunes, and as they left he did not protest. Those who remained, caught by the furnishing system, could not rise to lead. They were bound hand and foot—so firmly bound that the high price of cotton during the World War led them deeper into the money economy instead of freeing them.

As a result, up to the entrance of the United States into this war the farmer was trying unconsciously to live by two antithetical economies. In spite of his dual existence he managed to secure many good things from the soil, for his life was still largely ordered after his agrarian inheritance. The next, the fatal step, is to become a progressive farmer, for then he must reverse this dualism and think first of a money economy, last of a farmer's life. The new emphasis puts him in a critical condition; the precedence of the money economy means the end of farming as a way of life.

II

On a certain Saturday, a group of countrymen squatted and lay about the Rutherford County court-house yard, three-quarters of a century after Abner L. extended his invitation to Van Buren. One remarked to the others that "as soon as a farmer begins to keep books, he'll go broke shore as hell."

Let us take him as a type and consider the life of his household before and after he made an effort to industrialize it. Let us set his holdings at two hundred acres, more or less—a hundred in cultivation, sixty in woods and pasture, and forty in waste land, too rocky for cultivation but offering some pasturage. A smaller acreage would scarcely justify a tractor. And that is a very grave consideration for a man who lives on thirty or fifty acres. If the pressure becomes too great, he will be forced to sell out and leave, or remain as a tenant or hand on the large farm made up of units such as his. This example is taken, of course, with the knowledge that the problem on any two hundred acres is never the same: the richness of the soil, its qualities, the neighborhood, the distance from market, the climate, water, and a thousand such things make the life on every farm distinctly individual.

The house is a dog-run with an ell running to the rear, the kitchen and dining-room being in the ell, if the family does not eat in the kitchen; and the sleeping-rooms in the main part of the house. The dog-run is a two- or four-crib construction with an open space between, the whole covered by one roof. The run or trot gets its name from the hounds passing through from the front to the rear. It may or may not have a floor, according to the taste or pride of the occupant. This farmer will have it floored, because his grandfather, as he prospered, closed in the dog-run with doors, making it into a hall; added porches front and rear, weather-boarded the logs, and ceiled the two half-story rooms. His grandfather belonged to that large number of sturdy freemen who owned from three to five hundred acres of land and perhaps a slave or two in better days. But owning a few slaves did not make him a planter. He and his sons worked alongside them in the fields. Of farmers so situated in the South there was one to every twelve and one-tenth of free population.

There is a brick walk running from the porch to a horse block, lined on either side with hardy buttercups. From the block a road marked off by tall cedars goes out to the pike gate, two hundred yards away. The yard is kept grazed down by sheep, and occasionally the stock is turned in, when the pastures are burned in a drought. The house needs paint, but the trees are whitewashed around the base of the trunks to keep insects off and to give a neat appearance to the yard.

Over the front doorway is a horseshoe, turned the right way to bring luck to all who may pass beneath its lintel. The hall is almost bare, but scrubbed clean. At the back is a small stairway leading to the half-story. This is where the boys sleep, in their bachelorhood definitely removed from the girls. To the left is the principal room of the house. The farmer and his wife sleep there in a four-poster, badly in need of doing over; and here the youngest chillurn sleep on pallets made up on the floor.

The large rock fireplace is the center of the room. The home-made hickory chairs are gathered in a semicircle about it, while on the extreme left of the arc is a rough hand-made rocker with a sheep-skin bottom, shiny from use, and its arms smooth from the polishing of flesh, reserved always for "mammy," the tough leather-skinned mother of the farmer. Here she sets and rocks and smokes near enough for the draught to draw the smoke up the chimney. On the mantel, at one end, is dry leaf tobacco, filling the room with its sharp, pungent odor. A pair of dog-irons rests on the hearth, pushed against the back log and holding up the ends of the sticks which have burnt in two and fallen among the hot ashes. The fire is kept burning through the month of May to insure good crops, no matter how mild and warm its days turn out to be. The top rock slab is smoked in the middle where for generations the wind has blown suddenly down the chimney, driving heavy gusts to flatten against the mantel and spread out into the room. A quilting-frame is drawn into the ceiling, ready to be lowered into the laps of the women-folks when the occasion demands, although it is gradually falling into disuse. Beneath it, spreading out from the center of the floor, a rag rug covers the wide pine boards which, in turn, cover the rough-hewn puncheons that sufficed during the pioneer days. From this room, or rather, from the hearth of this room, the life of the dwelling moves.

If this is the heart of the house, the kitchen is its busiest part. The old, open fireplace has been closed in since the war, and an iron range has taken its place. This much machinery has added to the order of the establishment's life without disrupting it. Here all the food is prepared, and the canning and preserving necessary to sustain the family during the winter is done.

The cooking is a complicated art, requiring mastery over all its parts to burden the table with victuals that can be relished. Each meal is a victory over nature, a suitable union between the general principles of cookery and the accident of preparation. The fire must be kept at the right temperature (without a thermometer), or the bread won't rise; too much lard, or too little, will spoil the pastry; and since the test of all cooking is the seasoning, which can never be reduced to exact rules but is partly intuitive, too many pinches of salt may ruin the dish. The farmer's wife learns to satisfy the tastes of her particular family, but she can never set two meals on the table exactly alike. She never overcomes nature; her victories are partial, but very satisfying, for she knows her limitations.

The kitchen leads out to the back ell-shaped porch. Upon its banister, or, if there is no banister, upon the wash-table, a bucket of water and its gourd, a tin pan, soap, and towel wait to serve the morning toilet. The towel will hang on a folding rack fixed to the wall. This rack may also serve long strings of red peppers drying in the air. A bell-post rises up near the kitchen to ring the boys in from the fields at dinner-time. In the back, behind the kitchen, is the smokehouse and several outhouses. Iron kettles for washing tilt to one side in the ashes of an old fire, some distance away. An ash-hopper made from a hollow log, no longer in use, lies up against the buggy-house, having gone the way of the kitchen fireplace. The lye for soap- and hominy-making is now bought in town.

Convenient to the kitchen is the woodpile, made of different-sized sticks, some for the stove, split and cut to the right length, and some for the fireplaces, back logs and front sticks. The wood has been cut in the early fall, just as the sap begins to go down, not too early and not too late, but just at the right time, so that the outer surface will be dry and will catch quick, while the inside remains sappy and hard, burning slowly. It takes a great deal of study and intelligence to keep the fires going steadily.

Before dawn the roosters and the farmer feel the tremendous silence, chilling and filling the gap between night and day. He gets up, makes the fires, and rings the rising bell. He could arouse the family with his voice, but it has been the custom to ring the bell; so every morning it sounds out, taking its place among the other bells in the neighborhood. Each, according to his nature, gets up and prepares for the day: the wife has long been in the kitchen when the boys go to the barn; some of the girls help her, while the farmer plans the morning work and calls out directions.

One or two of the girls set out with their milk-pails to the barn, where the cows have been kept overnight. There is a very elaborate process to go through with in milking. First, the cow must be fed to occupy her attention; next, the milker kneels or sits on a bucket and washes the bag which will have gotten manure on it during the night (she kneels to the right, as this is the strategic side; the cow's foot is somehow freer on the left). After the bag is clean, the milking begins. There is always a variation to this ritual. When the calf is young, the cow holds back her milk for it; so the calf is allowed to suck a little at first, some from each teat, loosening the milk with uniformity, and then is pulled off and put in a stall until his time comes. There is one way to pull a calf off, and only one. He must be held by the ears and the tail at the same time, for only in this manner is he easily controlled. The ears alone, or the tail alone, is not enough.

This done, the milking begins. The left hand holds the pail, while the right does the work, or it may be the reverse. The hand hits the bag tenderly, grabs the teat, and closes the fingers about it, not altogether, but in echelon. The calf is then let out for his share. If he is young and there are several cows, it will be all that is left, for careful milkers do not strip the cow until the calf is weaned. The strippings are those short little squirts which announce the end, and they are all cream.

The milk is next brought back to the house, strained, and put in the well to cool. This requires a very careful hand, because if it happens to spill, the well is ruined. The next step is to pour up the old milk and let it turn—that is, sour—for churning. Some will be set aside to clabber for the mammy whose teeth are no longer equal to tougher nourishment. What she does not eat is given to the young chickens or to the pigs.

After breakfast the farmer's wife, or one of the girls, does the churning. This process takes a variable length of time. If the milk is kept a long time before it is poured up, the butter is long in coming. Sometimes witches get in the churn and throw a spell over it. In that case a nickel is dropped in to break the charm. The butter, when it does come, collects in small, yellow clods on top. These clods are separated from the butter-milk and put in a bowl where the rest of the water is worked out. It is then salted, molded, and stamped with some pretty little design. After this is done, it is set in the well or the spring to cool for the table.

The process has been long, to some extent tedious, but profitable, because insomuch as it has taken time and care and intelligence, by that much does it have a meaning.

Industrialism gives an electric refrigerator, bottled milk, and dairy butter. It takes a few minutes to remove it from the ice to the table, while the agrarian process has taken several hours and is spread out over two or three days. Industrialism saves time, but what is to be done with this time? The milkmaid can't go to the movies, read the sign-boards, and go play bridge all the time. In the moderate circumstances of this family, deprived of her place in the home economy, she will be exiled to the town to clerk all day. If the income of the family can afford it, she remains idle, and therefore miserable.

The whole process has been given in detail as an example of what goes on in every part of an agrarian life. The boys, coming in to breakfast, have performed in the same way. Every morning the stock must be fed, but there is always variety. They never shuck the same ears of corn, nor do they find the mules in the small part of the stall, nor the hogs in the same attitudes, waiting to be slopped. The buckets of milk did not move regularly from cow to consumer as raw material moves through a factory. The routine was broken by other phenomena. Breakfast intervened. One morning the cow might kick the pail over, or the milkmaid might stumble over a dog, or the cow come up with a torn udder. It is not the only task she performs, just as feeding the stock is not the only task done by the boys. The day of each member of the family is filled with a mighty variety.

After the morning work is over, the family gathers about the breakfast table. Thanks are returned and the meal is served, one of the daughters or the mother waiting on the table; and then, without undue haste, the men go to the fields and the women about their dishes. If it is spring, the women can be of great help in the garden. Very likely the cut-worms will be after the young corn. The cut-worm does not like heat. If some one gets into the garden before the sun gets hot, the worm can be found under a clod near the top of the ground and mashed. In another hour he will have gone far below the surface. It is imperative to go at the right time, for of all the thousands of insects and varmints on the land, he has the distinction of his own habits. By learning these habits, and not those of some other pest, can he be overcome.

Before going to the fields the farmer consults the signs. If the smoke from the chimney is blown to the ground, there will be rain. Lightning in the north early in the night means rain before morning. If there is enough blue in the sky to make the Dutchman a pair of breeches, the weather will turn fair. Lightning in the south is a sign of drought. If the moon lies on its back, it is holding water; if it is tilted so that the water can run out, the season will be dry. Charms, signs, and omens are folk attempts to understand and predict natural phenomena. They are just as useful and necessary to an agrarian economy as the same attempts which come from the chemist's laboratory in an industrial society, and far wiser, because they understand their inadequacy, while the hypotheses of science do not.

According to these signs the work is hard or leisurely.

If the fish are biting, the boys might knock off a day and go fishing, or hunting. Their father has not begun to keep books, so their time is their own.

At eleven o'clock the dinner bell rings. The ploughmen take out and come to the house. So regular is this ritual that a mule on the farm of Gen. Joseph E. Johnston's quartermaster used to square his feet in the furrow and answer the bell with a long, loud bray. Nor was anybody ever able to make him, by beating or pleading, plough a step farther. The teams are watered and put into their stalls, where so many ears of corn are shucked into the troughs, and a section of hay is thrown into the racks.

If the corn is low in the crib, the boys are likely to shuck carefully, keeping their eyes open for the king snake. This snake is worth ten cats as a ratter, and careful, economical farmers always throw one in their cribs if one is to be found. But not only as a ratter is he valuable. He makes war on all poisonous snakes and drives them from his presence. His invincibility is believed to be due to his knowledge of snake grass, an antidote for poison; for after bouts in which he has been bitten by venomous snakes, he has been seen to wiggle toward this grass and chew it. There is only one time of the year when he is to be avoided. He goes blind in August; and, feeling his defenseless condition, he will leg you—that is, charge and wrap his strong body about your leg, squeezing and bruising it.

The midday meal, like all the meals in the country, has a great deal of form. It is, in the first place, unhurried. Diners accustomed to the mad, bolting pace of cafeterias will grow nervous at the slow performance of a country

(225)

table. To be late is a very grave matter, since it is not served until everybody is present. But only some accident, or unusual occurrence, will detain any member of the family, for dinner is a social event of the first importance. The family are together with their experiences of the morning to relate; and merriment rises up from the hot, steaming vegetables, all set about the table, small hills around the mountains of meat at the ends, a heaping plate of fried chicken, a turkey, a plate of guineas, or a one-year ham, spiced, and if company is there, baked in wine. A plate of bread is at each end of the table; a bowl of chitterlings has been set at the father's elbow; and pigs' feet for those that like them.

And they eat with eighteenth-century appetites. There is no puny piddling with the victuals, and fancy tin-can salads do not litter the table. The only salad to be seen on a country table is sallet, or turnip greens, or if further explanation is necessary, the tops of turnips cut off and cooked with a luscious piece of fat meat. It has the appearance of spinach; but, unlike this insipid slime, sallet has character, like the life of the farmer at the head of the table. The most important part of this dish is its juice, the pot licker, a rich green liquid, indescribable except as a pot-licker green. Mixed with corn bread, it has no equal. Particularly is it fine for teething babies. If the baby is weaned in the dark of the moon and fed a little pot licker, he will pass through the second summer without great trouble. This will not relieve the pain of cutting. To do that a young rabbit must be killed, its head skinned, and the raw flesh rubbed on the gums. If this fails, tie a spray of alderberries around its neck, or hang a mole's foot. But sallet will do everything but cut the pain.

His table, if the seasons allow, is always bountiful. The abundance of nature, its heaping dishes, its bulging-breasted fowls, deep-yellow butter and creamy milk, fat beans and juicy corn, and its potatoes flavored like pecans, fill his dining-room with the satisfaction of well-being, because he has not yet come to look upon his produce at so many cents a pound, or his corn at so much a dozen. If nature gives bountifully to his labor, he may enjoy largely.

The dishes of food are peculiarly relished. Each dish has particular meaning to the consumer, for everybody has had something to do with the long and intricate procession from the ground to the table. Somebody planted the beans and worked them. Somebody else staked them and watched them grow, felt anxious during the early spring drought, gave silent thanksgiving when a deep-beating rain soaked into the crusty soil, for the leaves would no longer take the yellow shrivel. A townsman can never understand the significance of rain, nor why an agrarian will study the signs with so much care and often with so much pain, for to him it has no immediate connection. The worst it can do him is to interrupt a picnic, and the best to beat from the asphalt of its streets and its tall buildings for a few moments the enervating heat peculiar to such places. The fullness of meaning that rain and the elements extend to the farmer is all contained in a mess of beans, a plate of potatoes, or a dish of sallet. When the garden first comes in, this meaning is explicit. If the yield has been large and rich, it will be openly and pridefully commented upon; if the garden has burned and it has lost its succulence to the sun, some will remark that sorrier beans have been seen, while others, more resentful of nature's invincible and inscrutable ways, will answer that better, also, have been seen. But aside from some such conservative expression, in its formal tone masking a violent passion, no other comment will be made. And as the enjoyment of the garden's produce becomes more regular, this particular meaning which the dishes at a country table has for its diners settles into the subconscious and becomes implicit in the conduct of the household.

The description of this particular board is by no means general. Just as no two farms are managed alike, so no two tables will be set alike. It is better than most, and slightly changed from ante-bellum days. It is more stable, as it has had a century in which to harden its form. But this form, troubled by the dualism, is less strict than it would have been if nothing had happened to disturb the direction of its growth. This farmer, being a Tennessean, perhaps has some advantage over other Southwesterners except Kentuckians of a tradition less shaken during the hard years. Tennessee has never been given over to any one money crop. It has looked upon its land to sustain its culture, and from the beginning has diversified according to its needs. Serving as a furnishing state to the cotton regions, when these regions were overturned, it naturally stood the shock better than they. In consequence the table will be more formal, its meals better, than in those places where the small upland farmer moved down upon the segments of the broken plantations. He can never have the same respect for the sow-belly and corn-meal furnished him by the merchant, and actually a large body of these farmers in Alabama, Mississippi, Georgia, South Carolina, and West Tennessee did not vary a great deal this diet, as he could for the vegetables and meat brought to the table by his own hand.

After the midday meal is over the family takes a rest; then the men go back to the fields and the women to those things yet to be done, mending clothes, darning, knitting, canning, preserving, washing or ironing or sewing. By sundown they are gathered about the supper table, and afterward set before the fire if it is winter, or upon the porch in warmer weather. One of the boys will get out his guitar and play "ballets" handed down from father to son, some which have originated in the new country, some which have been brought over from the Old World and changed to fit the new locale. Boys from the neighborhood drop in to court, and they will jine in, or drive away with the gals in hug-back buggies. If they are from another neighborhood, they are sure to be rocked or shot at on the way over or on the way home.

If the gathering is large enough, as it is likely to be when crops are laid by, it will turn into a play-party.[1] Most of these games practiced by the plain people have maintained the traditions brought from England and Scotland, while the townsmen lost their knowledge of them in a generation. For example, "The Hog Drovers" is a version of the English folk-game, "The Three Sailors." The Southern country, being largely inland, could only speculate upon the

[1] The play-parties were to be found in operation much later in Mississippi and Arkansas than in Tennessee.

habits of sailors, but they knew all about the hog drovers. Every year droves of razorbacks, with their eyelids sewed together to hinder them from wandering off into the woods, were driven ten or eleven miles a day toward the Eastern markets. They would be stopped at private farms along the route, where pens had been put up to receive them, to feed. The drovers, nomadic and as careless as sailors, could not be made to keep promises. Parents, therefore, were careful of their daughters.

The game comes from, and is a copy of, the life of the people. A boy seats himself upon a chair in the middle of the room with a gal in his lap. He is the head of the house, and she is his daughter. The other gals are seated around the walls, waiting their turns; while the boys, representing the hog drovers, enter two abreast in a sort of a jig, singing the first stanza:

> "Hog drovers, hog drovers, hog drovers we air,
> A-courtin yore darter so sweet and so fair,
> Can we git lodgin' here, oh, here,
> Can we git er-lodgin' here?"

They stop in front of the old man, and he answers:

> "Oh, this is my darter that sets by my lap,
> And none o' you pig-stealers can git her from pap,
> And you can't git lodgin' here, oh, here,
> And you can't git er-lodgin' here."

The boys then jig about the chair, singing:

> "A good-lookin' darter, but ugly yoreself—
> We'll travel on further and sit on the shelf,
> And we don't want lodgin' here, oh, here,
> And we don't want er-lodgin' here."

(230)

They jig around the room, then return. The old man relents. Possibly it has as its genesis a struggle between greed and the safety of his daughter's virtue:

"Oh, this is my darter that sets by my lap,
And Mr. *So-and-so* can git her from pap
   If he'll put another one here, oh, here,
   If he'll put another one here."

The boy who is named jigs to one of the gals, brings her to the old man, takes his darter to the rear of the line, and the game starts over. After every couple has been paired off, they promenade all and seek buggies or any quiet place suitable for courting.[1]

This and other games, "Fly in the Buttermilk," "Shoot the Buffalo," "Under the Juniper Tree," will fill an evening and break the order of their lives often enough to dispel monotony, making holidays a pleasure; and not so frequent nor so organized that they become a business, which means that games have become self-conscious, thus defeating the purpose of all playing. As they play they do not constantly remind one another that they are having a good time. They have it.

Besides these play-parties people pleasured themselves in other ways. There were ice-cream socials, old-time singings, like the Sacred Harp gatherings, political picnics and barbecues, and barn dances. All of these gatherings which bring the neighborhood together in a social way are unlike the "society" of industrialism. Behind it some ulterior purpose always lurks. It becomes another province of Big Business and is invaded by hordes of people who, unable

---

[1] A complete version and account of the Hog-Drovers game song will be found in A. P. Hudson's *Specimens of Mississippi Folklore.*

to sell themselves in the sterner marts, hope to catch their prey in his relaxed moments and over the tea tables make connections which properly belong to the office. This practice prostitutes society, for individuals can mingle socially from no motive except to enjoy one another's company.

The songs of the Sacred Harp, like negro spirituals, are without accompaniment. The tune is pitched by the leader in the neighborhood schoolhouse under the shadows of oil-lamps. There is a grand meeting at the county seat once a year, and here the neighborhoods sing against each other and in unison under one general leader, who always remembers to turn the meeting over to each district leader for one song. This is a privilege jealously looked after; and if anyone is by chance overlooked, he will rise and make himself known. These songs of the Sacred Harp are songs of an agrarian people, and they will bind the folk-ways which will everywhere else go down before canned music and canned pleasure.

At the square dances, unlike round dancing, the stage is set for each individual to show the particularity of his art. Each couple is "out" in turn, swinging every other couple separately, ending up at "home" when the whole line swings "partners," then "corners." In this way a very fine balance is reached between group and individual action. Everybody is a part of the dance all the time, but a very particular part some of the time. There are no wall-flowers, no duty dances, no agonizing over popularity, and the scores of such things which detract from free enjoyment at the round dancings. "First lady out" means that she must step, cheat, and swing and show her superiority over the ladies who will follow; and likewise with the gentlemen. And the prompter, the one who calls the "figgers" (which happens still to be the proper English pronunciation of figure), is an artist and wit whose disappearance will leave the world much the poorer. Such calls as

> "Swing the gal you love best;
> Now cheat and swing."

> "Partners to yore places
> Like mules to the traces."

and from Mississippi,

> "Women swing hard, men swing harder,
> Swing that gal with the buckskin garter."

are metaphors and imperatives with full connotation for the dancers, and in an agrarian society will be as applicable a hundred years hence. But so will the fiddlers' tunes, "Leather Breeches," "Rats in the Meal Barrel," "Frog Mouth," "Guinea in the Pea Patch," "Arkansas Traveler," "Cotton-eyed Joe," "No Supper Tonight," "Hell Amongst the Yearlings," "Got a Chaw of Tobaccy from a Nigger," "All My Candy's Gone," and "Katy, Bar the Door." With a list of such dances as a skeleton, if all other records were lost, some future scholar could reconstruct with a common historical accuracy the culture of this people.

Before the farmer decided to keep books, the structure of his neighborhood culture had not been moved, and his sons and daughters, and he and the old woman, were a part of these things. Even mammy, if the rheumaticks had not frozen her jints, would put on her hickory-staved bonnet, a fresh-starched apron, and mount the waggin with the rest and drive to the singing and lift her cracked voice as the leader "h'isted" the tune, or at the barbecue pat her feet in time with the whining fiddle and think of better days when she and her old man balanced to "Cairo ladies, show yoreself," or "Jenny, the Flower of Kildare," until the sweat poured from her strong back, gluing the gray linen dress to her shoulders and ballooning it in places with air caught in the swing.

III

The Agrarian South, therefore, whose culture was impoverished but not destroyed by the war and its aftermath, should dread industrialism like a pizen snake. For the South long since finished its pioneering. It can only do violence to its provincial life when it allows itself to be forced into the aggressive state of mind of an earlier period. To such an end does bookkeeping lead. It is the numbering of a farm's resources—its stacks of fodder, bushels of corn, bales of cotton, its stock and implements, and the hundreds of things which make up its economy. And as the only reason to number them is to turn them into cash—that is, into weapons for warfare—the agrarian South is bound to go when the first page is turned and the first mark crosses the ledger.

The good-road programs drive like a flying wedge and split the heart of this provincialism—which prefers religion to science, handcrafts to technology, the inertia of the fields to the acceleration of industry, and leisure to nervous prostration. Like most demagoguery, it has been advertised as a great benefit to the farmer. Let us see just what the roads have done and who they benefit? They certainly can be of no use to the farmer who cannot afford to buy a truck. He finds them a decided drawback. The heavy automobile traffic makes it hazardous for him even to appear on the main highways. But if he has the temerity to try them, they prove most unsatisfactory. Besides being a shock to his mules' feet, it is difficult for the team to stand up on the road's hard, slick surface.

The large farmers and planting corporations who can afford to buy trucks are able to carry their produce to market with less wear and tear than if they drove over rougher dirt pikes. But this is a dubious benefit, for the question is not between trucks on good or bad roads, but between teams on passable roads and trucks on arterial highways.

But in any case the farmer receives few direct profits. Asphalt companies, motor-car companies, oil and cement companies, engineers, contractors, bus lines, truck lines, and politicians—not the farmer—receive the great benefits and the profits from good roads. But the farmer pays the bills. The states and counties float bonds and attend to the upkeep on the highways and byways, and when these states are predominantly agricultural, it is the people living on the land who mortgage their labor and the security of their property so that these super-corporations may increase incomes which are now so large that they must organize foundations to give them away.

But the great drain comes after the roads are built. Automobile salesmen, radio salesmen, and every other kind of salesman descends to take away the farmer's money. The railroad had no such universal sweep into a family's privacy. It was confined to a certain track and was constrained by its organization within boundaries which were rigid enough to become absorbed, rather than absorb. But good roads brought the motor-car and made of every individual an engineer or conductor, requiring a constant, and in some instances a daily, need for cash. The psychological pressure of such things, and mounting taxes, induce the farmer to forsake old ways and buy a ledger.

The great drain continues. The first thing he does is to trade his mules for a tractor. He has had to add a cash payment to boot, but that seems reasonable. He forgets, however, that a piece of machinery, like his mules, must wear out and be replaced; but the tractor cannot reproduce itself. He must lay aside a large sum of money against the day of replacement, whereas formerly he had only to send his brood mare to some jack for service.

The next thing it does, it throws his boys out of a job, with the possible exception of one who will remain and run it. This begins the home-breaking. Time is money now, not property, and the boys can't hang about the place draining it of its substance, even if they are willing to. They must go out somewhere and get a job. If they are lucky, some filling station will let them sell gas, or some garage teach them a mechanic's job. But the time is coming when these places will have a surfeit of farmer boys.

He next buys a truck. The gals wanted a car, but he was obdurate on that point, so he lost them. They went to town to visit kin, then gradually drifted there to marry or get a job. The time comes when the old woman succumbs to high-pressure sales talk and forces him to buy a car on the installment plan. By that time he is so far gone that one thing more seems no great matter.

He then has three vehicles which must be fed from the oil companies, several notes at the bank bearing interest, and payments, as regular as clock strokes, to be made on the car.

He finds his payment for gasoline, motor oil, and power for his tractor is tremendously higher than the few cents coal oil used to cost him. Formerly he bought it by the lampful; he now buys it by the barrelful. In fact, he no longer uses coal oil for lighting. He has installed a Delco-plant. Besides giving illumination it pumps his water, turns the churn, washes the clothes, heats the iron to press them, and cooks the victuals. If his daughters had not already moved away, he would have had to send them, for Delco has taken their place in the rural economy. The farmer's wife now becomes a drudge. As the mainstay of the structure she was content to bear the greatest burden, but now she grows restive. She has changed from a creator in a fixed culture to an assistant to machines. Her condition is miserable because her burdens are almost as great without the compensation of the highest place in the old scheme. Her services cannot be recompensed with gold, and gold has become the only currency.

Gradually the farmer becomes more careless of his garden. Each year he cuts down on the meat—the curing takes too much time. He may finally kill only a hog or two, and, under the necessity of paying interest, sell all his cows but one.

(237)

He has concentrated on the money crop, and as bought fertilizers and war-time prices have brought cotton to Tennessee, he chooses cotton. This sinks him deeper into the money economy. He must buy highly productive, and also highly priced, seed, and artificial fertilizers. He used to haul manure from the barns, but this is too slow and too unscientific now. But the outlay of money is not ended. There are fertilizer-distributors, cultivators, and improved ploughs of all kinds, with a value arbitrarily inflated by the tariff. He is now as completely on the money basis as a farmer can ever get, and each day he buys more and more from the town and makes less and less on the farm.

Being in the race for wealth, he begins to learn that a farmer can only make war successfully by beating his ploughshare into a sharp-cutting weapon. He cannot match the plough against the wheel. When he bought the various machines which roll where the mules stood and shivered the flies from their backs, he was told that he might regulate, or get ahead of, nature. He finds to his sorrow that he is still unable to control the elements. When it fails to rain and his fields are burning, he has no God to pray to to make it rain. Science can put the crops in, but it can't bring them out of the ground. Hails may still cut them down in June; winds may damage them; and a rainy season can let the grass take them. Droughts still may freeze and crack the soil. Dry weather does not greatly injure cotton, but if this farmer had happened to become a dairyman, his withered pastures and dry springs would have made him suffer.

The pests and insects are still with him. He may partially control them by poison: the army worm—possible; the boll weevil—evade by putting in early; flea—impossible! Neither can he control the tariff, nor a complete crop failure, nor a drop in prices. Since he cannot control these variables, his crop is not predictable; therefore his income is uncertain. But debt, the price of machinery, repairs, merchandise are all certain and must be met, if not by his crops, then by his land.

It is true that labor-evicting machines will give a greater crop yield, but a greater yield does not necessarily mean a greater profit. It means over-production and its twin, price deflation. Those who insist on the progressive-farmer ideal realize this, and for a long time the Federal Bureau of Agriculture and other agencies have insisted that he diversify his crops. In many instances this has brought relief, but it is not permanent. The diversification is always the money crop. The farmer is no better off when he has two or three money crops, if they are all over-produced, than he is with one. He has three crops, instead of one, to worry with.

There are farmers who manage to remain in the race, but they are few who actually make fortunes. When the land is very rich, the direction good, and the economy frugal, this is possible. Those places situated close to cities and towns may be turned very profitably into dairy, or poultry, farms; or a few acres may be turned advantageously into trucking. But where there is one like these there are thousands of others, one-horse, two-horse, or four-horse men, who suffer from these progressives who have made good.

Another way of growing rich on the land is to develop a new seed. Les Bedezer[1] is an example of this. A few make enormous returns on their outlay; others hear of their success, study the methods, and slowly make the effort to do likewise. By the time their crop is ready for the market there is too great an abundance, a fall in price, and the distress it always brings with it. Such farmers are enemies to the agricultural body. The horse-cropper, in attempting to follow their ways, puts his entire acreage in this crop, buying his feed elsewhere on credit at exorbitant interest. In Alabama 20 per cent is the usual demand. When the time comes to settle up, if he makes any money, it goes for luxuries instead of discharging his debt. He is always optimistic and hopes that next year will be as good, and on this wish he gives a lien on his land, which under such circumstances means a sale.

But even for those who succeed the disadvantage is too great, and for the less fortunate who enter the conflict without the advantages of science, it is overwhelming. At the outset there is the great burden of direct and indirect taxation. Because land cannot be hidden away in strong boxes it bears the greatest part of the national, state, and county expenses. According to Governor Lowden, a considered authority on taxation and the farmer's problems, real property, which is largely farmlands or property dependent upon farming produce, bears 90 per cent of the

[1] A Japanese Clover, splendid as a land builder, excellent for pasture or hay.

taxation and receives 10 per cent of the income. Since Wilson's administration gave way to Harding's normalcy, taxes have been increased on land four times and decreased on great wealth four times, making a ratio of sixteen to one against the farmer. The tariff, which he has borne a century, grows heavier rather than lighter, and apparently the Republicans have every intention of further increasing it.

The factory can close down to meet over-production and feed the market with its stock on hand; but the farmer is unable to do this because of the perishable quality attached to everything but cotton, tobacco and sugar; and when he sells these crops, he is an individual competing with large organizations.

Thanks to applied science, the factory can concentrate stupendous power in one place and fabricate its commodities serially; that is, a hundred yards of cloth can be reproduced exactly as a previous hundred yards, or a hundred Ford cars with the same uniform strokes, but the product of the farm cannot be so reproduced. There can be but approximate, and very general, organization to agriculture. Certain seasons require certain kinds of work: there is a breaking season, a planting season, a cultivating season, a laying-by time, and a marketing time. This very loose organization is determined by nature, not by man, and points to the fundamental difference between the factory and the soil. When the farmer doubles his crop, he doubles his seed, his fertilizer, his work, his anxiety . . . all his costs, while the industrial product reduces in inverse ratio its costs and labor as it multiplies. Industrialism is multiplication. Agrarianism is addition and subtraction. The one

(241)

by attempting to reach infinity must become self-destructive; the other by fixing arbitrarily its limits upon nature will stand. An agrarian stepping across his limits will be lost.

When the farmer, realizing where all this is leading him, makes the attempt to find his ancient bearings, he discovers his provincialism rapidly disintegrating. The Sacred Harp gatherings, and to a less extent the political picnics and barbecues, have so far withstood the onslaught; but the country church languishes, the square dance disappears, and camp meetings are held, but they have lost their vitality. Self-consciousness has crept into the meetings, inhibiting the brothers and sisters and stifling in their bosoms the desire to shout. When shouting ceases and the mourner's bench is filled up by the curious from the rear, the camp meeting may count its days, for they are numbered.

He finds that there is a vast propaganda teaching him, but particularly his children, to despise the life he has led and would like to lead again. It has in its organization public schools, high schools, the normals, and even the most reputable universities, the press, salesmen, and all the agents of industrialism. It has set out to uplift him. It tells him that his ancestors were not cultured because they did not appreciate the fine arts; that they were illiterate because their speech was Old English; and that the South will now come to glory, to "cultural" glory, by a denial of its ancestry.

This is the biggest hoax that has ever been foisted upon a people. It is nothing but demoniacally clever high-pressure sales talk to unload the over-producing merchandize of industrialism on the South. New England began it with her carrying trade. The shrewd Yankee skippers realized that if they could persuade prospective buyers that the bric-à-brac which they had brought from the Orient and elsewhere was "culture," their cargoes would fetch a fancier price. This brought about the overthrow of their own theocracy by 1830; but so long as the South had the planters for defenders the peddlers made no great headway. But now, in the hands of the industrialists everywhere, it is making very great headway.

And unless the agricultural South, like this farmer, wakes up to the fact that he is swapping his culture for machine-made bric-à-brac, there will be an absentee-landlordism far worse than that which afflicted the continent at the breakdown of mediæval society. When the nobility flocked to the court of Louis XIV, leaving the tenants the burden of land without the compensation of local government, conditions were bad enough, precipitating the French Revolution. But, even so, the French nobility retained certain ties to their estates. They were descendants of men who had ruled there.

But what of this absentee-landlordism of capitalism? Mortgage companies, insurance companies, banks, and bonding-houses that are forced to take over the land of free men . . . what will be the social relationship? What can an abstract corporation like an insurance company, whose occupation is statistics and whose faro-bank can never lose, know of a farmer's life? What can their calculations do before droughts, floods, the boll weevil, hails, and rainy sea-seasons? What will be the relationship between tenants who formerly owned the land and their abstract selves?

To avoid the dire consequences and to maintain a farming life in an industrial imperialism, there seems to be only one thing left for the farmer to do, and particularly for the small farmer. Until he and the agrarian West and all the conservative communities throughout the United States can unite on some common political action, he must deny himself the articles the industrialists offer for sale. It is not so impossible as it may seem at first, for, after all, the necessities they machine-facture were once manufactured on the land, and as for the bric-à-brac, let it rot on their hands. Do what we did after the war and the Reconstruction: return to our looms, our handcrafts, our reproducing stock. Throw out the radio and take down the fiddle from the wall. Forsake the movies for the play-parties and the square dances. And turn away from the liberal capons who fill the pulpits as preachers. Seek a priesthood that may manifest the will and intelligence to renounce science and search out the Word in the authorities.

So long as the industrialist remains in the saddle there must be a money crop to pay him taxes, but let it occupy second place. Any man who grows his own food, kills his own meat, takes wool from his lambs and cotton from his stalks and makes them into clothes, plants corn and hay for his stock, shoes them at the crossroads blacksmith shop, draws milk and butter from his cows, eggs from his pullets, water from the ground, and fuel from the woodlot, can live in an industrial world without a great deal of cash. Let him diversify, but diversify so that he may live rather than that he may grow rich. In this way he will escape by far the heaviest form of taxation, and if the direct levies

(244)

grow too exorbitant, refuse to pay them. Make those who rule the country bear the burdens of government.

He will be told that this is not economical, that he can buy clothes for much less than he can weave them, and shoes for half the labor he will put into their creation. If the cash price paid for shoes were the only cost, it would be bad economy to make shoes at home. Unfortunately, the matter is not so simple: the fifteen-hundred-dollar tractor, the thousand-dollar truck, the cost of transportation to and from town, all the cost of indirect taxation, every part of the money economy, enters into the price of shoes. In comparison, the sum he hands over to the merchant is nothing more than a war tax.

So long as he lives in a divided world he is rendered impotent in the defense of his natural economy and inherited life. He has been turned into the runt pig in the sow's litter. Squeezed and tricked out of the best places at the side, he is forced to take the little hind tit for nourishment; and here, struggling between the sow's back legs, he has to work with every bit of his strength to keep it from being a dry hind one, and all because the suck of the others is so unreservedly gluttonous.

As for those countrymen who have not gone so deeply in the money economy, let them hold to their agrarian fragments and bind them together, for reconstructed fragments are better than a strange newness which does not belong. It is our own, and if we have to spit in the water-bucket to keep it our own, we had better do it.

ROBERT PENN WARREN

THE BRIAR PATCH

I N 1619 twenty negroes were landed at the colony of
Jamestown and sold into slavery. Probably they came
from the Indies; in such case they were torn from the servitude of the Spaniard to be delivered into that of the Eng-
lishman in America. The ship that brought them—she was
named the *Jesus*—touched history significantly, but only
for a moment. When she again put to sea, with the price
of twenty slaves added to the profits of her venture, she
disappeared forever into the obscurity from which she had
brought those first negroes to American shores.

The number of negroes in the country increased slowly
until the eighteenth century, but they had come to stay.
Long before the Civil War, when Northern philanthropy
and Southern interest raised money from Sunday schools
and societies to colonize the negroes in Africa and thus
solve the problem which distressed the nation, the negroes,
in so far as they were articulate concerning their fate,
usually opposed any such scheme. They might be mobbed
from their farms in Ohio or be forced to spend their days
in the cotton-fields under a blazing Mississippi sun, but
America, after all, was home. Here they knew where they
stood; the jungle, though not many generations behind,
was mysterious and deadly.

At Appomattox, in the April of 1865, Lee's infantry

marched past the close Federal ranks to the place of surrender and acknowledged with muskets at carry the courtesy of the enemy's salute. The old Emancipation Proclamation was at last effective, and the negro became a free man in the country which long before he had decided was his home. When the bluecoats and bayonets disappeared, when certain gentlemen packed their carpet-bags and silently departed, and when scalawags settled down to enjoy their profits or sought them elsewhere, the year of jubilo drew to a close and the negro found himself in a jungle as puzzling and mysterious, and as little answering to his desires, as the forgotten jungles of Africa.

The negro was as little equipped to establish himself in it as he would have been to live again, with spear and breech-clout, in the Sudan or Bantu country. The necessities of life had always found their way to his back or skillet without the least thought on his part; the things had been only the bare necessities, but their coming was certain. He did not know how to make a living, or, if he did, he did not know how to take thought for the morrow. Always in the past he had been told when to work and what to do, and now, with the new-got freedom, he failed to understand the limitation which a simple contract of labor set on that freedom. It is not surprising that the idea of freedom meant eating the cake and keeping it, too. In the old scheme of things which had dwindled away at Vicksburg, Gettysburg, and Chattanooga, he had occupied an acknowledged, if limited and humble, place. Now he had to find a place, and the attempt to find it is the story of the negro since 1865.

The Reconstruction did little to remedy the negro's defects in preparation. Certainly, he discovered himself as a political power, but he was also to discover that the fruits of his power were plucked by some one else, by the friends who gave him big talk and big promises. Sometimes he got an office out of it all and smoked cigars in the chair of a legislature. The political training which he received, however, was the worst that could possibly be devised to help him; it was a training in corruption, oppression, and rancor. When the earth shook and the fool, or scoundrel, departed after his meat, leaving his bankrupt promises, the negro was to realize that he had paid a heavy price for the legislative seat and the cigar. He had been oppressed for centuries, but the few years in which he was used as an instrument of oppression solved nothing. Instead, they sadly mortgaged his best immediate capital; that capital was the confidence of the Southern white man with whom he had to live. The Civil War had done much to show the negro's character at its best, but, so short is human memory, the Reconstruction badly impaired the white man's respect and gratitude. The rehabilitation of the white man's confidence for the negro is part of the Southern white man's story since 1880.

Some people in the North thought that the immediate franchise carried with it a magic which would insure its success as a cure-all and fix-all for the negro's fate. Corresponding to them was the group in the South whose prejudice would keep the negroes forever as a dead and inarticulate mass in the commonwealth—as hewers of wood and drawers of water. Between these extremes of prejudice on the subject there lay a more realistic view that the hope and safety of everyone concerned rested in the education of the negro; the belief might spring from a democratic ideal of equal opportunity, or it might be, in the mind of a person who had witnessed the Reconstruction, an expedient insurance against the repetition of just such a disaster. On the surface, however, the intention appeared the same.

The process of fulfilling that intention has been a slow one, and the end is far from in sight. The poverty of the South for a generation after the Civil War played heavily against it. Educational efforts could not be concentrated on the negro, for the plight of the poor white, in both the mountains and the lowlands, was but little better. Money has trickled down from the North to be invested in the negro's education. Southern states have doled out money from their all too inadequate educational funds. The increasing prosperity of the section may give considerable hope for the future, but the process has scarcely begun. To realize this one has only to see the negroes in the deep South, or even in the middle South, sitting before the cabin, stooping over the cotton row or tobacco hill, or crowding the narrow streets of a town on Saturday night in summer.

But with the accelerated process of negro education a question will certainly be asked again. For what is the negro to be educated? It is a question that must be answered unless one believes that the capacity to read and write, as some believed concerning the franchise, carries with it a blind magic to insure success. In the lowest terms the matter is something like this: are most negroes to be

(249)

taught to read and write, and then turned back on society with only that talent as a guaranty of their safety or prosperity? Are some others, far fewer in number, to be taught their little French and less Latin, and then sent packing about their business? If the answer is *yes*, it will be a repetition of the major fallacy in American education and of one of America's favorite superstitions.

The most prominent man in negro education of the past, and probably the most prominent negro of the past or present, answered the question otherwise. "I am constantly trying to impress upon our students at Tuskegee—and on our people throughout the country, as far as I can reach them with my voice—that any man, regardless of color, will be recognized and rewarded just in proportion as he learns to do something well—learns to do it better than some one else—however humble the thing may be. As I have said, I believe that my race will succeed in proportion as it learns to do a common thing in an uncommon manner; learns to make its services of indispensable value." Booker T. Washington realized the immediate need of his race; he realized that the masses of negroes, both then and for a long time thereafter, had to live by the production of their hands, and that little was to be gained by only attempting to create a small group of intellectual aristocrats in the race. The most urgent need was to make the ordinary negro into a competent workman or artisan and a decent citizen. Give him whatever degree of education was possible within the resources at hand, but above all give him a vocation. This remains, it seems, the most urgent need.

An emphasis on vocational education for the negro is

not, as has sometimes been thought and said, a piece of white man's snobbery. In the first place, the principle applies equally well to the problem of white illiteracy in the South and elsewhere. In the second place, everyone recognizes that there is a need for negroes in the professions, especially medicine and teaching, just as there is opportunity if the negro combines a certain modicum of patience and unselfishness with his ability. But the general matter of so-called higher education for the negro in the South is a small factor in relation to the total situation.

There are strong theoretical arguments in favor of higher education for the negro, but those arguments are badly damaged if at the same time a separate negro community or group is not built up which is capable of absorbing and profiting from those members who have received this higher education. If this does not occur, if the negroes in the South cannot support their more talented and better equipped individuals, the unhappy process of the past will continue, and the educated negro will leave the South to seek his fortune elsewhere. This process is peculiarly unhappy in two respects. The less fortunate negro who stays at home is deprived of immediate example and understanding leadership among his own people, and his contact, if any, with his lost leader is through the medium of rumor or the printed page. Moreover, the leader himself loses his comprehension of the actual situation; distance simplifies the scene of which he was once a part, and his efforts to solve its problems are transferred into a realm of abstractions. The case is not dissimilar to that of the immigrant labor leader or organizer who has in the past left the life he understood and come to this country whose life he did not wholly understand. Both have shown a tendency toward the doctrinaire.

The reason given, and accepted, for the educated, ambitious negro's move from the South is the lack of opportunity which is there offered and the discriminations which exist against him. In its broadest aspects the question is that of "equality." The question is an extraordinarily complicated one, but certain very clear issues can be disentangled. The simplest issue, and probably the one on which most people would agree, is that of equal right before the law. At present the negro frequently fails to get justice, and justice from the law is the least that he can demand for himself or others can demand for him. It will be a happy day for the South when no court discriminates in its dealings between the negro and the white man, just as it will be a happy day for the nation when no court discriminates between the rich man and the poor man; and the first may be a more practicable ideal than the second. The matter of political right carries repercussions which affect almost every relation of the two races, but again the least that can be desired in behalf of the negro is that any regulation shall apply equitably to both him and the white man.

The other aspects of equality, which present themselves every day and which spring to most people's minds when the matter is mentioned, are more subtle and confused. When the educated Southern negro says that he cannot stay at home because no opportunity exists there, he may mean one or both of two things. Let us take the case of a

(252)

negro who has satisfactorily prepared himself for a profession. Does he simply regret, if he hangs out his shingle or puts up his plate, that his negro clientele will be small and many of its members too poor to pay him a living commensurate to his talents and training? Or does he protest against the fact that the white man will seek out another white man—a man whose professional abilities may possibly be inferior to the negro's own? Certainly in the North there are cases where a negro with a normal-school education has protested because he or she has not received a white school appointment when no negro school vacancy occurred. If our professional man, however, means the first thing, he states a problem whose solution has been slow but can be envisaged with some degree of clarity; it is a race group that will support and demand such services as he can offer. The first step in this solution is obviously the economic independence of the race. If he means the second, the answer is more roundabout, but depends to a great extent, as we may see, on the same factors.

This same professional man would probably add to his first reason that of the more general discriminations which necessarily surround him in the South. He has money in his pocket, but he is turned away from the white man's restaurant. At the hotel he is denied the bed which he is ready to pay for. He likes music, but must be content with a poor seat at a concert—if he is fortunate enough to get one at all. The restrictions confront him at every turn of his ordinary life. But his answer to another question might do something to clear both his and the white man's mind. Does he simply want to spend the night in a hotel as comfortable as the one from which he is turned away, or does he want to spend the night in that same hotel? A good deal depends on how this hypothetical negro would answer the question.

Again, as in the former complaint, if he wants the first thing the fulfillment of his want finally depends on the extent to which the negro makes himself economically free. But the negro radical, or the white radical in considering the race problem, would say that he wants the second thing —he wants to go to the same hotel, or he wants the right to go to the same hotel. The millennium which he contemplates would come to pass when the white man and the black man regularly sat down to the same table and when the white woman filed her divorce action through a negro attorney with no thought in the mind of any party to these various transactions that the business was, to say the least, a little eccentric. To such a radical the demand for less is treason to his race; to simply look forward to a negro society which can take care of all the activities and needs of its members is a feeble compromise. When Booker T. Washington at the Atlanta Exposition of 1895 lifted his hand and said, "We can be as separate as the fingers, yet one as the hand in all things essential to mutual progress," the hand he raised, in the eyes of such a radical, was the hand of treason.

"My friend," Washington might well reply to such a critic, "you may respect yourself as a man, but you do not properly respect yourself as a negro." To him the critic would be suffering from a failure to rationalize his position, from the lack of a sense of reality, and from a defect in self-respect, for the last implies the first two deficiencies. The critic's condition would be like that of the individual of any color who consumes himself in "desiring this man's art, and that man's scope"; and his principles would be those of the doctrinaire.

Many negroes undoubtedly possess a self-respect; in others something else, such as fatalism or humor, may partially serve its purpose in making the situation comfortable. But the more dynamic attitude is to be expected when, and only when, the negro is able to think of himself as the member of a group which can afford an outlet for any talent or energy he may possess. And much will have been accomplished to bring this about when Juvenal's remark will no longer apply with such force to the negro's condition as it does today.

> "nil habet infelix paupertas durius in se,
> quam quod ridiculos homines facit."

It has been the custom to some degree in the South, and probably to a greater degree elsewhere, to look forward to industrial progress as the factor which would make the Southern negro's economic independence possible. This industrial progress, which one sees heralded in the census reports, in announcements of chambers of commerce, and in the gaudy full-page advertisements of national magazines, is to strike off the shackles and lift the negro from his state of serfdom, ignorance, and degradation. Such an expectation involves an exorbitant act of faith—an act of faith, not in the negro's capacity, but in the idea of industrialism. Possibly industrialism in the South can make some contribution to the negro's development, just as to the development of the section, but it will do so only if it grows under discipline and is absorbed into the terms of the life it meets. It must enter in the rôle of the citizen and not of the conquerer—not even in the rôle of the beneficent conqueror.

But whether industrialism comes in the rôle of the citizen or the beneficent conqueror, bearing the Greek's gifts, what is the negro's relation to it? A factory or mill is built in a certain district and offers wages which appear attractive to him. He does not ask himself the very pertinent question as to why the factory has been built there, and nobody is at hand to tell him that he himself is one of the most significant reasons. The factory may have come to be near its requisite raw materials, but it has also come to profit from the cheap labor, black and white, which is to be had there. The negro labor is unorganized and unable to bargain effectively with its employer, and the white labor is in little better state.

Even if the policy of the factory is to employ white labor only, the negro is still a telling item in determining its location; his mere presence is a tacit threat against the demands which white labor may later make of the factory owner. It is an old situation in the North where the negro, cut off from the protection of the unions in time of peace, made an ideal scab in time of trouble. This fact and the related fact of the negro's lower standard of living have been largely responsible for the race riots which have occurred in the North since the days of the war, when pillars of smoke from Northern factory chimneys first summoned the Southern negro out of the land of Egypt. It is sometimes boasted in the South that the section has been spared such race riots as those of Chester, Washington, Youngstown, East St. Louis, and Chicago. It is to be wondered how much longer that boast can be made if the manager of a factory in the South can look out of his office window on a race of potential scabs. It will be a new era of the carpet-bag.

No blame is to be attached to the negro himself if his mere presence swells a stockholder's dividends at the expense of a white workman, or if he takes that white workman's job in time of strike. There is no good reason why he should fight the white man's battles if at the same time there is no proper provision for him in the system. In 1919 at the Atlantic City Convention the struggle to gain equal protection for the negro in the American Federation of Labor was won; at least, it was won on paper. But there is a vast difference between that paper victory and a workable system which would embody its principles.

There are two factors which will retard the development of such a system. Not infrequently in the South one meets a conservative temper which carries a naïve distrust of most types of organization. It is a temper somewhat similar to the eighteenth-century English squire's cynical regard of government. The antebellum "squirearchy" of the South did not have such an attitude, but its origins in both cases are the same; in both it springs from a certain individualism. The English squirearchy arose from a century of commotion and internecine war, while the Southern squirearchy expired in our Civil War, leaving in its relics the same dubieties.

But this attitude is not to be taken as a simple economic conservatism which would find a congenial supplement in capitalistic theory; its conservatism bears a more philosophical inflection which subjects the organization of capital to the same skeptical regard.

The potential danger is that in being forced to accept a certain degree of industrial development it will overlook the relation of white and black labor to each other and to the capital which makes that development possible. If this industrialism is to bequeath anything except the profit of the few, the conscious or unconscious exploitation of racial differences, and a disastrous rancor, an enlightened selfishness on the part of the Southern white man must prompt him to encourage the well-being and possibly the organization of negro, as well as white, labor. His safety and that of all concerned lie in a timely strategic adjustment of his position rather than in a tactical defense, however stubborn and expert, of point after point. Not many generations ago the South made just such an error in the conduct of a war.

The second obstacle is in the attitude of the "poor white," whose history shows him to be just as much the victim of the slave system as the negro.[1] In a clumsy, inarticulate

[1] The term "poor white" is an inexact one. Sociologists have used it— or, Southerners would say, misused it—to apply to almost any Southern whites, especially unskilled laborers, who happen to be poor and underprivileged in the cultural and economic sense; and the term is rather loosely applied by Northern writers even to mountaineers and to small farmers who live on a precarious footing. But in the Southern conception, not everybody who is both poor and white is a "poor white." To the Southerner, the "poor white" in the strictest sense is a being beyond the pale of even the most generous democratic recognition; in the negro's term, "po' white trash," or so much social débris. But the term is used here in the later and not the strictly Southern sense.

fashion the "poor white" realizes this fact, and from it comes much of the individual violence, such as lynching, which sometimes falls to the negro's lot. An unchecked industrialism will mean a hopeless aggravation of this attitude. The only way out, except for a costly purgation by blood, is in a realization that the fates of the "poor white" and the negro are linked in a single tether. The well-being and adjustment of one depends on that of the other. When Booker T. Washington said that the salvation of his race will come if the negro "learns to do something well—learns to do it better than some one else," he was stating a condition of free competition between the negro and the white engaged in the same pursuit. He offered no solution for this conflict beyond a vague optimism that the world would pay in money and respect for a thing well done; in fact, he scarcely hinted of the conflict.

But the world also likes to pay as little as possible for a thing. If a negro mason lays a brick as well as a white mason and asks less pay for the job or is content with longer hours, the negro mason in the end will get the job and keep it. The white mason can enter on a period of cut-throat competition with the negro in the labor market, to discover that the negro is better equipped to win. He can attempt to erect artificial barriers against the negro workman in the trade, such as a compact with the employer, only to discover that in a crisis the employer, whether Northern or Southern, will look at a balance sheet and not at the color of the hand which holds the trowel. The white workman, seeing his job in the hands of a negro at a wage which he himself could not possibly live on, can resort to a program of vio-

(259)

lence, sabotage, and persecution; then no bricks will be laid and the ranks of militia will meet him in the street. But the white mason can learn, either by these expensive and bitter experiences or by an exercise of simple intelligence, that color has nothing to do with the true laying of a brick and that the comfort of all involved in the process depends on his recognition and acceptance of the fact.

If the white laborer does not learn this the negro will be in the perpetual rôle of the cat who pulls chestnuts out of the fire for the smiling employer; but it will be no fault of the employer. A multitude of minor difficulties will necessarily arise in giving the negro the protection to prevent this. Their solution will demand tact on the part of the employer, judgment and patience on the part of both the negro and white workman, effective legislation, and the understanding by the ordinary citizen of the several possibilities of the situation. Something else may be added: what the white workman must learn, and his education may be as long and laborious as the negro's, is that he may respect himself as a white man, but, if he fails to concede the negro equal protection, he does not properly respect himself as a man.

But this is not the whole matter, and hardly even the major issue. In the past the Southern negro has always been a creature of the small town and farm. That is where he still chiefly belongs, by temperament and capacity; there he has less the character of a "problem" and more the status of a human being who is likely to find in agricultural and domestic pursuits the happiness that his good nature and easy ways incline him to as an ordinary function of his being.

Once he worked the land as a slave; now he operates on his own account a considerable part of it. Sixty-five years ago he was disappointed in his forty acres and a mule and began his life of freedom with only the capital of his bare hands; but now, only a few generations after, he operates on his own account in the deep South, either as tenant or owner, about one-third of the land. In the border states, of course, the proportion is much smaller. Over a quarter of the rural negro population lives on land which it owns. In Florida and border states over half of the negro population engaged in agriculture lives on owned land, but farther down, where the bulk of negroes are concentrated, the proportion is about one-fifth. Without capital, without education, and with only the crudest training in agricultural methods, the negro has demonstrated his capacity to achieve a certain degree of happiness and independence on the land, and there is every reason to expect that the process will be accelerated from year to year.

Even under the present circumstances, which fall far short of an ideal, not to say decent, adjustment, there are certain compensations in this way of life for the negro and for society in general. It affords a slow way, but the readiest and probably the surest way, for the greater number of the negroes to establish themselves. In the past it has been accepted in most cases simply because no other was at hand, but now if it can be made attractive enough and can offer enough opportunity, it will serve as a ballast to an extravagant industrial expansion. If both the negro and the poor white can find a decent living, there will be no new crowded and clamoring slave auction ready for exploitation by the first bidder. In the last place, it means that the racial distribution in the larger towns and cities can more or less naturally adjust itself and the municipal sections of both societies can develop peacefully without that clash which the relatively sudden influx of negroes has caused in certain Northern cities.

All relations between groups in the city tend to become formalized and impersonal, and such is especially true in those of the two races. But the condition outside of the city is somewhat different and infinitely more desirable. With all the evils which beset the tenant system in the South there is still a certain obvious community of interest between the owner and the "cropper"; profit for one is profit for the other. The relation between the white owner and the negro owner is not so crudely apparent, but it does exist, as anyone who is familiar with a rural community in the South can testify. In one sense it is their common consciousness of depending for the same external, unpredictable factors for the returns on their labor; it rains on the just and the unjust, the black and the white. But in all cases—owner, cropper, hand—there is the important aspect of a certain personal contact; there is all the difference in the world between thinking of a man as simply a negro or a white man and thinking of him as a person, knowing something of his character and his habits, and depending in any fashion on his reliability. The rural life provides the most satisfactory relationship of the two races which can be found at present, or which can be clearly imagined if all aspects of the situation are, without prejudice, taken into account.

But if the negro in the country finds his garden and his cotton patch pleasant enough to make him decline the offers of industrialism, the difficulty of competition between the two races is not finally disposed of; it is only transposed into terms which are more readily ponderable. With the negro's increase of ability and equipment there is the chance of a condition such as that which existed in California between the white and Japanese growers. In competition with the small white farmer the negro would have the same advantages as the negro mason in competition with the white mason. And the buyer of strawberries or cotton or tobacco would care as little whether the product came from a white man's land or a negro's land as the employer would care whether a brick had been laid by a white or black hand; indeed, he would care less.

If the Southern white man feels that the agrarian life has a certain irreplaceable value in his society, and if he hopes to maintain its integrity in the face of industrialism or its dignity in the face of agricultural depression, he must find a place for the negro in his scheme. First, there is the education of the negro—and this applies with equal force to the poor white—in a productive agricultural technique. At present both the landowner and the cropper are victimized by the methods which the cropper employs, but that is the grossest and most immediate aspect. If the negro farmer who owns his land cannot work it profitably there will be in the end that perpetual bait of cheap labor dangling before the factory-owner's eye. Again, in any coöperative or protective enterprise the white man must see that the negro grower receives equal consideration; he must remember that the strawberry or the cotton bale tells no tales in the open market concerning its origins. These, from one point of view, are the more purely selfish parts of the program.

The Southern white man may conceive of his own culture as finally rooted in the soil, and he may desire, through time and necessary vicissitude, to preserve its essential structure intact. He wishes the negro well; he wishes to see crime, genial irresponsibility, ignorance, and oppression replaced by an informed and productive negro community. He probably understands that this negro community must have such roots as the white society owns, and he knows that the negro is less of a wanderer than the "poor white" whose position is also insecure. Let the negro sit beneath his own vine and fig tree. The relation of the two will not immediately escape friction and difference, but there is no reason to despair of their fate. The chief problem for all alike is the restoration of society at large to a balance and security which the industrial régime is far from promising to achieve. Inter-racial conferences and the devices of organized philanthropy, in comparison with this major concern, are only palliatives that distract the South's attention from the main issue. Whatever good they do, the general and fundamental restoration will do more.

JOHN DONALD WADE

THE LIFE AND DEATH
OF COUSIN LUCIUS

HE REMEMBERED all his life the feel of the hot sand on his young feet on that midsummer day. He was very young then, but he knew that he was very tired of riding primly beside his mother in the carriage. So his father let him walk for a little, holding him by his small hand. On went the carriage, on went the wagons behind the carriage, with the slaves, loud with greetings for young master. In the back of the last wagon his father set him down till he could himself find a seat there. Then his father, still holding his hand, lowered him to the road, and let him run along as best he could, right where the mules had gone. The slaves shouted in their pride of him, and in their glee, and the sport was unquestionably fine, but the sand was hot, too hot, and he was happy to go back to his prim station next the person who ruled the world.

That was all he remembered of that journey. He did not remember the look of the soil, black at times with deep shade, nor the far-reaching cotton-fields running down to the wagon ruts in tangles of blackberry bushes and morning-glories. He knew, later, that they had forded streams on that journey, that they had set out with a purpose, from a place—as travelers must—and that they had at last ar-

(265)

rived. But all that came to him later. In his memory there
was chiefly the hot sand.

What he learned later was this—that in 1850 his father
had left his home in lower South Carolina and followed an
uncle of his—Uncle Daniel—to a new home in Georgia.
His father was then only twenty or so, and when he
inherited some land and slaves he decided to go on to
Georgia, where land, said Uncle Daniel, was cheap and
fresh, and where with thrift one might reasonably hope to
set up for oneself almost a little nation of one's own.

The next thing actually in his memory was also about
slaves. In South Carolina, Aunt Amanda, an aunt of his
mother's, had lately died. What that might mean was a
mystery, but one clear result of the transaction was that
Aunt Amanda had no further use for her slaves, and, in
accordance with her will, they had been sent to him in
Georgia. Their arrival his memory seized upon for keeps.
They were being rationed—so much meal, so much meat,
so much syrup, so much rice. But not enough rice. "Li'l'
master," said one of his new chattels to him, "you min'
askin' master to let us swap back all our meal for mo'
rice?" He remembered that he thought it would be delightful to make that request, and he remembered that it was
granted.

Next he remembered seeing the railway train. There it
came with all its smoke, roaring, with its bell ringing and
its shrill whistle. It was stopping on Uncle Daniel's place
to get wood, the same wood that all that morning he had
watched the slaves stacking into neat piles. It seemed to him
indeed fine to have an uncle good enough to look after the

(266)

hungry train's wants. That train could pull nearly anything, and it took cotton bales away so easily to the city
that people did not have to use their mules any longer, at
all, for such long hauls.

But in some things the railroad did not seem so useful.
For when it nosed farther south into the state, after resting
its southern terminus for a year or two at a town some
miles beyond Uncle Daniel's, the town went down almost
overnight, almost as suddenly as a blown bladder goes
down, pricked.

Then a war came, and near Uncle Daniel's, where the
road crossed the railroad and there were some little shops,
some men walked up and down and called themselves
drilling. That seemed a rare game to him, and he never
forgot what a good joke it seemed to them, and to him, for
them to mutter over and over as they set down their feet,
corn-foot, shuck-foot, corn-foot, shuck-foot—on and on. At
last the men went away from the crossroads, and Cousin
James and Cousin Edwin went with them—Uncle Daniel's
son and his daughter's son. His own father did not go and
Lucius was very glad, but very sorry, too, in a way. He did
not go, he said, because he could hardly leave Lucius's
mother and the baby girls—for somehow two baby girls
had come, from somewhere. Lucius thought his father very
considerate, but he wondered whether the girls were, after
all, of a degree of wit that would make them miss their
father very much.—But before he had done wondering, off
his father went also.

That war was a queer thing. It was away, somewhere,
farther than he had come from when he came first to

Georgia. He heard no end of talk about it, but most of that talk confused itself later in his mind with his mature knowledge. He clearly remembered that there were such people as refugees, women and children mostly, who had come that far south because their own land was overrun by hundreds and hundreds of men, like Cousin James and Cousin Edwin, who were up there fighting hundreds and hundreds of other men, called Yankees. They were really fighting, not playing merely. They were shooting at one another, with guns, just as people shot a beef down when time came. But after they shot a man they did not put him to any use at all.

One day he went with Uncle Daniel to see a lot of soldiers who were going by, on their way north to help whip the Yankees. Uncle Daniel said that the soldiers were the noblest people in the world, and Lucius understood why it was that he took his gold-headed cane and wore his plush hat, as if he were going to church, when he went to say his good wishes to such noble people. As the train stopped and as he and Uncle Daniel stood there cheering, one of the soldiers called out to Uncle Daniel, boisterously: "Hey," he said, "what did you make your wife mad about this morning?"—"I was not aware, sir," said Uncle Daniel, "that I had angered her."—"Well," the soldier said, and he pointed at the plush hat, "I see she crowned you with the churn." Lucius wished very much that Uncle Daniel would say something sharp back to him, but he did not. He simply stood there looking a little red, saying, "Ah, sir, ah, sir," in the tone of voice used in asking questions, but never coming out with any question whatever.

Once Lucius was with his mother in the garden. She was directing a number of negro women who were gathering huge basketfuls of vegetables. The vegetables, his mother told him, were being sent to Andersonville, where a lot of Yankees the soldiers had caught were being kept in prison. He asked his mother why they had not shot the Yankees, but she told him that it would have been very un-Christian to shoot them, because these particular Yankees had surrendered, and it was one's duty to be kind to them.

Years later he searched his mind for further memories of the war, but little else remained. Except, of course, about Cousin Edwin. He was at Cousin Edwin's mother's, Cousin Elvira's. It was a spring morning and everything was fresh with new flowers, and there were more birds flying in more trees, chirping, than a boy could possibly count. And at the front gate two men stopped with a small wagon.

He called to Cousin Elvira and she came from the house, down to the gate with him to see what was wanted. She was combing her hair; it was hanging down her back and the comb was in her hand so that he had to go round and take the other hand. What those men had in that wagon was Cousin Edwin's dead body. Cousin Elvira had not known that he was dead. Only that morning she had had a letter from him. He had been killed. How Cousin Elvira wept! He, too, wept bitterly, and the wagon men wept also. But Cousin Edwin was none the better off for all their tears. Nor was Cousin Elvira, for her part, much better off, either. She lived forty years after that day, and she told

(269)

him often how on spring mornings all her life long she went about, or seemed to go about, numb through all her body and holding in her right hand a rigid comb that would not be cast away.

He was a big boy when the war ended, nearly fifteen, and the passing of days and weeks seemed increasingly more rapid. As he looked back and thought of the recurrent seasons falling upon the world it seemed to him that they had come to the count, over and over, of Hard Times, Hard Times, Hard Times, more monotonous, more unending, than the count of the soldiers, muttering as they marched, years before, in the town which had before been called only the crossroads.

He went to school to Mr. and Mrs. Pixley, who taught in town, some three miles from his father's plantation. Both of them, he learned, were Yankees, but it seemed, somehow, that they were good Yankees. And he took with him to Mr. Pixley's his two sisters. There was a brother, too, and there was a sister younger still, but they were not yet old enough to leave home.

One day his mother was violently ill. He heard her cry aloud in her agony—as he had before heard her cry, he remembered, two or three distinct times. She was near dying, he judged, for very pain—but they had told him not to come where she was and he waited, himself in anguish for her wretchedness. That day as she bore another child into the world, that lady quit the world once and for all. He thought that he would burst with rage and sorrow. Wherever he turned, she seemed to speak to him, and he cursed himself for his neglect of her. Surrounded by a

(270)

nation of her husband's kin, she had not always escaped their blame. She had known that times were hard, well, well; but she had insisted that some things she must have while her children were still young. She had saved her round dollars and sent them to Philadelphia to be molded into spoons; she had somehow managed to find some books, and a piano she *would* have. Well, she was dead now, and it seemed to Lucius that the world would be always dark to him, and that things more rigid, more ponderous, more relentlessly adhesive than combs are, would drag his hands downward to earth all his life.

It would not do, then, he decided, to take anybody quite for granted. Already he had learned, as a corollary of the war, that *things* are not dependable; even institutions almost universally the base of people's lives could not, from the fact that they were existent in 1860, be counted upon to be existent also in 1865. He knew now that people also are like wind that blows, and then, inexplicably, is still.

He examined his father, coldly, impersonally, for the first time—not as a fixed body like the earth itself. His father had obviously many elements of grandeur. He was honest and kind and capable. He was introspective, but not sure always to arrive by his self-analysis at judgments that Lucius believed valid. By the Methodist church, which he loved, he was stimulated wisely in his virtues and led to battle against a certain native irascibleness. But in that church such a vast emphasis is set on preaching, that the church is likely to be thought of as little more than a house big enough for the preacher's audience. Lucius learned before long that many of the preachers he was expected to emulate might with more justice be set to emulate him, let alone his father. But his father could not be brought to such a viewpoint, and indeed, if Lucius had dared to suggest his conclusions very pointedly, it might have proved the worse for him.

Soon Lucius was sent to a college maintained by Georgia Methodists, and he stayed till he was graduated. The college was in a tiny town remote from the railroad, and it was such a place that if the generation of Methodists who had set it there some forty years earlier had looked down upon it from Elysium, they would have been happy. Whatever virtues Methodism attained in the South were as manifest there as they were anywhere, and whatever defects it had were less vocal. The countless great oaks on the campus, lightened by countless white columns, typified, appropriately, in his mind the strength and the disciplined joyousness that life might come to. His teachers were usually themselves Methodist ministers, like those who had come periodically to his father's church at home, but the burden of their talk was different. The books they were constantly reading and the white columns among the oaks and the tangible memories thereabout of one or two who had really touched greatness, had somehow affected all who walked in that paradise.

In his studies the chief characters he met were Vergil and Horace and other Romans, who seemed in that atmosphere, as he understood them, truly native. More recent than they were Cervantes and Shakespeare, and the English Lord Byron, the discrepancies of whose life one could overlook in view of his inspiring words about liberty. Hardly dignified enough, because of their modernity, to be incorporated into the curriculum of his college, these writers were none the less current in the college community.

Lucius knew many other boys like himself. In his fraternity, dedicated to God and ladies, he talked much about their high patron and their patronesses, and in his debating society he joined in many windy dissertations on most subjects known to man. In spite of all the implication about him regarding the transiency of earth, in spite of the despair evident in some quarters regarding the possible future of the South, Lucius and his fellows and even his teachers speculated frequently and long on mundane matters. They were large-hearted men, in way of being philosophic, and they felt a pity for their own people, in their poverty and in their political banishment from a land that they had governed—no one in his senses would say meanly —through Jefferson and Calhoun and Lee.

Once he went as a delegate from his fraternity to a meeting held at the state university, where an interest in this world as apart from heaven was somewhat more openly sanctioned than at his own college. The chief sight he saw there was Alexander Stephens, crippled and emaciated and shockingly treble. As he spoke, a young negro fanned him steadily and gave him from time to time a resuscitating toddy. That man's eyes burned with a kind of fire that Lucius knew was fed by a passionate integrity and a passionate love for all mankind. He was obviously the center of a legend, the type to which would gravitate men's memories of other heroes who had been in their way great, but never so great as he was.

(273)

Many young men whom Lucius met at the state university acknowledged the complexities of that legend when they attempted to follow it; when they rose to speak—as people were so frequently doing in those days at such conventions—they behaved themselves with a grandiloquence and declaimed with a gilded ardor that matched the legend of Stephens better than it matched the iron actuality. But Lucius did not know that. He admired the fervid imitations. He regretted that he could never send a majestic flight of eagles soaring across a peroration without having dart through his mind a flight of creatures as large as they, but of less dignified suggestion. He was sure that he could never speak anything in final earnestness without tending to stutter a little. His virtues were of the sort that can be recognized at their entire value only after one has endured the trampling of years which reduce a man to a patriarch.

When Lucius finally had A.B. appended to his name with all the authority of his college, he went home again. Hard Times met him at the train. For indeed the stress of life was great upon his father. Cotton was selling low and the birth rate had been high. Sister Cordelia was already at a Methodist college for girls, and Sister Mary would be going soon. And behind Mary was Brother Andrew. Lucius's father had married again, his first cousin, the widowed Cousin Elvira. And in the house was Cousin Elvira's ward, her sister's daughter, Lucius's third cousin. Her name was Caroline, and she was nineteen, and she had recently, like Lucius, returned home from college.

It was time for Lucius to go to work, and there was not

much work one could do. The cities had begun to grow much more rapidly than in times past, and some of his classmates at college had gone to the cities for jobs. The fathers of some of them were in a position to help their sons with money till they could get on their feet, but Lucius felt that it would be unjust, in his case, to his younger brothers and sisters for him to expect anything further from his father. About the only thing left was to help his father on the farm, but his father was in the best of health, and as vigorous and capable an executive as ever. He really did not need a lieutenant, and the thought of becoming a private soldier of the farm no more entered Lucius's mind than the thought of becoming executioner to the Tsar. While he was still undecided where to turn, he heard one day of the death of Mr. Pixley. Temporarily, then, at least, he could be Mr. Pixley's successor.

So with his father's help he took over Mr. Pixley's academy, naming it neither for its late owner nor, as his father wished, for Bishop Asbury. Instead he named it for the frail man with the burning eyes whom he had seen at the state university, Stephens.

All that fall and winter and into the next spring he managed his academy—one woman assistant and some eighty youngsters ranging from seven to twenty-one. And just as summer came round the year following he married Cousin Caroline.

So life went with him, year in, year out. Children came to him and Cousin Caroline in God's plenty, and children, less intimately connected with him, flocked to the academy. He was determined to make all these youngsters come

(275)

to something. After all, his lines were cast as a teacher. At least he could make a livelihood at that work, and very likely, there, as well as in another place, he could urge himself and the world about him into the strength and the disciplined joyousness which he had come to prize and which he believed would surely bring with them a fair material prosperity. If the children were amenable, he was pleased; if they were dull, he was resolute, unwilling to condemn them as worse than lazy. When night came he was tired—like a man who has spent the day ploughing; but perhaps, he thought, in a little while the situation would become easier.

After the war, nearly all the owners of plantations moved into town, and land that had formerly made cotton for Uncle Daniel gradually turned into streets and building lots. Lucius felt that the thing he had learned at college, and had caught, somehow, from the burning eyes of Mr. Stephens, involved him in a responsibility to that town that could not be satisfied by his giving its youth a quality of instruction that he, if not they, recognized as better than its money's worth. He organized among the citizens a debating society such as he had seen away at school, and he operated in connection with it a lending library. Shakespeare and Cervantes and the English Lord Byron were at the beck of his fellow townsmen—and Addison and Swift and Sterne and Sir Walter Scott, and even Dickens and Thackeray and George Eliot. Lucius managed to make people think (the men as well as the women—he stood out for that) that without the testimony and the comment of such spirits on this life they would all find this life less invigorating.

He found abettors in this work—his father and Uncle Daniel and others of the same mind—but he was its captain. His school, then, affected not merely those who were of an age appropriate for his academy, and it was not long before he was known almost universally in his village as "Cap"—for Captain.

His father turned over about two hundred and fifty acres to him as a sort of indefinite loan, and he became in a fashion a farmer as well as a teacher. That possibly was an error, for when word of his pedagogic ability and energy spread far, and he was offered an important teaching position in a neighboring city, he decided not to accept it because of his farm. But possibly all that was not an error. An instinct for the mastery of land was in his blood, and he knew few pleasures keener than that of roaming over his place, in the afternoons, when school was out, exulting in the brave world and shouting to the dogs that followed him.

There is no doubt that Lucius was gusty. He shouted not only to his dogs, but to himself, occasionally, when he had been reading alone for a long time, during vacations, on his shaded veranda. And he shouted, too, when the beauty of the red sinking sun over low hills, or of clean dogwood blossoms in a dense brake, seemed to him too magnificent not to be magnificently saluted.

Hard Times shadowed him night and day, thwarting in his own life more generous impulses than he could number. Hard Times also, singly or perhaps in collusion with other forces, thwarted in the lives of his neighbors activities that

(277)

he felt strenuously should be stimulated. What did people mean, in a land where all delectable fruits would grow for the mere planting, by planting never a fruit tree? His father had fruit trees, Uncle Daniel had, all of the older men, in fact, commanded for their private use, not for commercial purposes, orchards of pears and peaches, and vineyards, and many a row of figs and pomegranates. But only he of all the younger men would trouble to plant them.

Lucius pondered that matter. Of course there was the small initial expense of the planting, but it was very small or he himself could not have mustered it. Of course there was the despair, the lassitude of enduring poverty. He would shake his head violently when talking about this with his father—like a man coming from beneath water—but for all that gesture could find no clear vision.

It seemed to him, as he considered the world he was a part of, that common sense was among the rarest of qualities—that when it should assert itself most vigorously, it was most likely to lie sleeping. The prevalent economic order was tight and apparently tightening, yet the more need people had to provide themselves with simple assuagements—like pomegranates, for example—the more they seemed paralyzed and inactive. The bewildering necessity of actual money drove everyone in that farm community to concern himself exclusively with the only crop productive of actual money. The more cotton a man grew, the cheaper it went, and the more it became necessary to sustain one's livestock and oneself with dearly purchased grain and meat that had been produced elsewhere. Sometimes when Lucius considered these complexities, and ran

(278)

over in his mind the actual want of money of his friends, and the cruel deprivation that many of them subjected themselves to in order to send their children away to colleges which were themselves weak with penury—at such times he was almost beside himself with a sort of blind anger.

It was lucky that his anger saved him from despair. He was not built for despair, from the beginning, and he was, after all, the husband of Cousin Caroline, and between her and despair there was no shadow of affinity. In every regard he could think of except money, Cousin Caroline had brought him as his wife everything that he, or any man, might ask for.

She knew how to summon a group of people from the town and countryside, and how, on nothing, apparently, to provide them with enough food and enough merriment to bring back to all of them the tradition of generous living that seemed native to them. He often thought that she, who was at best but a frail creature, was the strongest hope he knew for the perpetuation of that bright tradition against the ceaseless, clamorous, insensate piracies of Hard Times. He was sure that the sum total of her character presented aspects of serenity and splendor that demanded, more appropriately than it did anything else, a sort of worship.

Cousin Caroline had religion. She was made for religion from the beginning, and she was, after all, the wife of Cousin Lucius, and in every regard she could think of except money, Cousin Lucius had brought her as her husband, everything that she, or any woman, might ask for. To many beside those two it seemed that Cousin Lucius, because he never quite accepted the Methodist Church, had no religion whatever, that, having only charity and integrity for his currency, he would fare badly at last with St. Peter as concerned tolls. But Cousin Caroline thought better of St. Peter's fundamental discernment than to believe he would quibble about the admission of one who was so plainly one of God's warriors.

Among the best things Cousin Caroline did for him was to bring him to a fuller appreciation of his father. Always fond of him, admiring him, always loyal to him, Cousin Lucius had never quite understood his apparent satisfaction with the offerings of Methodism. He was affected inescapably when the Methodists presented his father, on his completing twenty-five years as superintendent of their Sunday school, with a large silver pitcher. Most of the people who had helped purchase it were harried by need, and their contributions were all the fruit of sacrifice.

But it was Cousin Caroline's satisfaction, as well as his father's, with the offerings of Methodism that did most to quiet his misgivings in that quarter. Anything that two lofty souls—or indeed one lofty soul, he conceded—can be fain of, must itself be somehow worthy. And if it is worthy, an adherence to it on the part of one person should never stand as a barrier between that disciple and an honest soul who is unable to achieve that particular discipleship. As Cousin Lucius grew older, then, his love and admiration of his father, while no greater perhaps than they had been formerly, were certainly more active, less hampered by reservations. His father, he knew, had doted on him in a fashion so prideful that it had seemed a little ridiculous, but that surely could be no barrier between them, and the two men loved each other very tenderly.

Occasionally on trips to this or that city, he encountered friends whom he had known at college. Most of them were prosperous, and some of them were so rich and eminent that news of them seeped down constantly to the stagnant community that was his demesne. He was conscious, as he talked with some of them, of a sort of condescension for him as one who had not justified the promise of his youth. Friendly, aware soon that the old raciness and the old scope of his mind were still operative, one and another of them suggested his coming, still, to live in a city, where he might wrestle with the large affairs that somebody *must* wrestle with, and that he seemed so peculiarly fitted to control.

He learned pointedly through these people what was stirring in the great world. All of them recognized that the condition of Georgia, and of all the South, was indeed perilous, for acquaintance with Hard Times had taught them that Hard Times is a cruel master, who will brutalize, in time, even the stoutest-hearted victim. Somehow the tyrant must be cast down.

In the meantime Cousin Lucius saw the Literary and Debating Society, with its library, gradually go to pieces. It had lasted twenty years. People could not afford the bare expenses of its operation. He saw men resort to subterfuges and to imitations for so long that they at last believed in them; and he, for one, while opposed to anything that was not true, was too sorry for them not to be in part glad that they could persevere in their hallucination. He saw the negroes, inescapably dependent on the whites, sag so far downward, as the whites above them sagged, that final gravity, he feared, would seize the whole swinging structure of society and drag it fatally to earth. He saw the best of people, identified with as good a tradition as English civilization had afforded, moving, he feared unswervably, toward a despair from which they never might be lifted.

A small daughter of his, one day, chattering to him, said a thing that made him cold with anger. She used the word "city" as an adjective, and as an adjective so inclusively commendatory that he knew she implied that whatever was the opposite of "city" was inclusively culpable. He knew that she reflected a judgment that was becoming dangerously general, and he wondered how long he himself could evade it. For days after that he went about fortifying himself by his knowledge of history and of ancient fable, telling himself that man had immemorially drawn his best strength from the earth that mothered him, that the farmer, indeed until quite recently, in the South, had been the acknowledged lord; the city man most often a tradesman. "But what have history and ancient fable," the fiend whispered, "to do with the present?" Cousin Lucius admitted that they apparently had little to do with it, but he believed they *must* have something to do with it if it were not to go amuck past all remedy.

Some of Cousin Lucius's friends thought that the solution of their troubles was to adopt frankly the Northern way of life; and others thought that the solution was to band themselves with discontented farmer sections elsewhere in the country, and so by fierce force to wrest the national organization to a pattern that would favor farmers for a while at the expense of industrialists. On the whole, philosophically, he hoped that farming would continue paramount in his Georgia. He knew little of the philosophy of industrialism, but he knew some people who had grown up to assume that it was the normal order of the world, and he knew that those people left him without comfort. Yet he doubted the wisdom of fierce force, anywhere, and he disliked the renunciation of individualism necessary to attain fierce force. And he observed that in the camp of his contemporaries who relied on that expedient there were many who favored socialistic measures he could not condone, and more whose ignorance and selfishness he could not stomach. The only camp left for him, in his political thinking, was the totally unorganized—and perhaps unorganizable—camp of those who could not bring themselves to assert the South either by means of abandoning much that was peculiarly Southern or by means of affiliating themselves with many who had neither dignity nor wisdom nor honesty.

Cousin Lucius was nearly fifty by now, but he had not yet reconciled himself to the rarity with which power and virtue go hand in hand, leading men with them to an Ultimate who embodies all that our poor notions of virtue and power dimly indicate to us. When he was at college, among the great oaks and the columns, it had seemed to him that those two arbiters were inseparable, as he observed them along the shaded walks. And he had taught school

too long—Euclid and Plato were more real to him than
Ulysses Grant and William McKinley.

About 1890 one of Cousin Lucius's friends sent some
peaches to New York in refrigerated boxes. They sold well.
And slowly, cautiously, Cousin Lucius and all the people
in his community began putting more and more of their
land into orchards. It took a long time for them to adopt
the idea that peaches were a better hope for them than
cotton. Old heads wagged sagely about the frequent win-
ters that were too cold for the tender buds, young heads
told of the insect scourges likely to infest any large-scale
production; and every sad prophecy came true. In spite of
all, the industry proceeded. Farm after farm that had been
sowed to crops afresh each year since being cleared of the
forests was set now in interminable rows of peach trees.
In spring, when the earth was green with a low cover-crop
and each whitewashed stalk of tree projected upward to
the loveliest pink cloud of blossom, Lucius was like a boy
again for sheer delight. And in summer, when the furious
activity of marketing the fruit spurred many of the slow-
going Georgians to the point of pettishness, his own vast
energy became, it seemed, utterly tireless. What he saw
made him believe that the master compromise had been
achieved, that an agricultural community could fare well
in a dance where the fiddles were all buzz-saws and the
horns all steam-whistles.

An instinct, perhaps, made all of Cousin Lucius's children less confident of that compromise than he was. Without exception they revered him; and persuaded, all of them,

of his conviction that the test of a society is the kind of men it produces, they could not think poorly of the system that had him as a part of it. But they could not gain their own consent also to live in that system. And one by one they went away to cities, and they all prospered.

An instinct, too, perhaps, made the people of his community restive under the demands he made of school children. He had yielded to the community judgment to the extent of turning his academy into a public school, but he could not believe that the transformation was more than nominal. That is where circumstance tricked him. The people had lost faith in the classics as a means to better living, or had come to think of *better living* in a restricted, tangible sense that Cousin Lucius would not contemplate. And to teach anything less than the classics seemed to him to involve a doubt as to the value of teaching anything. He wondered why people did not send their children to "business colleges" and be done with it. So he was repudiated as a teacher, after thirty faithful years. The times, he thought, and not any individuals he knew, were responsible, and he was in no way embittered. It was, of course, a consideration that he would no longer draw his hundred dollars a month, but the farm was more remunerative than it had been since the Civil War. And before long the village bank was reorganized and he was made its president.

Money was really coming into the community, and it was sweet not to be stifled always with a sense of poverty. But sometimes he felt that money was like a narcotic that, once tasted, drives men to make any sacrifice in order to taste more of it. All around him, for instance, many gentlemen whom he had long recognized as persons of dignity were behaving themselves with a distressing lack of dignity. On the advice of New York commission merchants they were attaching to each of their peach-crates a gaudy label, boasting that peaches of that particular brand were better than peaches of any other brand. There were gentlemen who were actually shipping the same sort of peaches, from the same orchard, under two distinct brands. Cousin Lucius was sure that such conduct was not native with them, and he was at a loss to know what they meant. What if the commission merchants had said that such practice was "good business"? Who were the commission merchants, anyway?

Another by-and-by had come round and Hard Times was no longer knocking at the door. Cousin Lucius saw men and women, whose heads had been held up by a feat of will only, holding their heads high, at last, naturally. He thought they should hold them higher still. By the Eternal, these people were as good as any people anywhere, and it had not been right, he believed, nor in accord with the intent of God, for them to be always supplicants.

It made him glad to see the girls of various families with horses and phaëtons of their own. When a group of citizens promoted a swimming club, he exulted with the happiness of one who loved swimming for itself and who loved it in this special case as a symbol of liberation. The water that he cavorted in on the summer afternoons, while he whooped from time to time to the ecstatic shrieks of a hundred children, plopped no more deliciously upon his body than upon his spirit. For forty years he and his kind had wandered through a dense wilderness, with little external guidance either of cloud or fire. He told himself that by the light of their own minds they had wandered indeed bravely, but he was unashamedly glad that help had come, and that other men and cities were at last visible.

His father lived on, hale at ninety. He had become in the eyes of everybody who knew him a benign and indomitable saint. Shortly before his death he was in extreme pain and feebleness, and Cousin Lucius, for one, while he was saddened, could not be wholly sad to have the old man go on to whatever might await him. As he ran over in his mind the events of the long life just ended, one thing he had not before thought of stuck in his memory. His father had continued superintendent of the Methodist Sunday school until his death, and yet when he had rounded out his fifty years, though his flock was less hard pressed by far than it had been twenty-five years earlier, there was no silver pitcher offered in recognition of that cycle of effort. He believed that his father, too, had let the anniversary go unnoticed.

Yet Cousin Lucius felt that the omission meant something, most likely something that the people were not conscious of. To all appearances the Methodists were never so active. Like the Baptists—and as incompletely as he indorsed the Methodists, it truly grieved him for them to execute their reforms Baptistward—they had replaced their rather graceful wooden church with a contorted creation, Gothic molded, in red brick. Most of their less material defects remained constant. But the church's neglect of his father's fifty years of service made him know that in spite of its bustling works, it was bored upon from within by something that looked to him curiously like mortality. And the most alarming part of the situation was that the church could not be persuaded of its malady. People simply did not look to it any longer as to the center of all their real hopes. He felt that for the great run of men the church is an indispensable symbol of the basic craving of humanity for an integrity which it must aspire to, if it can never quite exemplify.

He dimly felt that in its zeal to maintain itself as that symbol it had adopted so many of the methods of the men about it, that men had concluded it too much like themselves to be specially needful. It had become simply the most available agent for their philanthropies. For its continued services on that score they paid it the tribute of executing its ceremonies, but they believed, in their hearts, if they were not aware that they did, that all those ceremonies were quite barren. Cousin Lucius, too, had felt that they were barren, but rather because they understated the degree of his humility than because they overstated it. It seemed to him that most of his contemporaries, who were in fact, by now, almost all his juniors, felt that those ceremonies needlessly belittled creatures who were in fact not necessarily little at all.

He did not solve those questions, but he held them in his mind, to couple them, if occasion came, with facts that he might run upon that seemed related.

So the new day was not altogether cloudless. Cousin Lucius felt that people were going too fast, that, villagers, they were trying to keep the pace of people they considered, but whom he could not consider, the best people in the great cities. He believed that the people who had represented in an urban civilization in 1850 what his family had represented at that time in a rural civilization, were most likely as little disposed as he was to indorse the new god, who was so mobile that he had lost all his stability.

Tom and Dick and the butcher and the baker and others were all shooting fiercely about in automobiles, and Europe was trying to destroy itself in a great war—and then America was driven into the war, too. As a banker, he urged Tom and Dick to buy government bonds to sustain the war, but most of them were more concerned to buy something else. Perhaps the older families in the cities were protesting as he protested—and to as little purpose. And people would not read any more. Well-to-do again, they would not listen to his efforts to reorganize the old Library. They would swim with him, they would set up a golf club, but they would not read Cervantes because they were too busy going to the movies.

That war in Europe, with the clamorous agencies that swung to its caissons, woman's suffrage and "socialism" and prohibition, was a puzzle to him. His knowledge of history taught him that most of the avowed objects of any war prove inevitably, in the event, not to have been the real objects. As for woman's suffrage, despite his fervor for justice, he was sure that the practice of a perfectly sound "right" often involves the practicer, and with him others, in woes incomparably more galling than the renunciation of that right.

(289)

Socialism meant to him at bottom the desire of the laboring classes for a more equable share of the world's goods, and the laboring classes that he knew were negro farm hands. It seemed to him that in all conscience they shared quite as fully as justice might demand in the scant dole of the world's goods handed down to their white overlords.

For many years Georgia had had prohibition, and he had voted for it long before it was established. He believed that it was mainly an expedient for furthering good relations between the whites and negroes. It was not practical for a rural community to command adequate police protection, and he was willing to sacrifice his right to resort to liquor openly, in order to make it less available to persons who were likely to use it to the point of madness.

But national prohibition, involving the effort to force upon urban communities, and upon rural communities with a homogeneous population, a system designed peculiarly for the rural South, seemed to him as foolhardy and as vicious as the efforts of alien New England to control the ballot-box in the South. The law was passed in spite of him, and for a while—stickler as he was for law—he grudgingly abided by it. But he soon learned that he was alone, with scarcely anybody except women for company, and that made him restless. He remembered his initial objection to the program, and reminded himself of the statute books cluttered with a thousand laws inoperative because people did not believe in them, and at last, so far as he was concerned, repealed the national prohibition law altogether and abided by the prohibition law of Georgia only, as he had before abided by it, with wisdom and temperance.

One day he was sitting in his brother's store, and he heard some men—they had all been students of his—talking lustily among themselves out on the sidewalk. "What this town needs," said one of them, "is looser credit. Look at every town up and down the road—booming! Look at us—going fast to nothing. What we need is a factory, with a big payroll every Saturday. Naturally we haven't got the capital to float the thing from the start, but, good Lord! how would anything ever start if people waited till they had cash enough to meet every possible expense? In this man's world you've got to take chances. The root of our trouble"—and here Cousin Lucius listened earnestly. He was president of the bank, and though he had not thought the town was disintegrating, he recognized that comparatively it was at a standstill—"the root of our trouble," continued his economist, "is old-man Lucius. Fine old fellow and all that kind of thing, but, my God! what an old fogy! I'll tell you, it's like the fellow said, what this town needs most is one or two first-class funerals!"

Cousin Lucius was pretty well dazed. He did not know whether to go out and defend himself, or to hold his peace, and later, when appropriate, to clarify his position as best he could for a race that had become so marvelously aggressive. He was afraid that if he went he would not be able to talk calmly. He had fairly mastered his trait of stuttering, but he felt sure that before any speech he might make just then he would do well to fill his mouth with pebbles and to plant himself by the roaring surf.

He knew well what that bounding youngster had in mind. He wanted, without effort, things that have immemorially come as the result of effort only. His idea of happiness was to go faster and faster on less and less, and Cousin Lucius was bound to admit that that idea was prevalent nearly everywhere. He did not know, for sure, where it had come from, but it was plainly subjugating Georgia, and if reports were faithful, it was lord everywhere in America. He did not care, he told himself, if it was lord everywhere in the hypothecated universe, it should win no submission from him. The true gods might be long in reasserting themselves, but life is long enough to wait. For that which by reason of strength may run to fourscore years, by reason of other forces may run farther. He would not concede that we are no better than flaring rockets, and he would never get it into his old-fashioned head that anything less than a complete integrity will serve as a right basis for anything that is intended to mount high and to keep high.

He would not say all that now. He believed that the peach business would be constantly remunerative, but he remembered that it had been in existence less than twenty-five years, and he knew that many things of longer lease than that, on men's minds, had suddenly crashed into nothingness. For that reason he was glad that his community had undertaken the commercial production of asparagus and pecans as well as peaches and the older dependence, cotton. He did not anticipate the collapse of all those industries. All that he insisted on was that the expansion of his community be an ordered response to actual demands— not a response so violently stimulated to meet artificial demands that it created new demands faster than it could satisfy the old ones.

The peach crop in 1919 was a complete failure—for reasons not yet determined. The fruit was inferior; the costs of production and transportation, high; the market, lax. And in turn other crops were almost worthless. Next year, everybody said, things would be better. And pretty soon it was plain to Cousin Lucius that his faith in the compromise between farming and industrialism had in its foundations mighty little of reality.

He was himself cautious and thrifty and he had not spent by any means all that the fat years just past had brought to him. He had saved money—and bought more land. He blamed, in a fashion, the people who had lived on all they had made, but against his will he had to admit to himself that he did not blame them very much. Gravely impoverished for years, holding in their land a capital investment that in theory, only, amounted to anything, they had toiled to feed and clothe a boisterous nation which had become rankly rich and which had reserved for itself two privileges: to drive such iron bargains with the Southern farmer that he could scarcely creep, and to denounce him from time to time for his oppression of the negro. Seeing all that, Cousin Lucius could hardly blame the grasshoppers for flitting during the short and, after all, only half-hearted summer of the peach industry. But he considered that he was weak not to blame them more, and he was torn to know whether he should promise the people a better day, which he could not descry, or berate them about the duties of thrift.

The towns in the peach area which had committed themselves to the looser credits he had heard advocated were in worse condition now, by far, than his own town. The same people who had called Cousin Lucius an old fogy began now to say that he was a wise old bird. And he accepted their verdict to this extent—he was wise in seeing the folly that a farm community surely enacts in attempting to live as if it were an industrial community. While he conceded that no community could in his day be any longer purely agrarian, he felt—when he heard people urging a universal acceptance of the industrial program—that that program was not suitable even for an industrial community if it was made up of human beings as he knew them. He recognized that his wisdom was only negative, that there were basic phases of the question that lay too deep for his perceiving.

The farmer, it seemed to him, was in the hard position of having to win the suffrage of a world that had got into the industrialists' motor-car and gone riding. He could run alongside the car, or hang on behind the car, or sit beside the road and let the car go on whither it would—with destination unannounced and, one might suspect, unconsidered.

The case was illustrated by some towns he knew. One of them had continued to grow cotton exclusively—and the world had forgotten it. Many of them had run as hard as ever they could to keep up with the world, and they had fallen exhausted. His own town had hung on as best it could, and though the industrialists might grumble, it managed not to be dislodged. That was a half victory indeed.

He thought as a matter of justice to the farmer and as a matter of well-being for the world, that that motor-car should be controlled not always by the industrialists but sometimes by an agency that would be less swift, more ruminative. A truly wise bird would bring *that* about, and Cousin Lucius knew that that task lay clean beyond him.

One might speculate on these things interminably, but what Cousin Lucius actually saw was that the economic structure of his community was falling down, like London Bridge, or like the little town which, as a child, he had seen burst, bladder like, when the railroad pushed on beyond it. He heard doctrinaire persons, sent down by the government, explain that the trouble lay wholly in the commitment of the people to one crop only. That infuriated him. His community was not committed to a one-crop system; it had four crops. But he found the doctrinaire persons hopelessly obtuse.

Four crops! They had five crops, worse luck, for the countryside everywhere was being stripped of its very forests, so that the people in the cities might have more lumber. That was a chance of getting some money, and one could not let it pass. Woods he had roamed, calculating—as he had learned to do at college—their cubic content in timber per acre, were to his dismay being operated upon in actuality, as he had often fondly, with no thought of sacrilege, operated on them in fancy. It seemed that people could not be happy unless they were felling trees.

One day the young school superintendent began chop-

(295)

ping some oaks on the school grounds, for the high purpose of making an out-of-door basketball court. Cousin Lucius had not a shred of authority to stop the young man, but when he found that the persons who did have authority would not interfere, he interfered himself. At first Cousin Lucius reasoned with him calmly, but the superintendent would not be convinced. There was much talk.

"I have the authority of the Board of Education," said the superintendent, concluding the matter. But Cousin Lucius was determined that that should not conclude the matter. "Authority or no authority," said he, flustered, stuttering a little, "you will take them down, sir, at your peril." Then he walked away.

The superintendent knew that Cousin Lucius had no mandate of popular sentiment behind him, but knew also *one* person who did not mean to risk that old man's displeasure. The trees were spared.

The sacrifice of the forests was a symbol to Cousin Lucius, and a sad one. He knew by it how grave, once more, was the extremity of his friends—how fully it meant the arrival once more of Hard Times as their master. Even now they retained a plenty of most things they actually needed, but lacked the means of acquiring anything in addition. Of course they had wanted too much, and had curbed their desires in general less successfully than he had done, and they were consequently harder pressed. But they were a people not bred to peasant viewpoints. Traditionally they were property owners. They worked faithfully, they maintained holdings upon the value of which was predicated the entire economic structure of the nation. Society would not in either decency or sense deny that value, and it never did. What it did—by some process Cousin Lucius could not encompass—was to make the revenues from that value quite valueless—or a. least quite valueless as compared with the revenues from equal amounts of capital invested elsewhere.

Once again he saw inaugurated the old process, checked for a while, of people leaving their farms and putting out for the cities. And he observed that those who went prospered, while those who stayed languished. Formerly, the more or less gradual development of the cities made them incapable of offering work to all who came, and many of his younger neighbors kept to their farms through necessity. Now the cities were growing like mad—precisely, he thought, like mad—and most of the old families he knew were moving off, losing their connection with their old home. Some survived their difficulties, but many, after lapsing deeper and deeper into debt, finally turned over their holdings to one or another mortgage firm, and went away. And the mortgage firms turned over the land to aliens, people from here and yonder, whose grandfathers never owned a slave nor planted a pomegranate.

Even the negroes, conscious at last of the insatiate capacity of the new cities, were moving away. The Southern cities had absorbed as many negroes as they could use, but the Northern cities had much work of the sort they felt negroes were suited for. It saddened Cousin Lucius to see them go. Men and women whose parents had come with his parents from Carolina, and who had lived in the same

(297)

houses all their lives, were going away—to Detroit, to Akron, to Pittsburgh. Well, God help them.

The prospect was not cheerful, but Cousin Lucius thought that as a human being he was superior to any prospect whatever. When he preached that doctrine to some of his friends they taunted him with the idea that his particular bravery was sustained by certain government bonds he had, and it was true that he had the bonds. He and Cousin Caroline had not stinted themselves during the fat years all for nothing, and he had kept out a small share of his savings to go into Liberty Bonds. But he told those who mourned, and he told himself, that even if he had not saved the bonds, he would still have asserted his humanity over the shackling activities of mere circumstance.

It was a fine sight to see him early on a summer morning walking the mile-long street between his home and the bank. On one side there were great oaks bordering his path, and the other side was a row of houses. In front of nearly every house a woman was stirring among her flowers, and Cousin Lucius had some words for nearly all of them. "Nice morning, ma'am," he would say. "I hope you all are well this morning." And then he would pass on, and often he would sniff the cool air greedily into his nostrils. "My, my," he would say, "sweet! How sweet the air is this morning!" And when a breeze blew, he would stretch out his arms directly into it—for of all the good things to have up one's sleeve he considered a summer breeze among the usefulest.

The time came round when he and Cousin Caroline had

been married fifty years. And they gave a great party, and all their children came home, and people from all that section came to say good wishes to them. Cousin Caroline sat most of the evening, lovely in her black dress and with her flowers, and Cousin Lucius—sure that Cousin Caroline would pay for the two of them whatever was owing to propriety—sat nowhere, nor was indeed still for a moment anywhere. He looked very elegant, as young, almost, as his youngest son, and he was as vigorous, apparently, as anybody in all that company. Cousin Lucius had never lost a moment in his whole life from having drunk too much liquor, but he had always kept some liquor on hand, and he felt that that night surely justified his touching it a little more freely than was his custom. So he summoned by groups all the gentlemen present into his own backroom, and had a toast with them. Now the room was small and there were many groups and that involved Cousin Lucius's having many toasts, but he used his head and came through the operation with the dignity that was a part of him.

Not everybody was satisfied with his conduct. Some of the ladies especially who had men-folk less well balanced than they might have been, thought the situation scandalous. They had been indoctrinated fully with the dogma which says that life must be made safe for everybody at the cost, if necessary, of shutting the entire world into a back yard with high palings, and they believed that somebody prone to sottishness might be wrecked by Cousin Lucius's example. They did not realize the complexities of life which baffle those who have eyes to see, and make them despair at times of saving even the just and wise—much less the weak and foolish.

Those ladies were not shadowed—nor glorified—by a sense of tragic vision, and they were not capable—not indeed aware—of philosophic honesty, but they were good and angry with Cousin Lucius and they went to Cousin Caroline and told her that she should curb him. That lady was not dismayed. The thought of being angry with Cousin Lucius did not once occur to her, but for the briefest moment she realized that she was having to check herself not to be outraged against the little ladies who had constituted themselves his guardians. "Oh," she said, "you know Lucius! What can *I* do with Lucius? My dear, where *did* you find that lovely dress. You always show such exquisite taste. I am so happy to have you here. No friends, you know, like old ones. I am *so* happy."

That next winter Cousin Lucius and Cousin Caroline both had influenza, and Cousin Lucius's sister, who came to look after them had it, too. They all recovered, but Cousin Lucius *would* violate directions and go back to work at the bank before he was supposed to go. And as spring came on it was evident that something ailed him, very gravely. It was his heart, but he refused to recognize the debility that was patent to everybody else, and went on.

And when summer came, and the jaded people began again to market the peaches they felt sure—and rightly—would be profitless, he, with the rest, set his operations in motion. One of his sons, Edward, was at home on a visit, and early one morning the father and son went out to the farm, with the intention of coming back home for breakfast. Only the negro foreman, Anthony, was at the packing-house, where they stopped, and Edward strolled down into the orchard, leaving Cousin Lucius to talk over the day's plans with Anthony. A little way down one of the rows between the peach trees, Edward almost stumbled upon some quail. And the quail fluttered up and flew straight toward the packing-house.

He heard his father shout at them as they went by, the fine lusty shout that he remembered as designed especially for sunsets and clean dogwood blossoms. And then there was perfect silence. And then he heard the frantic voice of Anthony: "Oh, Mas' Edward! Help, help, Mas' Edward! Mas' Lucius! Mas' Lucius! O Lord! help, Mas' Edward!" Stark fright slugged him. He was sick and he could scarcely walk, but he ran, and after unmeasured time, it seemed to him, he rounded the corner of the packing-house and saw Anthony, a sort of maniac between grief and terror, half weeping, half shouting, stooping, holding in his arms Cousin Lucius's limp body. "Oh, Mas' Edward! Mas' Edward! Fo' God, I believe Mas' Lucius done dead!"

He *was* dead. And all who wish to think that he lived insignificantly and that the sum of what he was is negligible, are welcome to think so. And may God have mercy on their souls.

HENRY BLUE KLINE

WILLIAM REMINGTON:
A STUDY IN INDIVIDUALISM

I

WILLIAM REMINGTON'S education could not
have made him more unfit to live life on the terms
he found prevailing about him if it had been carefully calculated with this end in view. His college was largely
responsible but not to blame for him; for all the materials
were there with which he might have been shaped into an
engineer or lawyer or business administrator; but, being
none too sure of just what he did want to make of himself,
and finding that he loved literature and the arts and philosophy, he passed over the courses of study which would
have taught him how to earn a comfortable and morally
painless living, only to turn instead to the useless "humanities."

He left his college with a feeling that he had been exceptionally fortunate in having been permitted to carry on his
formal education under men singularly lacking in pedantry.
William had heard very little delivered *ex cathedra*; his
instructors' attitudes toward the eminently desirable things
known in a workaday world as facts and theories ranged
from an active indifference to a militant distaste. He had
been shocked at first by their consistent disregard of work-

ing and workable truths; now he found himself only grateful; for he knew himself well enough to perceive that his education could have been carried out successfully along no other lines, that instruction of the dogmatic variety would have compelled him to spend much of his mental and volitional energies on mistrust and overt rebellion; for he felt any ready-made opinion, unless he were given an opportunity to compare it with the experience of his race and his own self as he understood them, to be an unwarranted intrusion on and violation of his spiritual privacy—as such to be resented with all his might.

By temperament William Remington was something of a solitary idealist; and instead of trying to cure him, his professors had persisted in reinforcing a critical habit of mind which, considering the ideals of living in force outside of his college walls, was no less than a disease. He was graduated with two potentially weighty handicaps. The first was some knowledge and appreciation of literature, history, music, and the decorative arts. The second was a deeply rooted determination to live his life, in so far as he possessed free agency to control it, on terms dictated by his own critical intelligence, and by nothing else. He was no radical reformer, however; he was inclined rather to scoff at the anarchic young poets and philosophers of his college class, and to defend the forces of conservatism against their hot onslaughts; he was ready and willing to subscribe to conventions and standards, insisting only upon reminding himself, whenever they became too fantastic in comparison with his self-chosen norm of human experience and common sense, that they were *only* standards, not revealed religion or natural theology; and he reserved the right to condemn conventions based on any morality not founded solidly in the ethics of human worth.

In a word, he was due for a hard bump. He expected nothing else, for he had been taught what to look for.

II

After graduation William had to decide where he would live. His environment, he knew, would be a vitally important factor in determining both his subsequent material success and his satisfaction in existence; therefore the choice was no light one. Unable to judge the congeniality of all parts of his nation, he tried to find in that part of the country with which he had some acquaintance a typical cross-section which would represent all the important conditions of American life, in a form he could experiment with.

The cleavage, he decided after some study, could best be made between Detroit and New Orleans: not only did these two most comprehensibly represent the opposite extremes, but this particular line of cleavage possessed the additional advantage of continuity, the velocity of social life and economic activity increasing in proportion as one followed it northward.

The next step was to decide where to meet the line. The choice he made, of a city somewhat closer to Detroit than to New Orleans, was founded not on experiment, but on certain circumstances beyond William's control, which made this selection the easiest and the one fraught, as it seemed to him, with the least risks to himself.

Once away from his school associates, he found no great difficulty in making acquaintances among other young college graduates of his city. Presently he was well established as a member of their group. The prospect should have been cheering, and he knew that from a detached observer's point of view his social relations must have appeared eminently satisfactory; for he had an average talent for the arts of polite and pleasurable converse, and, moreover, knew himself to be not unpopular even if he was sometimes accused to being too much the lone eagle ever to become a perfectly gregarious animal. But judging himself from within, by his most acid test, he knew that he was far from being satisfied. His social behavior was substantially the same as that of his friends; but their behavior seemed to be instinctive and unconscious, whereas he was unable to dispel a disquieting feeling that his own was a theatrical illusion, that he was an actor impersonating William Remington as the world wished him to be, not William Remington himself. One name for his ailment was self-consciousness, he knew; and self-consciously he decided that most of his new friends belonged to an apathetic majority which included the most of men—to the "happy, obliviously blissful mob," he told himself with a slight twinge of regret for the complacent egoism of his thought —they seemed to have accepted unquestioningly a way of life to which his temperament and education rendered him alien. He enjoyed dancing and drinking and many of their other diversions; he could not understand, however, their desire to fill every waking moment with some physical and sensuous activity, for he could find only too little time at best for the leisurely arts of human society and self-cultivation he loved so well.

He found it easy to look metaphorically on his and his acquaintances' relative positions in the world—and mistrusted the metaphor because it could not be worked into a logical, ideal proposition. He was fairly convinced, though, that, as far as essentials went, there was more than a little of truth in his conception. Life as it was being lived about him was a vast stream into which one could enter, or, by an effort of self-denial, stay out of. Most of his new friends were far out in the current; nor was he sure that they could get out of it if they would. He was not alone on the bank, but most of his companions were older, and many of them dead, known to him only through history and literature. He felt too lively for such associates; and he valued his freedom to walk the dry land too well to join the group toward which his youth and natural sympathies were drawing him. He hit on a compromise—to enter the stream where he listed, keeping always close to the bank, however, in order that he might be able to get back to shore when he should come to wish it.

This was some satisfaction, but not much; it gave him a lower rate of acceleration than that of his friends; it made him feel his aloofness very keenly. He was neither fish nor fowl; he was lonely. In the stream he knew the helplessness of the born landsman, on the bank the hopelessness of a creature out of its native element. True enough, he knew a few persons of his own age who felt as he did; but most of these were in some kind of emotional revolt against or flight from their environment, whereas William sought neither revolution nor escape, but to be a part of his surroundings and at the same time to be free and distinct of all the other parts and of the substance as a whole.

Some persons would have adjudged themselves social misfits and given up at this point; indeed, William wondered whether resignation were not, after all, the only reasonable course. But not for him. With characteristic youthfulness—he was glad to find that he had youth in him, so few of his contemporaries were able to be young— he commenced to suspect that if his trouble lay in his temperament or critical equipment, at least he was not blameworthy alone, that society was largely at fault for his ambiguous, anomalous position. In so intense an individualist as William Remington felt himself to be this attitude could easily have gone over into a sort of practical solipsism; instead it attained to a certain hard objectivity when he discovered that the swimmers were no better off than the bystander.

First, however, he had the dubious satisfaction of finding that he did not stand alone—indeed, that his companions were many enough. Following contemporary poetry and fiction showed him that many thoughtful persons liked their surroundings no better than he liked his. But for the most part these were self-torturers of one sort or another, romantic idealists disillusioned by the sharp prick of reality, defeated by the unideal conditions of sensuous existence; their wish was not to shape a satisfactory environment but to escape the effort of adjusting themselves to any set of conditions whatever. William did not feel whipped; he wanted to feel strong. The escape mechanism was not for

his kind: romanticism of any pronounced sort seemed only
a little foolish and puerile. He was skeptical, too, of religion as an escape, and he and his generation had nothing
on which could be set up a positive religion of expression
and affirmation; religion even as great art could find no
sustenance in the arid wastes of contemporary thought, he
knew; and he knew that, in spite of his intense desire to
maintain spiritual autonomy, he was too much a product
of his time ever to attain quite to incorporeal well-nourish-
ment. However, he was determined to get what nourishment he could, to carry on some sort of satisfactory existence
in the face of come what would. If he was in a spiritual
desert, then from within himself he would have to create
his own cosmos and establish a pantheon of his most stable
desires. He recognized himself for an egoist, out of tune
with the provisional harmonies of purely sensuous existence
—and he deplored both the egoism and the discordance;
but, feeling himself still to be valuable in some vague way,
he was inclined to lay the egoism to his uncongenial surroundings instead of concluding that these surroundings became uncongenial only because of his egoism.

His withdrawal from social life was well advanced before
he came to a fairly comprehensive realization of an earlier
suspicion that social life, or at least what social life he had
partaken of, was itself out of tune according to any more
than transitory rule of harmony . . . and so out of tune
with any harmony at all. He had seen his little group in
their intervals of inaction. Normally they were vivacious,
these friends of his; but their normal state seemed to be a

condition of artificial stimulation, their vivacity synthetic: no real gayety welled up from within them. Superficially, God was in his heaven, all was right with their world. There was a plethora of banter and witty innuendo; a great plenty of cocktails to promote the pleasure of man; a quantitatively great if not very rich and profound body of sexual experience to be had; but these things failed of realizing on their great potentialities as elements of a satisfying existence, going instead to what seemed to William criminal waste. Convinced that his friends were inherently serious, he was constrained to conclude that their seeming excesses came of an urgent necessity to keep going. In seeing them in what would have been in other places and other times intervals of repose, he knew why this necessity was so potent; for there were pipers to be paid, and paid with usury. After the brawl were sore heads, after the dance fatigued bodies, after the assignation, languor; after stimulation—depression. When called by slightly different names, brawls, bacchanales, and assignations have their rightful place in the life of youth; they become "abnormal" and inhuman only when it is assumed that one is alive only in the intervals of excitement and that ideal living would consist in a series of good times unbroken by interludes of no place to go. The devotee of such a program must needs be happy only so long as he is in action; in the inescapable intervals of inaction he is infinitely worse off than the prudent, detached William Remington felt himself to be.

His obvious place was on the bank of the stream of

turbulent sensational life; it was no less obvious that most if not all of his more vivacious acquaintances would have been happier had they joined him for a space now and then. But they had taken the world as they had found it; he had taken it only for the sake of argument and as a point of departure from which to shape an existence along more positive and purposive lines. In avoiding the swelling torrent he gained the spiritual satisfaction of being his own man; he missed the spiritual satisfaction of having a multiplicity of companionships with persons of his own age.

In the higher reaches of social life—William took his young-alumni group to be one of them—the stream-of-life (or progressivist, as he had learned to call it) manner of existence was a failure when judged by its social consequences, for it brought no ponderable happiness to those who partook of it. There was, he believed, some kind of happiness which is a part of the man and cannot be taken from him by a new eddy or torrent of fortune; he suspected that he wasn't getting very far in his pursuit of it; but at least he was getting somewhere, while his more active contemporaries hadn't even made a start—some of them had given up already; their names could be read on the first pages of newspapers almost every day. He wasn't very well satisfied with his existence; but at least he was spared the horrible emotional strain of periodic stimulation and depression. It was not pleasant to find his soul turning gray in the revealing light of introspection; even this, however, was to be preferred to an incessant flickering between red and blue.

With this thought he met an *impasse*; the dilemma seemed inescapable.

III

After making the first tentative adjustments to a new and strange environment, one of the first things William Remington had to thresh out was the question of what to do with himself. Manifestly his education had given him nothing to go by: he was not lawyer, engineer, business man, doctor; only a bachelor of arts. Aristotle was one of his gods. Did that mean that he must become a teacher-philosopher? He felt curiously unfit for such a career. How, for example, did one begin? To become a teacher was perhaps easy enough—indeed, he felt prepared to become nothing else; but was the teacher without the philosopher worth while? The answer was unqualified—No. Another god was Socrates. But William was not quite so naïve as not to know that modern Socrateses are given the hemlock cup not at the end but at the beginning of their careers; and he had no lust after martyrdom. He thought Jesus the most ethical man the world had ever known; and nowhere in the world William knew would any man be suffered to practice Jesus's ethics; moreover, William himself had no inclination to go the whole Christian road. Brightest perhaps of all deities, according to his way of thinking, was Shakespeare. The very thought made him laugh wryly. William Shakespeare and William Remington!

And yet, in intervals of complete intellectual honesty and self-candor, he knew that he did hanker to be the Shakespeare of his day and place. Unfortunately, there were two cogent and sufficient reasons why he could not hope to attain to a place in the canon of literary immortals. In the first place, he simply *was* no Shakespeare. For the sake of his *amour propre* he chose to think of this consideration as the less important, since the second was sufficient without it. The spiritual sustenance his time and place had to offer had produced James Branch Cabell, and could possibly produce even a Shelley or a Keats, but never a Shakespeare or a Chaucer: creative artists were no longer the articulate archetypes of great ages describing in painting or music or poetry what they saw and heard and felt of the life about them; twentieth-century artists were solitary watchers who, finding nothing a man could keep hold on in the aimless procession of change going on all about them, were turned inward to a fruitless contemplation of their own beings. This introspective practice seemed to William the most futile of pursuits; it revolted every classical and orderly instinct he possessed. Was self-expression the aim and end of life and of the art whose place it was to picture and interpret life? Then he preferred to express himself in more animal fashion, to let his emotions find their natural outlet in physical activity. Was the unique purpose of art to show the purposelessness of everything outside of one's own ego? Much better, then, to surrender all of oneself to the impersonal stream of uncritical sensuousness. . . . And yet, in the midst of his impatience, he thought he saw how a modern artist must make the apotheosis of self his cardinal aim—or else be no artist at all—which led him to believe that creative activity was the most bootless of occu-

(312)

pations. The inevitable conclusion of this line of thought seemed to be that, staging a one-man rebellion against a Kingdom of Whirl, the modern practitioner of the fine arts must needs become a bit of an egomaniac. A contemporary aspirant to greatness must be his own cosmos; being a solitary soul, viewing life exclusively *sub specie mortalitatis*, he is then unable to *know* life richly and thoroughly enough to wrench some communicable meaning from it; and, having nothing to communicate but his own particular and transitory states of feeling, any real artistic greatness, excepting the doubtful eminence of a supreme mysticism devoted to the cult of selfhood, becomes impossible. The curve closed in on itself with geometrical nicety. William's aim, unfortunately, was not to describe vicious circles, but to make something of the life he had before him to live. Certainly he could not make it a life of Shakespeare, nor either of Aristotle. . . . A cherished illusion of his school days had given up the ghost.

That it had reasoned out very nicely was no comfort, for it left him feeling more lonely than ever before. He wanted to give up, declare life futile, and attain thereby to companionship with the large company of the disenchanted. But he couldn't do it convincingly; for when he had assured himself that the fruit was not worth the picking, his faculty of self-criticism broke in on his mood and made him laugh at the callowness of a melancholy he had been determined to think of as the height of ultimate maturity. But the pessimistic views remained even though in a mitigated form; and to air them in talk or print seemed the most shocking kind—indeed, to his importunately generalizing mind the only kind—of spiritual immodesty. The dignified and manly thing to do was to keep silence. William had chosen his alternative: unable to be an artist of the old-fashioned kind, he was resolved to be no artist at all.

Still, faced with the necessity of doing something for his living and to keep him busy, he had to decide on something more positive than what he would *not* do, knowing though he did that his program must be of only the most tentative and provisional sort, constantly to be recognized as such.

Not very reasonably but naturally he sought a closer communion with the ideal of life prevalent in his world, in order to find out its nature and how he did not measure up to it. This led him directly to the factory. The ideal of industrial progress, he had been told rather convincingly, was the Satan of the modern world; now he wished to find out for himself.

During one summer vacation he had worked in a steel mill. Unfortunate for the unfavorable easy generalization his impatient mind wished to make, his recollections of the period were pleasant. He had lived close to his mill acquaintances—"Americans," Scandinavians, Irishmen, Italians, Hungarians, Poles; and with one or two exceptions they had been humorous, intelligent, quick-witted, kindly, and pityingly contemptuous of the world outside of the mill, and, under an undercurrent of grumbling that runs strong where men like the work they do, well satisfied with their existence and unwilling to exchange it for anything

short of actual wealth. On the other hand, from three summer vacation periods of employment in another factory—the
self-styled model factory, and with some justice behind the
boast—he had brought away nothing more than a rather
poor epigram: The machines were "almost human," their
operators "almost mechanical."

Some basis of comparison should have existed between
the pleasant steel mill and the unpleasant factory, and from
this comparison, if it were properly made and evaluated,
would come the answer to the question of what ailed the
industrial society William lived in. He thought he sensed
the answer, but could not explain it even to himself; and
even had he been the inspired intellectual giant who could
have made the feeling articulate and rational, the answer
would have given him no working plan for the conduct of
his own life. He knew only that the model factory and the
steel mill were alike out of the question as possible em-
ployers of his energies; in the former he would have enjoyed the perverse pleasure of seeing himself go mad of
ennui; in the latter, with his hardly acquired abilities in
abstract thought and creative pursuits, unextraordinary
though they were, he would have seemed to himself a
moral coward evading a personal destiny in which he still
believed. (If only it were a manifest destiny! he wished.)

Every remunerative and social work he could think of
seemed to be subject to one or the other of these disabili-
ties. The dilemma was unpleasant. But it had to be faced,
for he needed to find some gainful occupation, and for the
good of his soul he needed still more to work at something

(315)

he could feel to be worth more than the price of ministering to his merely physical needs and desires.

IV

Already forces were at work to resolve his difficulty, although he knew of them only long after the precipitating events. The system which he thought tended to bring about individual spiritual starvation and social madness was faced at long last by a real crisis. In a clear sky appeared of a sudden ominous portents: factories were closed down, men thrown out of work. The portents realized in cataclysm: the condition continued, grew worse, showed no signs of growing better. Hunger and cold stalked abroad in the land until premonitory shivers ran down the spines of the fattest and warmest. A bad state of affairs became steadily and rapidly worse.

Beyond feeling a rather abstract social pity for the victims of the disaster, William took only an academic interest in the phenomenon. He thought it reasonable and possibly logical to see the situation as a crisis in the life of the ideal of industrial progress. And now that a crucial time was come, certain questions tacitly ignored in times of material prosperity and social optimism seemed to demand answers coolly meditated and courageously spoken even where they might be found to show the central ideal itself to be a superstition, a heathen fetich, an adventitious postulate with no roots in human values. How, for example, could the votaries of prosperity solve unemployment and extirpate its consequent poverty? How explain away the rise of organized crime in the strata of society most immediately affected by the advancement of the industrial revolution? How defend the evils of Prohibition, a by-product of the established order? Above all, how explain why in the service of the industrial ideal was no work William and many others considered worth their doing?

His interest became less academic when he saw the form of the solution worked out by those in high places. "In the name of Prosperity, Patriotism, and Charity, *buy*—buy to the limit! The present depression is only temporary; it will pass very quickly if only everybody will do his part to reduce swollen stocks and so make room for the workers to return to their machines and provide funds to pay them with."

He now found himself—with some pleasure, for he had deplored the self-conscious detachment he had fallen into —taking spirited exception to such a program. No doubt the solution would work temporarily; even then he could see no possibility of a new dispensation being brought in under which would be a task to which he could give himself body and soul. And though the solution might bring present relief to the ails of the economic order, he perceived that under such a system of control without cure the disaster must necessarily be repeated later and on a larger scale, for the germs of the earlier disorder would have been fertilized, not rooted out. He detected an analogy—not a very critical one, perhaps, but jibing with all the experience he had had—and pursued it with all the concentration he could command. His friends lived in alternations of stimulation and depression; the economic order was beginning to show signs of being subject to just such a cycle; having passed from a long initial state of intoxication, it was now feeling the inevitable morning-after *Katzenjammer* . . . the cycle to go on according to some series of infinite extension, until something should occur to break it.

Very soon it became evident that the leaders and led of the nation were not going to play the game according to William's rules. Economic optimism was to continue; so too was the progressivist negation of human worth and suppression of individual personality. The dilemma now came very close to home: William found himself in the unpleasant though not entirely unhumorous predicament of being ignored and evaded completely out of existence. He lived in a highly industrialized city; he would have felt less lonely on Selkirk's isle. His position in social life was anomalous and generally unsatisfactory, his position in the economic race worth the creature-needs it enabled him to minister to, and nothing more.

But at least the anti-individualistic forces had at last shown themselves unmistakably for what they were, and so had given him a conception of something eminently worth doing—namely, to wage an individual civil revolt against the established economic fetich. For now he had a fuller realization that the prevalent order affected not only those who had become "almost mechanical" at their machines or office desks, but, in a lesser degree, perhaps, but still visibly, affected any person who subsisted where this order was generally accepted. William understood himself well enough to know that not all of his ego was active; that there was a lazy part being catered to, invited to partake of manufactured products of which he had no real need, and, what seemed a thousand times worse, was being invited to renounce the ardors of individualized leisure for the effortless diversions of seeing motion pictures chaste from having had no carnal connection with life, reading boiler-plate fiction on the run, professing a travestied Christianity so nicely abstracted as to require little effort, and that only intellectual, hearing tasteless music and lyrical soap advertisements from a horn as one ate or read or solved cross-word puzzles, and, all other pastimes failing, riding in the ubiquitous automobile. These blandishments were strong for William; no one knew it better than he himself. He had a decided taste for the material luxuries of life—but a selective one.

In his very selectivity he thought he espied his salvation; for the active part of him became increasingly wary of material benefits: they could too easily be sops thrown to pale creatures that once were men, in order to reimburse them for the loss of their souls. This mistrust he kept secret from his friends as a matter of policy; he did not care to be scoffed at as a Puritan ascetic; he chose, rather, to think of himself as a critical skeptic. A line from a useless classic haunted him to sound the fundamental tone of his spiritual state: *"Timeo Danaos et dona ferentes."*

Perversely, he felt warmly grateful to the college which had done so much to isolate him from active participation in human affairs.

v

Having no hankering after an ivory-tower existence, William next sought some means to conclude his voluntary isolation. He had already become so far involved in mundane matters as to pass from his pristine vague deploration to a very definite resentment directed against his environment. His next move, then, was to seek a practical, concrete, practicable program for the conduct of his life in relation to that environment.

He was back where he had started from, but much richer in experience and better acquainted with himself and his needs.

The environment was assumed, as before, to be constant. So, too, did he assume William Remington; he felt that he had to, that any other assumption would have led him into irresolvable chaos. In spite of the presence of these two apparent irreconcilables, however, he managed to commence his program realistically, with the candid admission that he would do better to make intelligent use of the fruits of material progress than to carry out any fairly complete renunciation of them. Motor-cars, talking pictures, the radio, labor-saving devices, possessed amazingly great potentialities for the extension and enrichment of the leisure one might devote to humane pursuits. At some point, however, one would commence to regard these things not as means, but as ends in themselves, to become dependent upon them to *be* one's leisure and social activity; beyond this point it could be reasonably expected that one would only become progressively enslaved to them. Between complete moral freedom without leisure to enjoy it and maximum leisure with a minimum of freedom there was some critical eutectic point at which one could hope to attain to one's fullest powers and find the richest of satisfactions consonant with one's nature. William had no way of knowing just where his own crucial point lay; he did know beyond the slightest doubt that it was far away on the side of spiritual freedom and relatively simple material culture from the point that had been reached by the society in which he was living.

His individual and personal program was then very simple. He pledged himself to himself to maintain his "sales resistance" at a very high level: he would not starve the body and its senses into submission to his will, but he would insist on being an *active* party in any transaction which might involve him. He would be fair game for no high-pressure salesmen and no high-pressure propaganda, and would look with a fishy eye on every blessing that was heralded to his notice through advertising and other media of "sales education." He would become a monkey wrench in the wheels of progress, a dissenter in word and deed from the dogmas of "high saturation" and "quick turnover."

In the practice of this creed—for he did practice it, rather consistently—he found a certain satisfaction and some self-pride. But the practice required much conscious exercise of will-power; and though he found the end worth the effort in any event, he preferred to save as much as possible of his to him precious energies from mere reaction for action in self-development and humane pursuits social, political, economic, and moral.

William Remington was still a constant; the environment then had to become a variable.

As a matter of fact, his abstracting intellect had much less to do with his next move than did his feeling of loneliness among worshipers of an alien god. All other considerations temporarily aside, it seemed manifest that, in some place where life was "simpler," where the clamor of progress was fainter than in the place where he then was, there would be people living more nearly by his values and sensing life with sympathies closer to his own; hence these people could give him the companionship for which he was in want.

Figuratively speaking—and geographically as well—the path he then set out on, some two years after his graduation from college, led away from "Detroit" toward "New Orleans." Made a little wiser by the additional experience he had gained of life, he found what he thought he was looking for after a not very long quest: still north of the southern cultural pole but much farther than he had been from the northern, he came upon a place where the social balance of progress and culture was for all practical purposes equivalent to his own eutectic balance.

And here, even as he had expected, he knew a new satisfaction, a sense that he "belonged" at last: for here was a social soil of just such a richness that he could take root and thrive therein; here was a people who thought in his terms and respected his traditions even when, exceptionably, they could not subscribe to them; here were young men who knew not only how to get drunk but also the finer art of staying happily sober: here were his own people. And, being satisfied in his new companions, he discovered the very interesting truth that many kinds of meat-and-drink labors which would have been distasteful and not worth doing in the houses of strangers may seem attractive and eminently worth while when one is able to maintain a feeling that one's efforts are in some way "all in the family." Furthermore, his self-imposed silence was broken at last; lifted out of the narrowly circumscribed area of self-hood into the richer realm of human relations by contact with a community life organized and conducted as a high and worthy end in itself, he now acquired that inner conviction which is the first condition of any artistic creation, no matter how humble. And here was an audience, not a very large one, perhaps, but in sympathy with his own sense of human values. He felt that he had set his foot on the highroad toward increasing happiness. . . .

VI

William Remington may live and die in his chosen place among his chosen people; for the missionary fervor to go through the world seeking proselytes does not burn high in him. He may not live in unbroken tranquillity, however; he speedily discovered that he and his friends would have to strive mightily and almost unremittingly to keep their terrestrial Thélème. With a central paternalistic government tending to reduce every metropolis and hamlet of the nation to a cultural common denominator, with cheap and rapid transportation and highly organized communications tending to extend the metropolitan areas and their indigenous ideals over most of the forty-eight states, with imperialistic industrial exploiters abroad in the land, any ideal of provincialism can be kept in force only by fighting for it.

So William will fight—with a mental qualification. He respects himself for a good citizen at last, and no effort now seems too great when it is for the maintenance of his social enfranchisement. He will try to muster up something like Roman fighting fervor to keep his chosen spot from falling ill of the "Detroit" malady; but, the reservation becoming operative, in the same way he will resist any tendency to go too far "back to the soil." And, most important reservation of all, should this society in which he now lives come of its own conscious desire to espouse ideals under which he finds existence unpleasant, or should his new friends become a party so small and so weak as no longer to afford the richness, variety, and multiplicity of social contacts he needs, or should he find that he has been mistaken in estimating his own eutectic point or that of his new home, then he will get out and seek more congenial surroundings . . . travel toward "Detroit" or "New Orleans," the direction to be determined by a future self-evaluation. For his devotion is to no cause, but only to a pleasant place to live in. He is candidly, brazenly, happily provincial—worshiping hearth and home, however, not because it is hearth and home, but because he is well content to abide there.

Avowed individualists though they are, William thinks that he and his new friends vindicate their larger social instincts by making common cause against what they conceive to be false ideals and inhumane practices. He is seeing the beginning of a general counter-revolutionary movement against the further diffusion of material culture. The battle is carried on in at least three major fields, as he conceives of it. The first is careful buying, which, in a large group, no matter how scattered its members may be, puts a decided crimp in the expanding markets for highly exploited and intrinsically valueless "comforts" and "benefits." The second is concerted civic and political activity to discourage promoters and exploiters from working their way in the section in which William's group lives and prefers to live. If the first two combats are waged in a relatively selfish interest, the third—and perhaps the crucial—one partakes of an unselfish motive as well. Using the adversaries' own strongest weapons of education and publicity, a determined onslaught is made here on the very holy of holies of the progressivist fetich, from the premise that not only would a minority of individualistic idealists live happier if the culture of aimless flux were brought to an end, but that the aimless-fluxers, too—the factory workers, the middle and professional classes, even a few millionaires after they should have got used to being half-millionaires—would find more joy in life if they would give more of themselves to being something and less to a perpetual becoming something else, more to the social arts and graces and less to going places and doing things, more to such strenuous activity as writing verses—no matter how bad ones—and less to such passive business as globe-trotting with one's sensations.

William's friends constitute a minority, and a small one; in no event does he expect to see them become a majority party. He is aware, however, that a militant minority has a leavening effect beyond its numerical proportion in the apathetic mass.

In this mass they propose no revolution, no prohibition, no violence save the devastation that critical and selective use of mechanical and mechanized facilities can bring about in the camps of idolaters, and the greater devastation wreaked by clear, honest thought expressed in terms familiar to the "median man."

And about this "median man": Though William finds him pretty consistently bovine-passive just now, he believes on the evidence of human history that a time would come, provided that social idolatries should continue to be practiced long enough, when a few hundred or a few hundred thousand median men would suddenly become aware that they had fallen into moral slavery . . . and so would set about a repetition of the Russian noble experiment. William's friends do not want this to happen. And although they can find no likelihood of armed rebellion coming to pass during their lifetime, the mere thought of such an issue ensuing at any time would make them have the less respect for the common sense of their race and so indirectly for themselves. To the individualistic way of thinking, communism, whether urban or rural, industrial or agricultural, is as bad as capitalism gone progressivist, and perhaps worse, as tending even the more to negate personality and to reduce critical individuality to the zero deadness of a mass-mind.

But because the beef cattle of the world have always some latent power to become Minotaurs which actualizes under sufficient goading; because all that is passive and human can become active and human in the bright dawn after an exceptionally dark night; because history has its multitudinous instances of apathetic masses being transformed into fighting units—William is encouraged to believe that individual men, no matter how much a part of the tepid and sterile stream of unethical, amoral existence, keep still, and will keep so long as humanity peoples the earth, some spark of rebellion which flares up when living by current rules becomes intolerable. To the notions of impetuous idealists social superstitions die out with maddening slowness; but the effort of speeding their demise through living example and social education is not hopeless. Though the effects of teaching and publicity and exemplary action may not at once be perceptible, their effects are no less real for their quietness. And William believes, in any event, that a calmly thoughtful reaction against an undesirable order is much less likely than is a bloody revolution to bring about a swing from the one antipode of fetichism to the other while freedom lies still somewhere between.

He is heartened by the proportions such a reaction has already attained, and can only hope that it will become general and that he will live to taste some of its maturer fruits.

STARK YOUNG

NOT IN MEMORIAM,
BUT IN DEFENSE

IF ANYTHING is clear, it is that we can never go back, and neither this essay nor any intelligent person that I know in the South desires a literal restoration of the old Southern life, even if that were possible; dead days are gone, and if by some chance they should return, we should find them intolerable. But out of any epoch in civilization there may arise things worth while, that are the flowers of it. To abandon these, when another epoch arrives, is only stupid, so long as there is still in them the breath and flux of life. In our American life today good things are coming in, which we should try to understand and to share, so far as our natures allow. But it is just as obvious that good things are going out. There was a Southern civilization whose course was halted with those conventions of 1867 by which the negro suffrage in the South—not in the North —was planned, and the pillaging began. But that does not imply that this Southern civilization, once the fine flower of men's lives, is wholly dead; for the core of our humanity lies in the belief that the essence of the soul is its mockery of death. It would be childish and dangerous for the South to be stampeded and betrayed out of its own character by the noise, force, and glittering narrowness of the industrialism and progress spreading everywhere, with varying degrees, from one region to another.

This discussion does not concern the peculiar devotion to their own part of the country, or at least their conscious sense of it, that Southerners exhibit, nor any catalogue or description of certain of our characteristics. What I have to attempt is far less redolent of time's sweetness and the old grace. It is, for a while at least, a problem practical enough: the defense of what we have drawn not from theory but from an actual civilization, and believe it necessary to remember. For us there are certain things, now endangered, that leave a kind of death to follow after them, and so must not be lost.

We cannot, save by an old, indomitable human hope, expect anything to rise higher than the life it comes from. But we may remark that the World War and its aftermath; the churches, trying to keep up with the times or to clinch all the ages; the schools; the moving-pictures; and, most of all, the press—have generalized our national thinking. We are plainly to infer that a hundred million people think the same about everything and that what they think is therefore right. How are we to know, then, what we do think? Not long ago I heard an old gentleman in Mississippi, a doctor of the old school, who has given most of his life to charity and is innocent of all money and business, say that a certain judge in the county ought to have known better than to announce a certain opinion, it would surely displease the man under whom he held office. My old doctor is himself the soul of principle, unable for the life of him to budge an inch from his honor for the sake of any sum of mere money, and yet he spoke like this. It was merely because he had picked up the tone of it from the national air, as it were, with its headlines, bang, boom, and doctrine of making-good, and from the newer riffraff who talk the idle mornings out in front of their little stores around the old town square. He talks the common talk like that at times, but in the midst of such a state of things he is untouched, confused, like a child watching the train passing.

The list of such Southern confusions would be endless, but there is one especially that has always seemed to me full of deadly import about the South; I mean the way in which so many of the Coolidge banalities, crudities, and arid White House silences, turned into virtues by his fortunate press, were accepted by Southern people whose every instinct about culture, manners, and eloquence these things grossly traduced. That such press-agent nonsense about Greatness, Simplicity, Silence, Economy, Fishing, Parallelism to Lincoln, Profundity and Deep Reserve, should be taken seriously by some of the South, simple people on one side and our newer vulgarians on the other, was natural enough; it was the kind of thing that reassures their piety, or soothes their minds, or flatters their origins, and avenges their spites. That Southerners of the older type should have swallowed all this, as many of them did, is a bad sign. The kindest thing to say of them is that they admire virtue and believe print. For a later view we may read a reporter's account of Mr. Coolidge's visit to San Antonio, this spring of 1930. In 1836, for twelve days General Santa Ana besieged the little mission of the Alamo, in which were the hundred and fifty Anglo-Saxon defenders who, refusing the escape that had been arranged for them by the Mexican commander in order to relieve him of this show of patriotism

(330)

and to clear the way to the rebellious colonies, stayed on. To the last man the garrison died. The Alamo is, then, naturally enough, the shrine of Texas independence and of pride in one of the glorious, inexplicable, heroic moments of all history. Mr. Coolidge, ex-President of the United States and guest of the city, would be sure to be taken there. When he got inside, he had, according to the report, only this to say, "What was the Alamo built for?"

Well, what we can say for that is that, in the first place, he need not have made a trip through Texas in a special coach; there was nothing official about his tour. But since he chose to do so, he was to some extent the guest of the state. Perfect consideration, or even the slimmest fruits of any civilization, indeed, would have led to his finding out ahead of time a few items about the town where he was about—shall we say?—to be met at the train. Or slipping from so high a level of courtesy, he might have waited a little and picked up a thread of information about the Alamo when he got there. At the hotel breakfast in his honor, the reporter said, he was asked if he had enjoyed his trip in Texas. To that effort at mere polite conversation, in favor of which there may have been some local prejudice, he replied, "I thought we had come here to eat." This, I gathered, did not appear to the company as humor, or if to be so taken, as a boorish form indeed, and there was, the account said, some silence afterward. And yet there are Southern people who, reading of this incident, and with the encouragement of a little journalism, may have taken it all as sincerity and rugged worth—people whose fathers were gentlemen and whose servants have good manners. All this might not be worth recording, if it were not so perfect an illustration of the confusion today among Southern people who know better and were born knowing better. It illustrates, too, how powerful words are, meaning different things to different people. To these people in San Antonio the Coolidge press talk about *sincerity* and *simplicity* and *reserve* meant something very different from this they heard when the great man visited their town.

Such instances of confusion and retreat are common all over the South. Among the minor decencies, one good instance is enough; we may take the pictures of Southern women seen—though rarely so far—in the advertisements confessing their addiction to some face cream or some mattress, with boudoir and garden snapshots, and footnotes from the advertisers stating the social importance of these ladies and their ancestors—who would have died at such vulgar exploitation of them. Many European and New York ladies have set the pace for this; many have not. The familiar excuse is money for one's favorite charity; and some at least of the checks paid by the manufacturers doubtless reach a charity; though, under the head of vulgarity, that is not much of a point—one might walk the streets for the benefit of the Marines. But in most cases the $2,500 or $5,000 is not the attraction so much as the strength of an idle, persuasive publicity mania, the wish to be seen, as others are seen. Obviously the entire Southern tradition is against this sort of thing, as it is, or was until lately perhaps, averse to giving the family name to a collar, a physic, hot-water bag, or what not; there was a time when the very servants would have despised you for it.

Well, along with this South, then, where we have much of the old life surviving, the old practices that belong with the land, the old beliefs and standards, the gradual blend of these with later ideas and conditions, the onrush of new powers in money, industry, and communication, and the confusion in what men do think, accept, or decline, as the case may be, there has sprung up these last few years a genuine interest in the South. This has taken the form of research, records, new statistics, fiction dealing with Southern life, written either by Southerners or outsiders, articles in newspapers; an influx, from the North, of touring, wintering and buying up the old places; and—significantly— an ever-growing mass of biographies of famous Southerners and of historical narrative, with a strong slant toward restating accepted accounts and vindicating tarnished causes.

This interest in the South is dictated, I believe, partly by the desire of historians for fresh fields and by the vogue of biographies; partly by the journalist's natural desire to follow where the public leads; and partly by the spreading news of the resources in the South for money-making. This behind-the-times, delightful, lazy land can make one rich, now that is quite another matter. But a good part of this general interest—quite aside from the financial interest— in the South, among people of many sorts, undoubtedly, I think, arises from a certain boredom at the flatness, excitement, and sterility of this American life that they have made for themselves. Not size, not the game of money or success, not even progress, seem to have solved the problem. They like to think of some state of living in which there is less exhaustion, colorless repetition, imitation, and joylessness, fewer well-dressed negligible persons; and, since the thought of Europe as a possibility is no longer satisfying, they ask themselves what, with America the richest country in the world, there is to do about living. Their thoughts turn, accordingly, to the South. In our problem of defense, all this is in our favor.

It is aristocratic to take things for granted, go your own way without comment, apology, defense, or self-consciousness. And, clearly, the greatest, most luminous defense of any point of view is its noble embodiment in persons. This is taking high and, just now, too abstract, ground, however. For such of us as wish to sustain certain elements out of the Southern life, our backs must be against the wall. The diverse and most manifest excellences, such as public improvements, exhilaration, money, and so on, that belong with the new state of things we should be only fools not to see and try to evaluate. But that does not mean that we have to swallow all the jargon, concessions, and simplicity of mind that fill the air. We are not necessarily old-fashioned because we stand by certain guns; it may mean only self-respect, proper pride, and distinguished scorn. But let us have no silence. A more conscious attitude is necessary for us. Not the usual attitude too often met in Southerners, and worse for our cause than silence would be. The mere hauteur, the supercilious, defensive high-headedness, the bursting bitterness, old tales, exclusive sentiment have been used up long ago; and have grown only flat or picturesque and endearing, or impolite or antagonistic, sometimes pathetic. In sum there is a campaign to consider.

At the start I must remember not to let myself disgrace

the thing I have set out to defend. I need not forget the grace I celebrate, nor the consideration for others that my boasts imply. This tendency—may I avoid it!—among Southerners at times to drive the shot home arises partly from hurt pride, a defensive tack after years of being poor and shut out from one's inherited way of living; but the display of it is useless and only offends. On the other hand, I should study when to inflame or offend, to be downright and hot, and so bring the opponent into such heat that he will plank down his idea, tell me what he thinks a civilization should be. If he has a solid theory, I can make an honorable argument. If he has only a jumble of puerile catchwords, he may be such as can be led to say:

"In our town we've got twenty thousand miles of concrete walks."

"And where do they lead?" I say.

He will not have thought of that.

I remind myself of diverse things. It is not necessary to make men, foolish or serious, agree with me, no matter what the principle is; they may have different faculties. Nor should I be over-anxious to justify our cause, lest I resemble those who, the more they act out of sheer sensation, the more they claim to live by reason's laws. And I must not make the mistake of saying that any of these qualities that I would promote has reason for its basis; it is based on preference only, and it achieves its consummation, or perfection, in becoming rational. It is then a thing complete in itself, making its own kind of sense.

It is important, too, that we do not make the mistake of thinking we are alone in the whole body of these qualities

(335)

that we admire and claim as Southern; it is easy thus to be uninformed if not absurd. Plenty of people in New England, for example, though cramped very often by Puritan aridities, resent certain tendencies in American life and wish to preserve certain elements on the same grounds that we do, and often more coherently and more intelligently; indeed, the statement of the New England quality by her nobler authors has won her a fine, solid presentation; and her good fortune in being celebrated in so much bad poetry has made her virtues popular. Many Jews share our Southern family instinct, the home, the sense of parents, the endless cousins, uncles, and aunts, the nostalgia for one's own blood. But such comparative points are too obvious to dwell on, as is the fact that there are gentle things, of course, that gentle people everywhere believe. Though the South, not these other parts of the country, is our subject, we must remember that we are concerned first with a quality itself, not as our own but as found anywhere; and that we defend certain qualities not because they belong to the South, but because the South belongs to them. The intelligent course sees first our Southern culture in relation to other cultures, and then in the light of its own sum.

At the outset we must make it clear that in talking of Southern characteristics we are talking largely of a certain life in the old South, a life founded on land and the ownership of slaves. Of the other people living in the South of that epoch we know less, the people who worked their own farms with their own hands, respectable and sturdy, a fine yeomanry partly, and partly the so-called poor whites, who were more shiftless or less self-respecting. They had certain pioneer virtues, common on all our frontiers, and they sometimes, doubtless, reflected certain traits from the planter class; but it is not they who gave this civilization its peculiar stamp. They have by now, of course, so widely mixed with the other Southern type that—without speaking of the descent and vulgarization of some members of good families which have brought them lower than many over whom they felt their superiority—the line of distinction is long since vague. It is not true, however, as many have said, that the higher class completely lost, along with other things, their social manners and customs. It is true, even at this day in the South, that the manners and customs of the South do not wholly arise from the bottom mass; they have come from the top downward. It is true that our traditional Southern characteristics derive from the landed class.

This leads us to another point. There have developed among us down South—as well as everywhere in the nation—certain of what might have been called in England once, chapel-going virtues. I mean by this a certain degradation of a once austere Puritanism, a whining on certain pious excellences that arise from goodness combined with natural dullness, and a certain half-conscious jealousy of all distinction. You are simple, for example, because you are a mixture of plain thinking and an incapacity for thought, you are praised for a sincerity that consists of boorishness and peasant egotism. There was always in the South a flourishing, social religion if you like. But this middle-class piety, platitude, canting, and ignorant assurance was not common to the better element, however much a certain

Scotch-Irish Calvinism was breaking the way for it. In the new South it is rampant. The lack of education after the Civil War, the neglect of ideas, the rise of people whose share in things had been restricted, these are some of the contributing causes to such a state. It is encouraged by democracy—all votes are equal—and is flattered by a commercial society. One of the odious traits of industrialism is that, even where there are men who know better, it defers to the mass, largely in order to exploit them, but partly because most of the leaders have few conceptions—barring business—beyond the mass at large. It is remarkable how far this whine has carried among Southerners born to more noble terms of conduct and the spirit. In my opinion the South should be told flatly and coldly that, with other sections acting as they choose, such moral canting, confidence, and whining belong to a village of cobblers and small traders, and are based on ignorance, commonness, and a sense of what will pay. Such a state may well be within our maudlin possibilities but it is not in our genuine tradition. Politicians may flatter the masses. But the ignorant do not possess every man of any intelligence, who should love and despise rather than indulge them; nor have elemental, narrow, stubborn convictions the right to infringe on private spiritual rights. We can put one thing in our pipes and smoke it—there will never again be distinction in the South until—somewhat contrary to the doctrine of popular and profitable democracy—it is generally clear that no man worth anything is possessed by the people, or sees the world under a smear of the people's wills and beliefs. Of this whining, canting simplicity the Southern quality that we fight to preserve must at the very outset disclaim all defense.

From such a paragraph the great question of education and religion in the South easily evolves. On this subject I would admit almost anything gracefully, trying to show at the same time that education, in the most endowed sense, is making great strides among us. Then I should add that the resounding education in the richer parts of the United States is already by many intelligent observers admitted to be mostly futile, and that I should like to hope that a return of confidence will lead the South to turn toward the general idea, held once in the old South and still in England, that education of the university sort, not professional or technical, is suited to a small number only.

This, at present, un-American idea of education may spread if in our schools and universities a less democratic, mobbed, and imitative course of things should come to be, with less booming and prating, organizing, unrest, babble about equipment, election of trustees from the Stock Exchange—all signs of an adolescent mentality and prosperous innocence of what culture may mean. I shall never forget the encouragement with which I saw for the first time that some of the dormitory doors at the University of Virginia needed paint, so sick was I at the bang-up varnishing, rebuilding, plumbing, endowing, in some of the large Northern institutions. If they learn little at these Virginia halls, it is doubtless as much as they would learn at the others, and they at least escape the poison of the success idea that almost every building is sure to show, the belief that me-

(339)

chanical surface and the outer powers of money are the prime things in living.

Then I should hasten to add, in some further defence of Southern education, that it has suffered from the Civil War, from the poverty due to chaos, bad methods at home and tariffs at Washington. I should also claim for what education we have in the South a few little virtues fairly implicit in it. I have seen hack-drivers at Sewanee, for instance, who showed a nicer sense of consideration toward others and better manners than, on numerous occasions, I have seen by full-fledged graduates of a certain old and famous university; just as I have seen some fellow in that larger institution battle with philosophy and the Lord for hours, where one of my country cousins would have dropped the matter automatically, merely as something beneath him. I had likewise the pleasure once of saying to the dean of a famous old New England college, upon his complaining of the lapses of the students on some matter about which he preached continually, that he should try giving some reason besides the moral wrong of it; there are certain things, I said, that, according to what I had always been taught, belong to decorum, to our *mores* rather than to our morals, and that we refrain from doing as we refrain from bodily odors or obscenity in company. He was too much inured to agreeing with influential alumni or affluent trustees not to agree to this also; but I felt that some faint streak at least had penetrated.

As to religion, I would merely ask what about organized religion in the rest of the country, and would then bewail the low ebb of religion in the South, as is shown by the vast growth of the denominations formerly associated with the most bigoted and ignorant classes, and as the preacher-ridden towns oftener than not confirm. The drift toward such a level is a trait inherent in the Anglo-Saxon, who naturally lacks taste; he is saved, if at all, only by a ruling better class, whose stately or unholy views keep the masses somewhat in awe, or else by an independent middle-class opinion, which we have not at present. We have but to remember that to convert the South to religion is only to convert religion to the Southern; our religion will depend on us. We must then add that we may desire a more modern religious thought for certain kinds of people; for others a chance to fulfill their religious needs without any loss of the old warmth in their hearts, or of the look on their gentle faces; and for the rest, in the organized churches, a return of whatever there was in the old that might lead to dignity, decent formality and tolerant social balance. At present, I may say that, with no great hopeful-ness either way, my own feeling is that I prefer a certain rude reality in the Southern drift toward religion, to the rude promotion of religiosity as an asset to restraint, pro-duction, and mental evasion.

There are kinds of criticism against which you can re-sort to foreign comparison, colonialism, or snobbery, all legitimate, if lighter, weapons in our campaign. In America the War left us much richer and more sure of ourselves, but we still have a share of colonialism, nevertheless, and such comparisons may have weight. We may, for instance, suggest that the English get on better with Southerners than with other Americans, the better class especially; most

Continentals do, the Italians, for example, who have our same family sense and the same proud taste for a friendly, semi-formal, complaisant living. If we are accused of being sentimental, or, at the other extreme, of being cynical and supercilious about the idealistic, sublimated haze in which some persons like to see life, well, the Latins are like us in that. If the Southern culture so often mentioned among us is assailed as perplexingly unlearned, say that the Duke of This or That and many of the English county families have a culture very much the same, and that one of its aspects is a certain indifference to mere attainments, which may be left to the professors, *arrivistes*, and paid performers. If the old habit of sitting back, talking hours on end, is the trouble, the same may be said of the Russian nobility, the Spanish, the French, or of any civilization whose ideal is social existence rather than production, competition, and barter. Nor has any aristocratic life in Europe, though it has its own comfort and an elaborate elegance, ever sought the mechanical perfection in domestic living—the vulgarities in plumbing competitions, for example—that flattens so much of America now, but in the South has never, despite the new progress there, seemed the greatest interest about the home. With the right opponent this foreign citation may prove something of a rout; it is at least a way of checking such as tend to measure everything by their own world, and of forcing them to speak not their own dialect, but Esperanto, a language that is international, whatever else. In the meantime it does us no harm to study our own ideas in the light of tried and ancient civilizations. Such study illumines and dilates our own opinion, not to speak of the mild pleasure of showing what some of our knowers do not know.

But the basis, of course, that all these Southern discussions must at last come to is conceptions. If you have no conceptions on which to base your claims, what you say may seem to others only personal prejudice, with no support beyond your fervor or charm. Certain characteristics we are free to indorse, to exhibit, to feel. But to champion them we must comprehend their grounds, we must know. Otherwise, among the average and incessant, we may be overcome with jargon, progress *clichés*, and views well backed with the arguments of success, which rain upon us from presidential speeches, captains of industry, promoters, journals, pulpits, every speaking source and possibility. Otherwise among the grim, prejudiced and hostile we may be dismissed as only hot and childish. Otherwise, among the courteous and reserved, we may serve only as a Virgilian illustration—

sed argutos inter strepere anser olores

and seem but "to hiss like a goose among the tuneful swans."

We shall have to find grounds, then, for these qualities we indorse—to take an example, provincialism.

Provincialism that is a mere ramification of some insistent egotism is only less nauseous than the same egotism in its purity, raw self without any province to harp upon. But provincialism proper is a fine trait. It is akin to a man's interest in his own center, which is the most deeply rooted consideration that he has, the source of his direction, health

(343)

and soul. A comparison between New York, the great city, and one's own town or country might mention the petty faults and secret vices of the provinces, the wear and tear, the limited chance, the fellowship of saints, the hairpulling of the wicked, and might also go on, if you like, to the poetry of echoes possible there, the quiet, the stream that reminds you of Carducci's verse where the nymphs' breasts beneath the water were silver like the moon; and then pass to the river of life in the city, the city's protection and privacy, or public stir, whichever you choose; the arts, the lively contacts, the chance to rise into big fortunes, the speed, the variety, or the wonder and enchantment of size and audacious enterprise, for both those who can feel such magic and those who can extract it from magazines. But such comparisons are only possibilities in preference and show how easily the point is missed. Provincialism does not at all imply living in the place on which you base your beliefs and choices. It is a state of mind or persuasion. It is a source. With or without knowing the rest of the world, you can, against all odds, defend your provincialism to yourself quite by simple inner necessity, as you think of your own nature, which you would not at bottom change with anyone else. You need not, for instance, live in the South, but you feel your roots are there. You love even the pain it has given you, and you exasperate some critical citizen elsewhere, who thinks the fact that you would not live in your beloved land a point against you and it, and never discovers that the vacancy in his own heart is partly his forgetfulness of the friendly verdure and first memory of his early years. No matter where you are, in any city or land or on the sea, and some old song suddenly heard again, or a childhood dish tasted, or some fragrance remembered from a garden once, or a voice or word, brings tears to your eyes because of its memory of some place, that place is your country. People who give up their own land too readily need careful weighing, exactly as do those who are so with their convictions. I am not sure that one of the deep mysteries, one of the great, as it were, natural beauties of the heart, does not lie in one's love for his own land. If there is a sadness, or old memory, added to this sense, it may become a part of the substance on which the soul makes its tragic journey.

The discussion of manners, affability, friendliness turns on the salubrity of people's living close together. An at-home-ness among others is implied; and a lack of suspicion—the most vulgar and humiliating of traits, I was taught by my elders—with regard to others and their intentions—it was better a thousand times, they said, to be deceived than to be common; a taste for the approval of others—how Southern!—derived from politeness, friendliness, and vanity; the belief that one of our most natural impulses is the wish that the other person may be happy in our company. As to manners and the accusations against Southerners of insincerity, floweriness, gush, and indirection, the answer is that such reproaches are the defensive arguments of selfishness, of meager natures, of self-conscious egotism, of middle-class Puritanism, or of laziness: it is easier not to consider the other man's feelings, or it is sinful to pretend to feelings that we do not feel. In those regions, however, where such non-flowering sincerity is most highly commended, you will not detect any lack of color when they are trying to sell something; it is a sin only when it merely makes life more pleasant for some one.

Manners and sincerity are matters understood only with reference to a state of society that assumes a group welfare and point of view rather than individual whims, a flow among a group of human beings, a life to which each single human being contributes and in which he lives. It is comically true that you may dislike meeting X on Monday, but you say, nevertheless, I'm glad to see you. This declaration may not be true to what you feel toward X on that particular day, but it is true to your feelings for him by the year, feelings that would have been falsified by your not saying on Monday that you were glad to see him; you are, therefore, in X's case, insincere by the moment but sincere by the year; only self-centered boors could think otherwise. As for those judgments and opinions on some person which you try to indicate by your manner toward him, such forms of sincerity are usually ill-bred egotism. "Use every man after his desert," as Hamlet says, "and who shall escape whipping? Use them after you own honor and dignity." Manners are the mask of decency that we employ at need, the currency of fair communication; their flower is a common grace, and their fruit not seldom friendship. To think otherwise than this is only peasant stolidity and middle-class confusion. The stress on the individual in such matters is only barbaric, mere tree-dwelling.

The Southern family sense, often onerous to aliens and not seldom one of our own domestic burdens, is nevertheless a good trait. Our tradition of family involves the fact that so many of our families came from the British Isles, with Scotch clannishness plentiful enough, and remained unmixed with other bloods, as did the French and Spanish of Louisiana, for a long time. And a sense of family followed our connection with the land, a gracious domain where the events of the day began with the sky and light, the bread you ate came from the fields around you, your father's, your own; and life has been led; where you have known man's great desire, that generation of himself in the body of life, of which the earth is the eternal and natural symbol; and where there was, of all occupations, the form of labor in which the mystery and drama of life—the seed, the flower and harvest, the darkness, the renewal—is most represented to us.

As for the notion in general of kin and family, in some men the source of so much proud and tender emotion, it goes back to one of the oldest racial instincts and is rooted in the most human poetry of the imagination. A man's thought of his mother, loving him before he was born, thinking of her own mother during this that has now come to her; his thought of his father, of his father's hopes for him, and of what his father as a young man felt in his warm, restless heart and troubled, glowing brain—And if, then, he loves his father and mother, how can he not love those who brought them into the world and loved them, and those yet farther back, this line of hopes and struggles and love? The nature and course of such love as parents give, no matter what imperfections may appear, is like no other that he will ever receive; and later he may come to say, "What I might have said to them! If only——" As I write I think of my own grandfather's father, whose memory is still so strong in my family, for his reserve and gentleness, his hidden, strong feeling, his authority and control, and find myself wishing that I had some faith by which I could say to him, if he be somewhere now and could hear me, "I know what you felt, I know that you loved me long before I was born, and that your power over me lies in my knowledge of your love and of the passionate gravity of your life." A man's love of these dead is only another love that is also in him: when his blood runs in other veins, not yet born, against the day when the house will be empty, the scene too unbroken; it has the same relation to unceasing life that his pulse has to unending time.

Suppose, as some research has declared, only three Virginia families were of any great importance back in England, there is nothing in that, be it true or false, to throw us off. You need only to say that it was not the memory of the British Isles, it was an attitude and point of view induced by the Southern way of life that we came to mean by *aristocratic*. Suppose your family, like most of the rest, never did anything alarmingly great, was merely a Southern family on Southern land. Be careful here, lest you expose us to the outside scorn of facts, or indulge some of us already too much given to the infirmities of sentiment! You must not begin about the fine house, which, after all, at the very best anywhere in the early American states would have been only pleasantly grand—we had no Caprarola, Strá, or Chenonceaux or Knole—or about china, silver and furniture. Your family lived in a big house, not without elegance, hospitality, and affection; and what made your position was not power necessarily or any eminence in the country's history, but rather your settled connection with the land; it was the fact that your family had maintained a certain quality of living and manners throughout a certain period of time, and had a certain relation to the society of the country. And in the same way, not unlike the British today, our meaning of culture—the Southern culture of which the orators used to spout, adding a dash about chivalry and honor—did not imply, not necessarily as it often did in New England, a learning, perhaps a trifle parochial, in philosophy, the Scriptures, or German, French, and other worthy knowledges. It implied, no doubt, some gentlemanly acquaintance with the classics, a whiff of the poets, or a respect for a polite degree of polish and cultivation, and a genuine taste for oratory, whose large flowers went, perhaps, with white columns and the great white moons of the magnolia. What it did imply is difficult to explain. It was one of those things half of whose mysterious virtue lies in their arbitrariness. Undoubtedly it had to do with a certain fineness of feeling, an indefinable code for yourself and others, and a certain continuity of outlook; but what it inherently implied was something like that which Lord Melbourne, the celebrated Minister to Queen Victoria, meant, when he observed that, of all the coveted orders in England, the one he admired most was that of the Garter— "there was no damn merit about it." In a curious way this defines our Southern notion of the aristocratic. It is a thing forever annoying to those who, from the outside of such traditions, wish to put them into reasonable terms, and it will never be understandable by those born in a different scheme of life.

The aristocratic implied with us a certain long responsibility for others; a habit of domination; a certain arbitrariness; certain ideas of personal honor, with varying degrees of ethics, *amour propre*, and the fantastic. And it implied the possession of no little leisure. Whether that was a good system or not is debatable. I myself think it, if we had to make a choice strictly between either one or the other, better than a society of bankers and bankers' clerks, department-store communities, manufacturers and their henchmen and their semi-slaves, and miserable little middle-class cities, frightened of one's position in the country club, snatching at the daily paper to see if one is all right. Good system or not, from this Southern conception of aristocracy certain ideas arose, about which this book to a fair extent, has been written. This way of life meant mutuality of interests among more people, an innate code of obligations, and a certain openness of life. It meant self-control that implied not the expression of you and your precious personality, not the pleasures of suffering or of denying your own will; you controlled yourself in order to make the society you lived in more decent, affable, and civilized and yourself more amenable and attractive. If in such a life the nature of it made you unhappy, restive under its pattern, you suffered all the more because the people around you were so gentle about it, but you might remember that same fineness and love as in itself some mode of assurance, as some guaranty of goodness, even, reflected from yourself.

In case you have believed lies about your family, which is

not so fine and grand as you had thought it, try saying to yourself:

"Is it not better that I should believe lies, believe in my family, desiring its luster for myself, shamed by its ideals and my own unworthiness, touched by the past of its affections and its standards, than to believe another special sort of modern American lie, such a one, for instance as believes Mr. Henry Ford's opinion on art to be of any importance, merely because of his success with wheels in a mechanical system that makes men constantly dryer, more thwarted and less exercised, and Mr. Ford richer and richer?"

It is a sad state of affairs when a Marylander, for example, is pleased merely because a plumber plenipotentiary from afar, or a Broadway broker with his restless wife, likes an old family mansion on the Sound. It is rather generous and pleasant that such persons like what they could never have inherited or created, and what may in time distinguish them from the mob of their successful friends back home. But the final results in the case of any of such patrons must depend on the amount of consideration, refinement, bloated confidence, machine-mindedness, and so on, that he displays; on whether the box walks prove bearable under his meditating feet, whether the ancient quiet is possible to his electric spirit.

As for the pride that people meet in Southerners, sometimes with amazement, and that even old friends and kinsmen at home must now and then be careful of, it is not pride in the boasting sense, though that sort happens in the South as it does everywhere. It is rather a kind of *amour propre*, sometimes a sort of mad self-respect and

(351)

honor complex, such as the Spanish traditionally have, though as a rule not so strong, foolish, and magnificent as the Spanish. Well, as Byron thought, sheer animal pride is one of the simplest and straightest ways of keeping the human animal decent and superior. I have heard cousins of mine say, "No, I don't do that sort of thing," and let it go at that, like a horse with water that he will not drink. Such pride, though it may take away from your sense of humor, may add to your manner and bearing. What it loses in amiable looseness it may gain in dignity. If it makes enemies it also banishes contempt; and it is sometimes, by its very retreat, capable of drawing others toward you, or by the rankling memory of some surrender they themselves have made, it rouses them in your defence.

This personal honorable, fantastic pride may also have a mad price. I have seen pathetic manifestations of that: a man walking out of an office rather than take some real or fancied slight; a poor cousin giving a third of his day's salary to a negro for a small service, too proud to be thrifty or to resemble the white trash, whom the negro despised and my cousin's family had never invited farther than the front steps. Or shall we take—there are several to be heard of—the poor and unknown writer, coming to New York from the South, uncertain of his work but sure of the vulgar rudeness of this publishing magnate with whom he has been granted an audience. He picks up the manuscript, throwing away his chance before he will accept such patronage, and leaves this publisher, who meant presently to accept the book, somewhat in the lurch and raging at these Southern authors, so huffy and difficult. If these were foolish acts, the glamor of high things, at least, lay upon them, some fine salvation or vain private pomp. Various souls need various nurtures, and there are worse things than refusing to take insults for a mere chance of profit, and worse things than walking out and leaving the dog with the bone.

It is clear that we have come now to where our discussion concerns no outside argument but strictly ourselves. As a matter of fact it has been from the first less a defense of certain Southern qualities than a strengthening of ourselves in them.

The South has long since made a start, now famous indeed, toward that industrialization for which she offers such manifest resources. We are an enthusiastic people and it is certain that, once having turned industrial, we shall be zealous about it. You cannot object to that, for we should be only dull not to respond to the sweep, the live force, the surge of possibility, youthful daring, change, architecture, and invention that America so displays that all other countries may seem to us flat and stale. But at the same time the South has one special advantage.

Voiced in newspapers, in magazines, especially those of success and personality—one and the same thing—and finally in moving pictures, plays, novels, and public utterances, there has arisen in the United States as naïve and limited a mode of thinking as has existed since the primitive epochs. In its simplest form this thought turns on a crude sense of money. But this is the smaller part of it. Our American love of money is both infantile and aimless compared with that of the older countries of Europe; they are far more rapacious than we are, but they have more conceptions of what money does, more wants, systems, and styles of living. What we love is the idea of fortunes, heads of corporations, adventures in competition and material development. Boyish fancy and empty pursuit like that has its lovable side, though it is a little less lovable and heartening when we see the average man produced by it. The primitive man had at least physical strength in his body, and in his mind fear, joy, and wonder at the earth, the elements, the shadows within himself. The type we have created is nervous, busy, softened physically, good-hearted, or easy-going at least, anxious for undisturbing sentiments, without conversation, without much idea of any enjoyment beyond a sort of violent leisure, not much left in him for friendship, too hurried and exhausted for passionate love, and without any taste for the music of women in his life. His wife goes to Europe for months, or with clubs and careers is trying to organize herself into affectionate unconsciousness. His friends compete with him, none of them with a great sense of what it all leads to. He does not care to know anything, but merely to know about it. He is less concerned with the truth than with what people will think. For such a state of civilization as such a man quite generally represents, it is only to be expected that a defensive philosophy, good or bad, should have been developed and that statements the thoughtful mind perceives to be almost comically incredible, time-serving and flattering to the general trend, are widely, eagerly, and fearfully accepted as true, economic, and truly patriotic.

It is just here that our special advantage comes in. Exactly as the factories in the South, erected so recently, are not much encumbered with obsolete types of machines and buildings, so in our passage today into a degree of industrial life we can, if we choose, escape at least some portion of the mentality and point of view that have accompanied the industrial development in so many parts of the United States. We must admit that in some Southern states where industrialism has already taken a foremost place, the public mentality, as events of the last two years have shown, has moved in the dark ages of American industrial history and has made the word "progressive," applied to them, a sickening epithet. There is no reason now that we should pass through quite the state of mind that went, in the rest of the country, with the mechanization of the past decades. We can begin close to where the better sort of thinking and better conditions have by now arrived. We can, if we only would, see industrialism as it spreads in the South, and study it, from the vantage ground of theory, criticism, and error elsewhere developed from experience and from longer observation. We can accept the machine, but create our own attitude toward it.

There is no reason why Southern people, however industrialized, should bolt the whole mess as it stands. Let them concur in whatever extent of industrialism may seem to them advisable, but look sharp to the doctrines they accept, and to the half-unconscious rot, evolved from a dissatisfied, eager and short-sighted state of society, that they blind their own eyes with. Let them remind themselves constantly that the front of this heralded affair is not so solid and unbroken as it may seem, and that there are people, scattered over

the country here and there, in some places a good many of
them, who watch this confident activity, crass loneliness,
and baffled egotism, and its bewildering, rich powers and
results, and ask what it is all about and what it will come
to. Such people already suspect the childish face-value of
this prosperous credo—though it is not so prosperous of
late—they suspect the monotony of the American mind.
They are bored at the celebrated uniformity of American
life, which they may excuse sometimes on the grounds of
the rapidity of our development but deplore on the grounds
of entertainment, variety, and vital detail in human life.
There are people who doubt if two million a year fills a
man's head with anything beyond an annual two million,
and who puzzle over such a man as delights in mere speed,
going faster than anybody for ten miles and unable to think
of anything when he gets there except going the next ten
miles. And there are those who are saddened at meeting up
and down the country the mind and innocence of a child,
without that softness and that participation in nature by
which the child is divine.

What's more, there are even people quite aware that the
reputation of some of the greatest leaders in these industrial
times has been created entirely—or else well cleansed—for
public consumption, by highly-paid press agents. The press
agent looks up stories of former popular heroes and fits
them to this monument of progress, or invents fishing tales,
biographical tales, charities, pet animals, or other delicate
inclinations for the sake of keeping the big name becom-
ingly in the papers. He even invents beguiling things to
do; an old magnate, for example, on the point of nation-

wide disfavor because of some fine scandal, may be instructed by his press agent to give every day a dollar bill to the first red-headed boy he meets; the photographs of which deed, appearing in the papers everywhere and every month or so, after a golf game, a fishing trip, or a banquet to Gold Star Mothers, will soon create the legend of the bounteous heart.

Even so few hints of the reactions of thoughtful people elsewhere should heighten the Southerner's spirits. Besides the more thoughtful virtues, there are in the South plenty of prejudice, pride, and scorn—each with its healthy uses—that will help toward short-cuts to our own position on the new state of things; and that, moreover, will quickly dispose of some of the heroes and superstitions of the day. The simplest way to put it you may often hear ready to hand, as I heard it once from an old Mississippi lady. She was speaking of one of our most headlined millionaires, a semi-comic old creature, whose career of single-mindedness, photography, bonded vulgarity, chicanery, and pious sterility she apparently had observed for a long time: "I don't care. He may have three hundred millions, but he's nothing but trash after all." A very good way to put it. St. Paul said, "Alexander the coppersmith hath done me much harm, the Lord reward him according to his merit"; but it took no divine omniscience to understand what St. Paul meant, and I should have thought him a healthier spirit and a more likable sort if he had sent Alexander to a sound damnation.

This old lady's words were only a whimsical way of relating the new order to our Southern use of it. To have it good for us we shall have to see it in the light of our own tradition, our conceptions, our preferences, the flower of another way of life, more of which is left within us than, in the heat of a new impulse, we may think. It is impossible to believe that a Southerner of good class, with a father who was a gentleman of honorable standards, pride, and formal conceptions, could regard many of our present leaders, however heroic they appear in the tabloids and in the unconscious lapses of great editorial writers, with quite the naïveté of some self-made foreman in a shoe factory, of some Bowery child, born out of a magnificent, ancient spiritual tradition, but muddled with the crass American life around him. For this inheritance of ours, together with all we have learned, all there is outside to profit by, the South must find its own use. It all comes down to the most practical of all points—what is the end of living? What is the end of living that, regardless of all the progress, optimism, and noise, must be the answer to the civilization in the South?

It is a question easy to ask but incorrigibly defensive, even if we lost the fight. It may be that the end of man's living is not mere raw Publicity, Success, Competition, Speed and Speedways, Progress, Donations, and Hot Water, all seen with a capital letter. There are also more fleeting and eternal things to be thought of; more grace, sweetness and time; more security in our instincts, and chance to follow our inmost nature, as Jesus meant when he said he must be about his Father's business; more of that last fine light to shine on what we do, and make the sum of it like some luminous landscape, all the parts of which are equable, distributed, and right. We shall have to think that out for ourselves, and not be fed headlines as seals tallow balls, to keep up the performance.

To arrive, then, at some conception of the end of living, the civilization, that will belong to the South, is our great, immediate problem. But in this case, as always in life, alongside a man's open course there moves a mystery, to him dark and shining at once. The mystery here is change, whose god is Mutability. In the shifting relation between ourselves and the new order lies the profoundest source for our living, I mean change in that almost mystical sense by which, so long as we are alive, we are not the same and yet remain ourselves. All things hate steadfastness and are changed, Spenser wrote, and yet, being rightly weighed:

> They are not changéd from their first estate;
> But by their change their being do dilate:
> And turning to themselves at length again,
> Do work their own perfection so by fate.
> Then over them change doth not rule and reign,
> But they rule over change and do themselves maintain.

That a change is now in course all over the South is plain; and it is as plain that the South changing must be the South still, remembering that for no thing can there be any completeness that is outside its own nature, and no thing for which there is any advance save in its own kind. If this were not so, all nature by now would have dissolved in chaos and folly, nothing in it, neither its own self nor any other.

VIRGINIA ROCK

THE TWELVE SOUTHERNERS:
BIOGRAPHICAL ESSAYS

The twelve southerners who took their stand in 1930 for a way of life they called "agrarian" and identified as southern are not to be explained merely as a collection of individuals loosely grouped through accidental convergence of place, birth, and heritage. Nor are they adequately or appropriately characterized by such flippant delineations as "unreconstructed rebels," "typewriter agrarians," "sufferers from nostalgic vapors." They saw themselves as "committed defenders of a tradition"—with a sharpened consciousness of the "dehumanizing and disintegrative effects" of the process of "progress"—determined, according to Warren on the occasion of the Fugitives' Reunion, to "relive something, to recapture, to reassess . . . a notion . . . fused with [their] own personal sentiments . . . and [their] personal pieties and [their] images of place and people that belong to [their] own earlier life."

The implications of biography, collective and individual, are fundamental in any analysis of the symposium and the cause it embodied. Clearly a flowering from a particular kind of milieu, one nourishing a family, social, cultural, and spiritual heritage, *I'll Take My Stand* was concerned with the strategies of an ancient war. To put it metaphorically, it was a call to arms to do battle for the cause of the spirit beleaguered by the insatiable expectations of the body; it was a campaign led by a small band of Agrarian generals (as they occasionally ad-

(361)

dressed each other in communiques) drawing upon the natural resources of faith in the family rooted in a symbiotic relationship with the land and a humane quality of life. Attacking a cult whose trust in "moreness," in "bigger and better" machines, in the acquisition of things as a means of somehow curing social ills, the Agrarians through their personal and sectional identity combined their aesthetics and political philosophy in a mythic, communal image—in essence, the artist's vision of a world he would create.

Men of conviction and sensibility, these twelve southerners for nearly a decade espoused a cause, in ways both subtle and explicit, that appeared in particular works and was reflected in the directions of their careers as well as in their thematic commitments as poets, novelists, social and literary critics, scholars and teachers. Emerging four years after the demise of the Fugitive group, this new gathering of southern men of letters, defined in part by the similarities and loyalties of their personal heritage and by the continuity of their values with those of the past, were sensitized to a realization that they must "do something about the South." All were born in the South, chiefly in rural areas or small towns; almost all at some critical point in their lives were connected with Vanderbilt University. The two "outsiders," John Gould Fletcher and Stark Young, were invited to join the group in part because their stature as men of letters was already well established outside the South and in part because their attachment to their region was consciously vital, even though they were not living in the South when *I'll Take My Stand* was published. These two were the most cosmopolitan in experience, perspective, and life style. Nine members of the group were engaged in the creation of literature; although three found themselves involved in writing biographies of historical figures, three viewed their professional interest in history, political science, and psychology as part of their commitment to the humane quality of life.

With a shared heritage of locale and regional tradition—imparting a respect for family, for a particular quality and character of education, for the arts, a code of conduct, and religion—these southerners united in a common cause. For most of them, education was both personal and traditional—including elements of classical and humanistic learning, a training in languages (Latin and Greek in several instances), education at home or by private tutors, private academies, and attendance at some southern university. As John Gould Fletcher observed in his symposium essay, a southerner's education was "classical and humanistic rather than scientific and technical"; we "employ our minds in order to achieve character . . . to make our lives an art." "The American craze for simplifying, standardizing, and equalizing the educational opportunities of all," to which the South was succumbing, Fletcher felt, was juxtaposed in his historical account against the traditional purpose of education: "to produce the balanced character—the man of the world in the true sense, who is also the man with spiritual roots in his own community in the local sense."

The Civil War, a source for a perspective on their collective past and for literary creation, was more than a historical abstraction; it was the most provocative and complex event against which southerners could measure their loyalty to the past in the context of their perception of the present. And for these men of letters it offered the raw material, themes, and symbols for biographies, novels, poetry, social criticism, and historical

(363)

interpretation. Allen Tate in 1929 announced a view that served as a description of how history was to be presented: "The past," he observed, "should be magnified to keep the present in its place." Through four narrative biographies of Civil War figures, four novels, two major poems, a number of historical essays, and a meditation on the Civil War, Tate, Warren, Lytle, Young, Davidson, Fletcher, Owsley, and Wade have recreated objective correlatives in images and metaphors interpreting historical events and their protagonists in a sweep of narration and commentary; thus these southerners found through their personal and regional history a "usable past" to communicate not only a political and social message but a reaffirmation of human values and pieties emerging out of history.

The fact that the contributors to the symposium were primarily teachers and men of letters has been commented on by critics who find their agrarianism a romanticized panacea. The reality is that a number of the Agrarians had a direct experience with farming and rural life: Nixon wrote of "plowing, hoeing or picking cotton, cutting sprouts or piling brush in newground"; Davidson represents his harvesting experience in a poem published before the symposium; Lanier lived and worked on a Tennessee farm until he was sixteen; Lytle managed his father's cotton farm before going to Yale and later returned there to grow tobacco and other crops while he was writing; Allen Tate lived at Benfolly, a farm in Tennessee, and supervised its operation by a tenant family. For most of the Agrarians, emotional attachment to the land and to an agrarian way of life was grounded in physical contact and personal experience with a rural or small-town community.

Probably of greater significance in understanding the elements of biography that led to the formation of a cohesive group was their affiliation with Vanderbilt University. Ransom, who had been at Vanderbilt the greatest length of time, was the teacher of Davidson, Warren, Lytle, and Tate, as well as a colleague later of Davidson, Tate, Lanier, Wade, Owsley, and Nixon. Four of the Agrarian group had been, from 1922 to 1925, the creators of and important contributors to *The Fugitive*, described by a contemporary anthologist as "the most distinguished poetry magazine in America." The poems of the Fugitives who were to become Agrarians constituted a significant proportion of the total number published: of the 517 appearing, one-third were by Tate, Davidson, Warren, and Ransom—with Ransom contributing the largest number (55). Through the four years of its existence, *The Fugitive* was a source for editorial commentary by Davidson, Tate, Ransom, and Warren. Publishing the journal was an activity that engaged not only the individual talents of the Fugitives, but also their considerable capacity to fight for art. It was, Ransom said in 1939, "a group effort beyond anything I have ever taken part in. Its quality was rare and fine as a piece of cooperation. . . . It was the best days I ever had."

Some form of group effort continued through the 1930s; following the appearance of *I'll Take My Stand* a vigorous campaign was waged with polemical publications and continued devotion to the creation of poetry, fiction, and literary criticism; five public debates drew thousands of southerners to hear Ransom or Davidson argue the cause of agrarianism as a way of life. In 1935 Tate and Herbert Agar edited a second plea for resisting the advance of industrialization in the distributistagrarian collection, *Who Owns America?*—to which all but four of the Agrarians contributed. It was the last concerted group effort to affect directly the political, economic, and social character of a nation bent on self-destruction—as they saw it—through "progress."

They continued, however, to pursue their own careers as men of letters, teachers, commentators on their southern–spiritual–American heritage and environment. Through the decades after the publication of *I'll Take My Stand*, these southerners as a group surpassed their impressive achievement to 1930, producing an astonishing body of serious, distinguished writing —more than a hundred works—in almost every field and genre: fiction, poetry, collections of literary and journalistic criticism, social commentary, studies in history, economics, and psychology; textbooks and anthologies with critical, introductory essays; translations and even a libretto for a folk opera; biography and autobiography, at times in the form of memoirs and letters, and collections of poetry. All of the poets —Fletcher, Davidson, Ransom, Tate, and Warren—have published retrospective selections from their volumes, most of them covering a period of three or four decades of writing.

The consciousness of personal identity and family continuity, of the relation between self and place, between experience and imagination informs all of the autobiographical writings of the Agrarians—whatever the particular mode: Fletcher's chronological autobiography, *Life Is My Song* (1935); Young's reminiscences evoking the past through recollections of place, atmosphere, and family relationships in *The Pavilion* (1951); letters by Davidson, Tate, Ransom, and Young in three recently published collections—*The Literary Correspondence* of Donald Davidson and Allen Tate (1974), *Stark Young, a Life in the Arts: Letters,* 1900–1962 (1975), and *Art as Adventure in Form: Letters of John Crowe Ransom,* 1923–1927 (1977)—disclose such autobiographical details as the writers' sense of personal identity; their values, perceptions, and tastes; their practices as artists; their responses to the social, cultural, and spiritual milieu. In yet another sense of autobiography, Tate and Lytle embarked on a course of rediscovering not only what their family and personal past was but how, in coming to understand that past as "the country of the living" in themselves, they might deepen the awareness of whoever might read what they had discovered. Wryness, humor, the unabated power of the concrete detail, the philosophical dimension—all are evident in Tate's *Memoirs and Opinions,* 1926–1974 (1975) and Lytle's *A Wake for the Living: A Family Chronicle* (1975). "The imaginative writer," said Tate, "is the archeologist of memory."

Critics of *I'll Take My Stand,* and there have been many, have difficulty reconciling their lack of respect for what they perceive as simplistic agrarian views of economic and political reality with the achievements of individual members of the group who have been honored with an array of awards not to be matched by any other collection of writers grouped in a common cause. Six—Ransom, Owsley, Tate, Lytle, Warren, and Wade—have had Guggenheim grants; Tate and Warren have held the Library of Congress Chair of Poetry; Ransom, Tate, and most recently Warren have won Yale University's Bollingen Prize in Poetry. Works by Fletcher and Warren have been named for Pulitzer Prizes: Fletcher's *Selected Poems* and Warren's *All the King's Men,* as well as his *Promises: Poems,*

1954–1956, a work also chosen for the National Book Award. (Warren is the only writer to have been named in two different genres.) Other honors have come for a lifetime of creative work: Andrew Lytle was chosen for the 1966/67 National Foundation of Arts and Humanities Award; Warren was selected in 1970 for both the National Medal for Literature by the National Book Committee and the Copernicus Award from the American Academy of American Poets for his lifetime achievement as a poet; four years later he was named by the National Foundation for the Humanities as recipient of the Jefferson Lectureship in the Humanities and his lectures appeared in published form as two essays in *Democracy and Poetry*. John Crowe Ransom's honors include the Russell Loines Award in Literature in 1951 from the National Academy of Arts and Letters, the Book of the Year Poetry Award in 1964 (for his *Selected Poems* published the year before), and the Gold Metal for Poetry awarded by the National Institute and Academy of Arts and Letters in 1973, the year before his death. Both Warren and Tate are among the fifty members of the Academy of Arts and Letters. Allen Tate has likewise been honored for his creative achievements as a man of letters, receiving the following awards since 1961: the Dante Society's Medaglio d'Oro, an award from the Academy of American Poets, the Ingram Merrill Foundation prize, the first Oscar Williams–Gene Derwood Award, and most recently, the National Medal for Literature from the American Academy of Arts and Letters in May, 1976. Special lectureships were another form of recognition: Tate and Owsley were Fulbright lecturers; Davidson inaugurated the special Mercer University Lamar Lecture Series in 1957 with his memoirs and history of the Fugitive and Agrarian groups (published as *Southern Writers in the Modern World*); John Donald Wade at the time of his death in 1963 was preparing his notes for the same Lamar lectures; Stark Young was invited to address the Southern Literary Festival in 1949 and was chosen in 1959 for the first award by the South Eastern Theatre Conference.

Although the Agrarians have been seen most consistently as sectionalists, regionalists, respectors of the southern heritage they sought to quicken and perpetuate for their contemporary world, they were in a deeper sense unmistakably American. Their affirmation of the humanity and dignity of the individual, their insistence on the importance of man's relationship to and harmony with nature were "right," said Warren, in a New York *Times* interview published early in 1977; it was, he insisted, a realization "arrived at through experience"—through "personal experience and Thomas Jefferson"—an affirmation of the importance of the biographical. Like other Americans— from the Transcendentalists to ecologists, philosophers, and hippies—the Agrarians' concern was, said Warren, for "the broad general idea of man's place in nature, his relationship to the whole natural world." Dramatically and metaphorically the Agrarians had presented their image of the whole man, imperfect, fallible, desirous of enjoying the good life, of realizing the potential of his "self." The values they perceived in a way of life expressive of aesthetic, religious humanism, of the enjoyment of work and the amenities of human relationships— "manners, conversation, hospitality, sympathy, family life, romantic love"—were the rallying points for their cause. From their common personal experiences, their friendships, they evoked a myth to serve, said Warren, "as a fifth column." *I'll*

Take My Stand, one metaphor for the artist's relation to his culture, represents after more than four decades, the power of a faith embodying a myth out of a timeless order of man's universal consciousness into the world of history. Perhaps it is like the "signatures" Tate remarked upon in his *Memoirs*, "pointing to persons and events once as real as Johnson's cane tapping the pavement, but now faded into another kind of reality."

Donald Grady Davidson (1893–1968)

For more than half a century Donald Davidson, considered the Agrarian who remained most consistently conservative, lived out an early self-characterization—the "old role of impassioned Idealist" who believes "anything is possible for determined men." An editor, literary journalist, historian, teacher, social and literary critic, and poet, Davidson was in some respects the most central to the Fugitive and Agrarian groups, yet in comparison with the other key members—Ransom, Tate, and Warren—he is the least known, the least read.

Born in Campbellsville, Tennessee, the son of teachers, Davidson acquired his lifelong interest in classical languages and music from his parents. His formal schooling began when he entered Lynnville Academy at the age of eight, a form and character of education that were reinforced by four years at the noted Branham and Hughes preparatory school at Spring Hill where he was trained in Latin, Greek, English, and mathematics.

Other important influences in his formative years were his friendships and the quality of his education at Vanderbilt University—begun in 1909 and interrupted by four years of teaching and World War I (he received a Bachelor's degree in

1917, a Master's in 1922). His exposure to foreign cultures through his service as a lieutenant in the war, and the effect of his separation from familiar surroundings—family, friends, and land—heightened his love for the South and for the culture and values it represented.

The following decade, 1921–1931, was perhaps the most significant in his life. From 1921 to 1925 he developed through his university studies, evening meetings discussing poetry, and the *Fugitive* experience a consciousness about the value, quality, and character of poetry in general and an awareness of what might be for him an appropriate subject matter, form, and voice for the poetry he would write. In this same period, responding to various attacks on the South (the most fierce of which was the Scopes trial debate), he became the uncompromising spokesman for the preservation of threatened values. Whatever subsequent activity or form of writing he chose— poetry, history, social and literary criticism, a libretto for a folk opera (*Singin' Billy*, 1952), even textbooks, the most successful of which was *American Composition and Rhetoric* (going into a fifth edition in 1968)—Davidson never abandoned his agrarian stance. For seven years, 1923–1930, he was editor of the Nashville *Tennessean's* book page, which has been described as the "best literary page ever published in the South." Syndicated for the last two and a half years of existence (it was stopped in November, 1930, the same month and year the Agrarian symposium was published), the weekly page exposed Davidson to a wide spectrum of intellectual and literary attitudes, issues, and practices. He reviewed more than 370 books—novels, poetry, history, biographies, social and literary criticism, and works concerned with music, economics, and political philosophy. At Davidson's request, the book page engaged the minds and reviewing skills of some of his Fugitive friends (among them, Ransom, Tate, and Warren), who, said Davidson, "were passing [with him] into their 'Agrarian phase' shortly afterwards." For Davidson, the "Book Page became more than a book page because of the ideas, hopes, pressures, enterprises, both individual and collective, that engaged us all from about 1925 to 1930."

By the end of the decade the Agrarian group had come into being, their principles were being formulated, and twelve southerners were engaged in writing for the symposium. Davidson was the catalyst in bringing the book to publication— handling contract details with Harper, maintaining correspondence among the contributors not at Vanderbilt, gathering and editing many of the essays. "Without his devotion and determination the symposium would not have been organized," said Tate. "He was the leader of the Southern Agrarians." Nor did he stop with the publication of the Agrarian call-to-arms. He defended their cause from the debate platform and wrote during the following nine years more than forty articles and review essays, most of which reflected some element of the Agrarian position. Several appeared in the conservative *American Review*, and at least half of the essays first published in journals as part of a deliberate campaign to solicit supporters for the Agrarian program were included in Davidson's first collection of social criticism, *The Attack on Leviathan* (1938).

A fierce spokesman for the values identified with a southern agrarian way of life, Davidson in both his early and late poetry and his critical essays focused on the themes of protest against a commercialized contemporary life inimical to the enjoyment and beauty of art, asserting that the poet should "retire more deeply within the body of the tradition," that "the cause of the arts . . . offers an additional reason . . . for submitting the industrial program to a stern criticism and for upholding a contrary program, that of agrarian restoration." Poetry itself must be seen as crucial to survival: "Nothing is more imperishable than poetry. In comparison, the material works of science and industry are but fleeting trifles. No civilization of the past has ever lived without poetry. Our civilization can hardly be an exception."

Through his five volumes of poetry, *An Outland Piper* (1924), *The Tall Men* (1927), *Lee in the Mountains and Other Poems* (1938), *The Long Street* (1961), and *Collected Poems, 1922–1961* (1966), Davidson as southerner and man of letters reflected the values he believed were essential for the artist to function: the preservation of a traditional society in which the organic relationship between man and nature could flourish. *The Tall Men*, created when he was becoming convinced that the poet must perceive his art as a weapon to be wielded in the political arena, was, said Davidson, "to be a dramatic visualization of a modern Southerner, trapped in a distasteful urban environment, subjecting the phenomena of the disordered present to a comparison with the heroic past." Honoring his Tennessee heritage and the pioneering men who stand tall symbolically, Davidson presents them in contrast to modern deracinated man in a dehumanized world of war, mechanization, and urbanization. For Davidson the hope for a healthy society lay in a return to an authentic folk culture, "true cherishers" of which "are . . . the family in its traditional role, securely established on the land . . . and . . . the stable community which is really a community, not a mere real estate development."

The same perspective and themes evident in the poetry appear in his prose. His scorn of objectivity is evident in the very titles he chose for his two collections of social criticism: *The Attack on Leviathan* (1938) and *Still Rebels, Still Yankees* (1957). His two-volume history, *The Tennessee* (1946, 1948) in the Rivers of America Series, reflects his immersion in and love for his region—rendered in a richness and character of detail, through research into historical records, geography, and folklore. As in his other prose, the style is distinguished: precise, vivid, evocative, gracefully lucid, persuasive, in short, as his biographers T. D. Young and M. Thomas Inge say, "faultless prose."

As a man of letters, Davidson has been chosen for honorary doctorates by three institutions: Cumberland University in 1946, Washington and Lee University in 1948, and Middlebury College in 1966, two years before his death.

Davidson's life and aesthetics were consistent with his values. He celebrated and enjoyed nature, as his letters and poetry reveal; he lived, when he could, in a rural, more natural environment, spending summers in Vermont after 1931, the year he was first invited to teach at the Bread Loaf School of English. The blight of "progress," the spread of the effects of industrialization and urbanization in a city like Nashville, Davidson found a disturbing contrast to John Donald Wade's Marshallville in Georgia, "a kind of Prospero's island, almost magically preserved from the tempests that so ruinously swept the land at large"—a wistful observation in the last published critical writing Davidson did, a historical-biographical introduction to the *Selected Essays and Other Writings of John Donald Wade* (1966). Even at the age of seventy-three, two years after his retirement from Vanderbilt in 1964, Davidson suffered no abatement of his concern for the preservation of humanistic values, no loss of control over his craft. Speaking of Wade, he said (and inadvertently described his own powers): "To have the gift of language that, when friends or casual guests are at hand, makes one room an everywhere and one small Georgia town a world garden—how difficult, how all but impossible in the skeptical, self-deluding twentieth century!"

As an Agrarian, a poet, a critic, Donald Davidson was, as Robert Frost said, firmly in the American tradition of insubordination. From his Fugitive days until his death in 1968, the "impassioned Idealist" lived a life of confrontation, a choice made when he was beginning his career as a poet. "It was necessary," he recalled at the Fugitives' Reunion in 1956, "for the poets to make an attack upon society."

John Gould Fletcher (1886–1950)

The place of John Gould Fletcher in American letters has remained uncertain. The complexity of his interests, the variety of his activities, the shifts in modes, qualities, and influences in his poetry make a description by labels impossible; indeed, some of the most appropriate appear contradictory: he was both experimenter and traditionalist; cosmopolitan expatriate and southern American; aristocratic disparager of "democracy," yet a supporter of the folk arts.

Born in Little Rock, Arkansas, the only son of a Confederate soldier, Fletcher began his education early with private tutors, studying Latin and German at the age of five, attending a pub-

lic school and the Phillips Andover Academy as preparation for
Harvard—an education considered appropriate to the position
and wealth of his father (he was one of the state's leading finan-
ciers). A senior at Harvard when his father died, Fletcher inherited an independent income, withdrew from the university
in 1907, a few months before graduating, and resolved—after
an unhappy experience with a summer archeological expedition
—to live abroad and "to try to acquire an education, to learn
something concerning aesthetic, moral, and spiritual values."
He had already realized at Harvard that he "disliked democracy," and "preferred, on the whole, the past to the present."
After some months in Italy, he settled in London in the spring
of 1909 where he was soon caught up in political and literary
circles; he joined the Fabian Socialist movement, marched
through the streets in a suffragette parade, met the editor of
the *New Age*, A. R. Orage, who stimulated him to write poetry by directing him to Walt Whitman and Ezra Pound.
It was Pound who agreed to promote Fletcher's verse by reviewing it in *Poetry*, and Fletcher's literary career was encouraged by Pound's introducing him to Amy Lowell and the new
Imagist poetry.

Fletcher remained in England for nearly twenty-five years,
returning for brief visits to the South and a two-year stay during World War I; in 1933 he resettled in his native Arkansas,
finding, as he saw it, a retreat from the confusions of the technological age in a pine-surrounded stone house near Little
Rock.

Before his repatriation, Fletcher had developed a wide variety of interests in addition to poetry; his was a career in the arts
—not only in the abstractions of aesthetic theory but in such

(376)

concrete manifestations as painting, sculpture, the graphic arts, music, the dance, cinema, and folk culture. As early as 1918 he was writing about art, planning at that time *Paul Gauguin: His Life and Art*. Between 1915 and 1930 he published nine books on poetry (five had simultaneously appeared in 1913, printed at his own expense); a study in folk history, *John Smith—Also Pocahontas* (1928); and a small book called *The Crisis in the Film* (1929). His interests also embraced history, political theory, psychology, economics, and social structure. During the last two decades of his life he published his comparative analysis in *The Two Frontiers* (1930), a neglected study of the psychology, economy, and social structure of the United States and Russia; *Arkansas* (1947), an eminently readable social and political history that had developed from his long poem, *The Epic of Arkansas* (1936), commissioned by a Little Rock newspaper in honor of the state's centenary; his revealing autobiography, *Life Is My Song* (1937); and *Selected Poems* (1938), for which he received the Pulitzer Prize, the first southern poet to be so honored. His art commentaries appeared in such journals as the *International Studio* (London), *The Print Collector's Quarterly, Art Work,* and the *Arts of New York*.

Evaluations of Fletcher's achievements in poetry too often begin and end with his early experiments in imagistic poems and polyphonic prose. (It remains the view of many critics that this poetry is the most likely to survive.) Yet he responded to other influences and forms of art and experience—music, symbolism, impressionism, mysticism, Oriental aesthetics, poetry, and philosophy. It has been suggested that Fletcher's poetic themes reflect his specific discoveries of ancient Chinese

(377)

painters and poets, the art and poetry of Japan, in particular the *haiku*, Zen Buddhism, Taoism, the mysticism of Blake, the French symbolists, and Saint Augustine. Fletcher's biographer-critic Edna Stephens notes that "Fletcher's work is . . . written in a highly individual esthetic, depending frequently upon a knowledge of music and painting for understanding, and following an alien tradition." Yet these elements, it should be observed, are absorbed into his consciousness and translated into a language of metaphor and image that can speak to any sensitive reader.

In considering Fletcher's entire body of work as a poet, critics must take into account a significant change in his interests —his shift to a concern for folk literature and history—that became evident after his return to his native environment. His later work is often consciously regional in subject, more traditional in metrical effects, and less fanciful in imagery. His return home was presaged by his participation in the Agrarian symposium; his contribution on education in the South was metaphorically a public declaration of a spiritual "going home" from a self-imposed exile (though three years were to pass before he actually reset his roots in Arkansas). He joined the Fugitive-Agrarians happily, finding that their "defense of the culture of the old South was in a way an answer to a prayer [he] had cherished since [his] going abroad in 1908"; it gave him hope that "some part of America might in some way be delivered from the incubus of the machine." His involvement in the Agrarian cause continued with his participation in a round-table conference on regionalism at the University of Virginia in 1931, "a lone hand battling against the tide of modernity." Despite his scorn for democracy—which he equated

(378)

with plutocracy and which seems to suggest his rejection of the common people who, he declared, did not support the great art of Sophocles or Aeschylus or Shakespeare (only "an intelligent and leisured class" can read and enjoy poetry, he asserted) —Fletcher nevertheless organized the Arkansas Folk Society in 1936 "in the hope of putting on a folk festival of mountaineer ballads and square dances, negro spirituals and folk plays."

His last two volumes of poetry, *South Star* (1941) and *The Burning Mountain* (1946), clearly reflect his concern for the history, values, and themes of his region in the context of his deep pessimism about the destruction of man and his civilization through mechanization and its most obscene manifestation, war. Evoking the peace and beauty of nature, the majesty of the elements, these poems manifest the tension that pervaded Fletcher's life and art.

A man of passionate loyalties and strong reactions, he suffered periodic emotional breakdowns during his lifetime. It has been said of the final one, when apparently he took his own life, that his death was the result of the rage and despair of a sensitive man confronted with "the Machine Age and its Machine Wars." He was found dead in a pool near his country home on May 10, 1950. Prophetically, and perhaps ironically, thirteen years before, Fletcher had ended his autobiography with the observation: "Yet life is in many ways unamenable to our efforts to find reason for it, to make it into a pattern of abiding significance. . . . I have not so far lived my life, that I need fear for my death."

(379)

Henry Blue Kline (1905–1951)

Close friends of Henry Blue Kline have described him as "a great bear of a man," with tremendous energy. A southerner who would have enjoyed a life of leisure and gracious manners, who had a passionate fondness for wilderness areas, who took pleasure in working with his hands, he has been called a rebel against the comfortable and the conventional, a New Deal agrarian who thought that a totally new approach—TVA, rural electrification, and the building up of small industries—was necessary for the South.

A Tennessean by birth and education (except for a few years in the North), Henry Blue Kline is unknown to the academic and literary world. He was of a later generation of Vanderbilt students, respected by Ransom and Davidson for his intellectual seriousness and his philosophical turn of mind, as well as for his desire to perpetuate the values of a culture that appreciated an enjoyment of the arts. At Vanderbilt University Kline completed his Master's degree in English in 1929. During the planning of the symposium, he wrote Davidson about a variety of matters—his own essay, statements in the manifesto, suggestions for titles.

After unsuccessful attempts to launch a career as a freelance writer or a teacher (he was at the Univesity of Tennessee from 1930 to 1933), Kline turned to government agencies—first the Civil Works Administration, then the Tennessee Valley Authority, where he held many posts. As an industrial economist, he planned and coordinated research and wrote an influential report, "Regionalized Freight Rates: Barrier to National Productiveness." Published as a House of Representatives document in 1943, it bolsters the Interstate Commerce Commission's protest of northeastern discrimination against southern shippers.

In 1944 Kline joined the St. Louis *Post-Dispatch*, where his special knowledge of economics and related areas was reflected in his editorials on railroad problems, fair trade laws, taxation, housing, tariffs, and education. From 1949 to 1951 he was information officer for the Atomic Energy Commission, his last position. He died of uremic poisoning in 1951.

After his death, a St. Louis *Post-Dispatch* editorial said of him: "It was characteristic . . . that when he found he was totally ill . . . he should dedicate his body to medical science. . . . Kline applied his own conviction that life has purpose and meaning in his desire to help others whom he will never know." Like his *persona* in his symposium essay, Kline revealed in his own life a search for "a closer communion with the ideal of life prevalent in his world," "a deeply rooted determination to live . . . on terms dictated by his own critical intelligence."

Lyle Hicks Lanier (1903—)

Born in Madison County, Tennessee, Lyle Lanier came from the farm, attended a one-room school, and after a year of preparatory study at Valparaiso University, entered Vanderbilt in 1920 to study philosophy. Advanced degrees and subsequent research in psychology at George Peabody College resulted in an important monograph, *Studies in the Comparative Abilities of Whites and Negroes* (1929).

A member of the psychology department at Vanderbilt while the Agrarian symposium was planned, Lanier became

involved with the group not only because of personal friendships and proximity, but also because his humanistic studies
had led him to question a blind faith in social science and a
"scientific attitude" as an easy means of solving human and political problems. Like his fellow Agrarians, Lanier has been
concerned with the unified human being in harmony with his
society, with the concrete realities rather than scientific abstractions. Science alone would not provide the answers. Lanier
saw philosophy and psychology as intrinsically related disci-
plines. In 1939 he observed in the *Southern Review* that dic-
tators, not the social scientists, are the end of the search for effective control over social events. "The scientist is forced to
contemplate the appalling paradox that science—the systematic use of intelligence—is found to have improvised its own
means of destruction." The solution, if it is anywhere, Lanier
said, lies within the democratic process.

An eminent psychologist in the areas of race, experimental
and physiological psychology, he is now retired from the University of Illinois where he had been executive vice president
and provost. Lanier had a distinguished academic career, teaching in the South, East, and Midwest. He has served as editor of
the *Psychological Bulletin* and as director of professional and
governmental organizations, including the Social Science Research Council, the Defense Science Board, the American Psychological Association, the Society of Experimental Psychologists, and the Office of Administrative Affairs of the American
Council of Education.

As a psychologist, Lanier considers himself a monist rather
than a dualist, for in his opinion the mind-body bifurcation
"constitutes one of the most serious impediments to sound

(382)

psychological progress." This split would suggest a parallel to the Agrarians' concern about man's dissociation of sensibility in a technological society. The relation of Lanier's scientific convictions to agrarianism becomes clearer: "Political leadership, informed social science and a definitive social philosophy," he noted in his symposium essay, seek to effect a synthesis of living "in an agrarian family and community."

Andrew Nelson Lytle (1902—)

Andrew Lytle has been a farmer, teacher, editor, and writer. Born in Murfreesboro, this Tennessean had a varied education: the Sewanee Military Academy, Vanderbilt University, a year of study in France, and two years of graduate work at the Yale School of Drama. For a time he considered making the theater his career; he wrote a few plays and acted professionally in New York, experiences that would later influence his craft as a novelist.

Although, as Lytle said, he was "no proper farmer," agrarian experiences have been a significant part of his life: for some ten years he managed Cornsilk, his father's cotton farm, the place he "loved most." During the Depression he tried to combine writing with farming, completing his first book, a prose celebration of his region and his people in his novelistic, dramatic biography, *Bedford Forrest and His Critter Company* (1931, 1960), and his first novel, *The Long Night* (1936).

Realizing that farming and writing were ultimately incompatible, Lytle chose, like his Fugitive-Agrarian friends, to become a teacher and to follow the pursuits appropriate to a man of letters. Over a period of forty-five years he wrote, in addition to the biography of Nathan Bedford Forrest, several distinguished short stories, a novella, four novels, book reviews, social and political commentary, a group of essays focusing on the craft of fiction and European and American authors (Tolstoy, Flaubert, Joyce, Stephen Crane, Henry James, Faulkner) —"not like any other literary criticism of our time," said Tate; and most recently he completed "a memoir of a society."

While teaching history at the University of the South (1947/48), he was managing editor of the *Sewanee Review*. Lytle taught at Southeastern College in Memphis, Tennessee; at the Writers' Workshop at the University of Iowa (1946–1948); and at the University of Florida (1948–1961). In 1961 he returned to the University of the South to teach creative writing and literature until his retirement in 1973. He served again as editor of *Sewanee Review* from 1961 to 1972, and in 1971 edited *Craft and Vision: The Best Fiction from the Sewanee Review*.

His devotion to his craft as a writer was recognized by a number of awards—Guggenheim Fellowships in 1940 and 1941; a Kenyon Fellowship in 1956 while he was completing his major work in fiction, *The Velvet Horn* (1957); and the National Foundation of Arts and Humanities Award (1966–1967).

In his essays and fiction, Lytle treats "reality" as image—heightening or selecting particular elements for their dramatic, symbolic, paradigmatic effect—evident, for example, in his Agrarian symposium, "The Hind Tit," which was a deliberate overstatement of the character of the yeoman farmer's life. Other essays and writing of the 1930s include: polemical reviews and articles on Civil War or southern figures—Lincoln, Lee, Calhoun, Robert Barnwell Rhett, Sherman—and a fine short story, "Mr. MacGregor." For these works, Lytle resorted to novelistic techniques that he would develop further in his more complex longer fiction: a skillful shifting of levels of language in narration and dialogue, the rendering of a sense of reality through dialect, the patterning of concrete, precise details, a sensitivity to the mythic or ritualistic dimension of the conscious and the unconscious in human experience.

His first novel, not surprisingly, focused on the period of the Civil War. *The Long Night* was widely reviewed and admired for its historical realism, its effective narrative focus on a vendetta carried out against the backdrop of the war, its remarkable depiction of the Battle of Shiloh, and its "vivid and powerful . . . visualization of a dead and gone countryside and culture." His other works of fiction are likewise set in the past. *At the Moon's Inn* (1941) and the novella *Alchemy* (1942), as a sequel or a prologue to the novel, portray the conquistadors, De Soto and Pizarro, as prototypes of modern Western man; motivated by an ambitious individualism, by pride and greed, they ultimately destroy themselves through self-deification, by insistence that human will is a mirror of God's will. His third novel, *A Name for Evil* (1947), focused on the restoration of an old southern mansion and evocative of Henry James's *Turn of the Screw*, has been described as "a recasting of the Edenic myth," a depiction of "a distorted private view of tradition" informed by reading in Jung and other psychologists, and reflective of techniques and themes in Henry James and James Joyce: archetypal symbolism, form and dramatization, epiphany and secular communion. Some of the same elements of form and substance, of the archetypal paradigm and Christian myth appear in his fourth novel, *The*

(385)

Velvet Horn (1957), a complex original work illuminated by "The Working Novelist and the Mythmaking Process," an essay Tate has called "the most brilliant example of . . . formalistic-historical criticism." The novel is rich in symbols, two of which link the themes of sexuality/knowledge and initiation (the Christian fall and pagan rites): the tree and the velvet horn, which are reinforced by other natural phenomena as symbols—the mountain and water. Woven into the fabric of the narration are themes central to Lytle's moral view: the redemptive power of the Christian heritage and the family as synecdochically representative of the larger community, extended to the family of man.

Both themes pervade Lytle's most recent work, *A Wake for the Living: A Family Chronicle* (1975), a personal narrative of anecdotes, legends, and the history of his family, their friends and community. Lytle ranges freely in the "presentness" of the past—from the living presence of his ancestors in the Revolutionary War to his own consciousness of coming "to live in the sense of eternity." Embodied in concrete details, his conversational memoirs reaffirm the distinctiveness of "a country society [his family's] which was, and is no more," which "by its habits and customs discovers the identity between the natural and the supernatural." The Agrarian persuasion has remained alive in Lytle, who acknowledges "that mystery which becomes ceremony to people who make their living by the land." Some forty years after the publication of the symposium, Lytle affirmed in an important *Sewanee Review* essay, "The State of Letters in a Time of Disorder": "Almost absolutely I would say that the great, at least lasting, literatures and repre-

(386)

sentative arts are found in either a pastoral or agrarian society. The images and references which the arts find to hand are to things natural and supernatural." Recognizing and accepting these elements as characteristic of the substance of lasting art, Lytle notes that what he has been saying "presupposes a traditional attitude, one which cherishes and sustains an inherited way of life." Hence his search into and celebration of a personal, familial past: "If you don't know who you are or where you come from, you will find yourself at a disadvantage. The ordered slums of suburbia are made for the confusion of the spirit. . . . For the profound stress between the union that is flesh and the spirit, they have been forced to exchange the appetites. Each business promotion uproots the family. Children become wayfarers. Few are given any vision of the Divine. They perforce become secular men, half men, who inhabit what is left of Christendom."

In 1966 a number of Lytle's most distinguished critical essays were collected under the metaphorical title, *The Hero with the Private Parts*. In his foreword for that volume, Allen Tate wrote from the perceptiveness and sensibility of a fellow artist and southerner, recognizing precisely the special problem Lytle as a novelist and critic faced: "to discover in his native *milieu* typical actions (he calls them mythical or archetypal) that permit him to write, not historical novels but novels as history," and a "high programmatic criticism that is . . . 'creative' . . . in a formal sense similar to that . . . in his best fiction." The convictions the Agrarians held as commentators on modern society served Lytle well as critic and novelist. Tate notes with admiration—"Lytle knows better than any writer today that there are no abstract techniques that can be taken down from the shelf, or provided by a computer, and superimposed upon the materials of fiction."

In his life as a man of letters, Lytle lived by the conviction that the work of the artist must be expressive of a man whose sensibilities and moral being reflect an awareness of the spiritual dimension. The artist, in the act of creating, in permitting an idea to turn flesh, thus giving it the illusion of life, experiences "the flash of miracle . . . the artist's reward." Art is created when "the conscious and the intuitive practice of the craft work together," when the "craft is overborne by the stroke of life." For Lytle the interest in myth and the act of creation are akin to a mystical spiritual experience—suggesting to him an understanding of what William Blake might have been thinking when he said the artist continues the act of God. Lytle's commitment to his Agrarian southern heritage is subsumed and shaped into his practice as an artist. From his being as a man and an artist whose sensibilities and moral quality belong to a Christian heritage, he draws and re-creates "the archetypal experience which forever recurs within the human scene."

Herman Clarence Nixon (1886–1967)

Historian, political scientist, analyst of economic and social conditions, and pleader for the "little people," Herman Clarence Nixon in attitude and activities failed to fit the uncritical characterization of Agrarians as "visionary" or "reactionary."

Born in Merrellton, Alabama, son of a landowner and country store proprietor, "a product of the folkways of the hills," Nixon was educated chiefly in the South: a one-room school, the State Normal School, the Alabama Polytechnic Institute. From army experiences, his service with the library of Wilson's Peace Commission in France, and his study at the University of Chicago, he gained a new understanding of and perspective on his Piedmont democratic heritage. His doctoral study of the Populist movement in Iowa (1926) had, he said, "injected [him] heartily into the liberal side of agrarianism."

Nixon devoted more than half a century to teaching history and political science in the South and Midwest, beginning at Jacksonville (Alabama) State College in 1910. He held other appointments at Louisiana State University, Tulane, the University of Missouri, and at Vanderbilt for eighteen years (1925–1928 and 1940–1955). After his retirement from Vanderbilt in 1955, he was "circuit riding" as a visiting professor at colleges in New York, California, Ohio, West Virginia, and Kentucky. In 1957 he received the John Jay Whitney Foundation Emeritus Award for teaching.

His books, sociological-economic-political studies, included interpretations of the rural and village South (*Forty Acres and Steel Mules* and *Lower Piedmont Country*), a plea for social planning (*Possum Trot*), and three text books: *A Short History of the American People* with Frank L. Owsley and Oliver Chitwood (1945), *American Federal Government: A General View* (1952), and *State and Local Government in America* with Daniel Grant (1963). To these may be added a score of articles and book reviews in professional journals. He was also an editorial board member of the *Journal of Politics*.

That Nixon endorsed a politically liberal position, one which disturbed some of his more conservative colleagues, is evident from his activities and writing. He was regional consultant for

the Civil Service Commission and director of the New Deal
Louisiana Rural Rehabilitation Corporation; he served as chair-
man of the Southern Policy Commission (1935) through which
he supported cooperatives, government ownership of natural
resources and public utilities, and socialization of medical and
hospital services. He lobbied in Washington for farm tenant
legislation. As an essayist, he examined the South's problems
of desegregation, urbanization, and industrialization. His position might best be characterized by his own statement: "I am
for constructive acceptance of the inevitable, with a maximum
effort for the preservation of human community and common
roots." He continued in his writings and activities to voice resistance to "an atmosphere of technological illiteracy, to reject
the worship of industrial gods and mere economic progress."
Thirty years after the publication of the symposium, he still
saw "agrarianism at its best as a Confucian element of balance
for civilization at its best" and the agrarian society as a "pre-
server of the arts, including the important art of living."

Frank Lawrence Owsley (1890–1956)

As a sectional historian, an influential teacher, and an Agrarian, Frank Owsley treated the past like a humane study and a
scholarly discipline. History was for him "an allegiance, an act
of faith in one kind of future rather than another."

Born in Montgomery County, Alabama, the son of a school
teacher–farmer–cotton buyer, Owsley grew up on farms and
was educated in country schools and at the Alabama Polytechnic Institute in Auburn, completing there both an undergrad-
uate and a graduate degree in history.

His long teaching career began in 1912 with appointments at the Fifth District Agricultural School and at Auburn. His continued interest in southern history took him north to the University of Chicago; there he worked under the outstanding southern historian, William E. Dodd, receiving an M.A. in 1917 and a Ph.D., *magna cum laude*, in 1924. For more than four decades, Owsley taught continuously, chiefly at Vanderbilt University, where he developed a strong graduate program in sectional and Civil War history, and at the University of Alabama.

Owsley's kind of scholarly research broke new ground. He was fascinated by the Civil War as a subject, absorbed in investigating its causes, events, and the reasons for the South's defeat. His first book, *States Rights in the Confederacy*, was published in 1925 and was considered revolutionary at the time. It was followed by other works similarly independent in their conclusions. Harriet C. Owsley, his wife and the editor of a posthumous collection of important essays, noted that her husband considered it his obligation as a scholar to correct certain misconceptions about the South, its people, and its history. The result was a variety of publications: in addition to a two-volume textbook, *A Short History of the American People* (1945, 1948), with Oliver P. Chitwood and H. C. Nixon, Owsley published *King Cotton Diplomacy* in 1931. A revised posthumous edition of this careful study of primary sources was published in 1959. Owsley's analysis of data and his emphasis in interpretation—a shift from the moral to the economic— led historian Henry Steele Commager to write: "[Professor Owsley's] massive volume not only challenges old beliefs and excites new controversies, but it supersedes all other studies of Confederate diplomacy by its thoroughness and its scholarship."

Through the 1930s and 1940s Owsley published a number of controversial essays in such journals as the *Southern Review*, the conservative *American Review*, the *Virginia Quarterly Review*, and the *Journal of Southern History*. A sectional allegiance, Owsley maintained, can sometimes result in an analysis that comes closer to the truth than an abstract uncommitted objectivity. Called a modern fire-eater by some historians and attacked for his "devil theory" of the causes of the Civil War, Owsley admitted that some of the Agrarian essays (including his) were "deliberately provocative." His Agrarian symposium contribution illustrates his distinction as a historian. Other such polemical stances by Owsley include "The Origins of the American Civil War" (1940) and "The Fundamental Cause of the Civil War: Egocentric Sectionalism" (1941). Such fierce commentaries should be seen, however, in the context of earlier and later Agrarian and historical writings—his essay-reviews and articles like "Democracy Unlimited," an analysis favoring a Constitutional construction of government, and "The Pillars of Agrarianism" proposing, as part of the Agrarian cause, to counter the crusade against the South, an Agrarian solution to some of the South's problems. The Agrarians sought, Owsley said at the time of the Fugitives' Reunion, to do something about the loss of "the basic values of civilization . . . the sense of community . . . the common courtesies of life." Most of these commentaries and some impressive review-essays on southern figures were included in a distinguished posthumous collection, *The South: Old and New Frontiers* (1969), edited by Harriet C. Owsley. Owsley's last book-length work was perhaps his most original piece of research, *Plain Folk of the Old South* (1949). This study, spanning ten years, involves diaries, wills, private correspondence, and a statistical analysis of census records and county tax rolls; the result was proof that the plain folk or yeomen farmers were a significant group of nonslaveholding whites of the antebellum South. Formerly lumped together and dismissed as "poor white trash," they now were perceived as important in establishing the varied character of the cultural pattern of the South.

Owsley's books on the Civil War and the South, though completed from a half to a quarter of a century ago, have not been superseded or undermined by more recent historical research. Both *States Rights in the Confederacy* and *King Cotton Diplomacy* have been republished since his death. Recognition of his achievements and honors accorded him as a historian include special lectureship invitations from Louisiana State University, the University of Kentucky, and the University of Mississippi; summer visiting professorships at the University of Illinois, the University of North Carolina, Duke and Columbia Universities; a Guggenheim Fellowship in 1927/28, a Social Science Research Grant, and a Fulbright lectureship in 1956 at St. John's College, Cambridge University, England. He was there completing research on the diplomatic history of the Civil War when he died of a heart attack in 1956.

Owsley's character as a teacher has been described by fellow historians: he was deeply interested in students and influenced a large body of young doctoral candidates, directing more than forty dissertations at Vanderbilt alone; he was a gifted teacher, in part, H. C. Nixon observed, because he was "never too judicious or too impartial." The best historians have been characterized as storytellers, men of letters who go beyond the mere analysis of fact. As such a historian, Owsley found Agrarianism congenial, for it embodied values that permitted, he said, "art, music, and literature [to] emerge from the dark cramped holes where industrial insecurity and industrial insensitiveness have often driven them." In practice and philosophy, Owsley as historian belongs to the humanities.

John Crowe Ransom (1888–1974)

"The artist," wrote John Crowe Ransom to Allen Tate during their *Fugitive* days, "can't . . . be the impartial spectator, the colorless medium of information, the carrier of a perfectly undirected passion. . . . The work of art must be perfectly serious, ripe, mature—full of heart, but with enough head to govern heart." And that rare combination of passion and rationality, of emotion and intelligence, of integrity and decorum is represented in Ransom's canon of work, in his lifetime as a teacher. The nature of Ransom's profound yet intangible influence on his students is perhaps best described by poet Robert Lowell as leaving them "with something inside us moving toward articulation, logic, directness, and complexity."

Born in Pulaski, Tennessee, the son of a Methodist minister, Ransom was graduated from Vanderbilt University in 1909. A Rhodes Scholar, he read widely in the classics and philosophy—marked influences in his poetry and critical theory. In 1913 he was granted a degree in *Litterae Humaniores*.

One of the most distinctive qualities of Ransom's thought and style as a poet, literary critic, and commentator on society is his irony, rendered in his use of the concrete image or situation and in his precise diction—archaic, Latinized, colloquial, and elegant. Through irony his central dualisms emerge: death in life, the past in the present, science *versus* art. His *Selected Poems* (1945, revised and republished in 1963 and 1969) contains the best of his earlier three volumes and reveals his artistic integrity, a sensitivity and control that represent an impeccable poetic taste.

After the late 1930s Ransom's influence derived chiefly from his criticism. His three collections of essays and the *Kenyon Review*, which he founded and edited until 1959, were the focus for discussion and for new critical analysis. The first collection, *God Without Thunder*, appeared in 1930. *The World's Body* (1938) is suffused with dualisms; and *The New Criticism* (1941), still highly influential in universities, is marked by a formalized, close analysis of the aesthetic experience, in part through a consideration of various modern critics. *Beating the Bushes*, a selection of Ransom's unpublished *Kenyon Review* essays, appeared in 1972.

In the early years of his Agrarian activity, Ransom's interest had extended from his poetry to religious, economic, and social matters. Drawing on his Protestant heritage and his Agrarianism, he sought "to recover the excellences of the ancient faith," to combat "scientism." This concern with nonliterary matters—which he linked to his involvement with aesthetics—found expression in his Agrarian essays in the mid 1930s. By 1945, however, Ransom had disavowed the assumption that the values of civilization would best be preserved in an agrarian culture.

Ransom clearly did not remain a static thinker—not in literary considerations or otherwise. His career was marked by respect for the fact, for the ambiguities and complexities of human existence. He will continue to be admired, not only for his identification with the South, but for the high order of his poetry and criticism; for the unremitting integrity with which he explored, as Tate has suggested, "the possibilities of an Aristotelian criticism of the poetic disorder of our age."

Allen Tate (1899–1979)

In the heat of the Agrarian battle against the forces of materialism, Allen Tate published an essay on Emily Dickinson and her "poetry of ideas." It stated, long before his conversion to Roman Catholicism, a conviction inherent in his social and literary criticism, his fiction, and his poetry: "I am . . . upholding a . . . rational insight into the meaning of the present in terms of some imaginable past implicit in our own lives; we need a body of ideas that can bear upon the course of the spirit and yet remain coherent as a rational instrument." Tate's southern background, classical education, and life-long devotion to the discipline and art of writing were part of his quest for this body of ideas and part of the discovery.

Born in Winchester, Kentucky, Allen Tate was educated in southern private schools and at Vanderbilt University, where he formed close friendships with Ransom, Davidson, Warren, and other Fugitives. Here he began his career as poet and editor. After unsatisfactory forays into the worlds of business and high school teaching, Tate fled to New York in 1924 to write poetry.

Extraordinarily productive in this six-year absence from his native region, Tate published more than fifty articles, his first volume of poetry (*Mr. Pope and Other Poems*), and two biographies (*Stonewall Jackson* and *Jefferson Davis*). In these works, two central themes emerge: the inviolability of art and the superiority of an organic, agrarian southern culture over a fragmented industrial, northern society. In his southern heritage Tate found a coherent body of ideas from which he and other writers identified with the southern renascence had converted the "southern legend of defeat and frustration into a universal myth of the human condition." Representing this metamorphosis are some of his finest poems, published during his Agrarian period, including "Ode to the Confederate Dead" and "The Mediterranean." His conscious use of the South as an image was implicit also in his antebellum novel *The Fathers* (which is being reissued by Louisiana State University Press in 1977) and in his literary and social criticism.

In view of the direction and themes of his later poetry, Tate's choice of religion as the subject of his Agrarian essay is meaningful. He had come to represent the sickness of the modern world not only as a "dissociation of sensibility" but also as a lack of a faith, which he later described as a "battle . . . between the dehumanized secularism . . . and the eternal society of the communion of the human spirit." This search for a faith became more explicitly religious in the early 1950s when Tate published three sections of a long, incomplete autobiographical poem: "The Swimmers," "The Maimed Man," and "The Buried Lake." His last volume of collected poems (1961) reveals that poetry has remained for Tate "the art of apprehending and concentrating our experience in the mysterious limitations of form."

As a critic and teacher of literature, Tate expressed a devotion to the art of letters, reflecting an intensity and insight rarely so well sustained. His *Collected Essays* (1959), *Essays of Four Decades* (1969), and *Memoirs and Opinions* (1975) exhibit his commitment to "absolute" standards and his attack on scientism.

In the opinion of his contemporaries, Tate's critical essays are among the most brilliant of his generation; his poetry has been called "seminal," its impact far-reaching. The poet, Tate has said, "is responsible to his *conscience* . . . the joint action of knowledge and judgment . . . [and] for the reality conveyed to him by his awareness." Perhaps these characteristics explain Tate's stature in the world of letters.

John Donald Wade (1892–1963)

The son of a country doctor and great-great grandson of the first governor of Georgia, John Wade was born in Marshallville and grew up in a tradition of humane living, with its roots in the land and church. After a Bachelor's degree from the University of Georgia in 1914, Wade went north for graduate study in English: he received the Master's degree in 1915 from Harvard University and completed his doctorate at Columbia in 1924 (his studies were interrupted by two years of World War I service and teaching at the University of Georgia).

From his first publication, *Augustus Baldwin Longstreet: A Study in the Development of Culture in the South* (1925), to his last major piece of writing, an unpublished narrative about his father, his "connections," and the past, Wade found biography a challenging and congenial genre. His *Longstreet*, a study ahead of its time, depicted the Georgia judge-clergyman-humorist in a lively, fresh, impartial manner; Wade captured

(398)

the personality of Longstreet and events of his life with humor and dramatic skill. With an uncommon interdisciplinary perspective, Wade viewed the backgrounds of southern literature and culture. His study of Longstreet's life, said Wade, was to be regarded as "an epitome in some sense, of American civilization." His second intensive involvement with biography began in 1926; with a Guggenheim grant, he left the University of Georgia, where he had been teaching since 1919, to do research in England on John Wesley. That biography was published in 1930, when Wade was teaching at Vanderbilt University; but before its publication, Wade was already immersed in research and writing of 116 biographical sketches for the *Dictionary of American Biography*. An assistant editor in 1927/28, Wade had developed in his compressed vignettes an astringent style with ironic judgments and an appropriate juxtaposition of facts. From this experience, Wade observed, "I came to know that some of our most revered heroes and evangels of Progress seemed to me to have been as regardful of their personal advancement materially, as with that of the Race in general"—a realization, he suggested, that served as a link with some thoughts the Vanderbilt Agrarians were having at the time he joined the English faculty in 1928.

The affinity Wade felt for biography was manifest also in the 1930s and 1940s in many fine critical essays on southern culture and southern political and literary figures like Joel Chandler Harris, Erskine Caldwell, Thomas Wolfe, Tom Watson, and Henry Grady. These were studies in which "he could come directly to grips with the motivating factors in his subjects' lives," says M. Thomas Inge of *Selected Essays and Other Writings of John Donald Wade* (1966)—"essentially studies in the human heart." Even his other writings—ostensibly not biographical—reflect the same interplay of the anecdotal and factual, enlivened by a wry, friendly humor and a subtle piquancy: his informal history of the Marshallville Methodist Church from its beginnings to 1950, a work involving research into diaries, church records, and family memories; his contributions to three symposia published in the 1930s—"Cousin Lucius" in *I'll Take My Stand*, drawing upon the life of his Uncle Walter; "Southern Humor" in W. T. Couch's *Culture in the South*, (1934); and "Of the Mean and Sure Estate" in *Who Owns America?* (1936). All in various forms reveal Wade's commitment to an agrarian way of life. Davidson, Wade's friend of many decades, found his "Cousin Lucius" a kind of *exemplum* or in the end, "one great metaphor" or "fable" of a culture and a man unwilling to compromise his integrity, having lived through the change from traditional values to the standards of a new order.

For nearly three decades Wade taught composition and literature at southern institutions, chiefly at the University of Georgia (1919–1926), where he was responsible for developing the graduate program in American literature. During his six years in Nashville (1928–1934), Wade encouraged the biographical dissertation, and a number of these important studies of southern figures, which bridge the gap between history and literature, were subsequently published. Wade's colleagues and students at the University of Georgia found him a distinguished teacher: with another member of the department he established the Fortnightly Club, an active forum for students and faculty to discuss and debate—as the Fugitives had done—matters literary and human. One product of his years of teaching was an important anthology, *Masterworks of World Literature* (1941), which he co-edited with two colleagues.

Wade retired from formal teaching in 1950, thereafter continuing to devote himself to activities he had begun in the 1940s: the Marshallville Foundation, created in 1944, and the *Georgia Review*, first published in 1947. His Marshallville Foundation was his personal effort to sustain in a practical way the vitality of the traditional elements in his community. His editorship of the *Georgia Review* established the journal as an important resource of writing about literature, history, and culture, especially as it related to his state. At the time of its founding, Wade announced its aim "to be alert not merely against the false and the stupid but against all manner of highbrow cliché, faddism, and tish-tosh." Originally conceived as a "review of Georgia, for Georgians," the quarterly became, according to Inge, "an outlet for some of the best creative writing and scholarship in the South and the nation."

Donald Davidson, in his memorial introduction to Wade's *Selected Essays*, speaks of him as a kind of Plutarch, "a Southern Thackeray, with Georgia and the South as his Vanity Fair." In a sense he was that—but much more. Not the distanced commentator on a people and culture being treated as *object*, Wade was a southerner for whom teaching and writing were only part of the whole of living and being and doing. In one of his *Georgia Review* editorials, Wade considered the implications of a proverb: "Stretch your legs to suit your quilt." Noting that the reverse might appeal, he repeated with new emphasis:

"Stretch your legs to suit *your* quilt." "Very many of us," he observed, "are always busy stretching or shrinking ourselves to suit somebody's quilt besides our own." Wade's life reveals his scorn for such unnatural accommodation.

Robert Penn Warren (1905—)

It is not an unimportant consideration that Warren was born in Guthrie, Kentucky, nor that in his childhood he watched troops establishing martial law over tobacco growers, nor that at Vanderbilt University he found chemistry "damned dull" and literature and composition under Ransom and Davidson exciting. Invited to join the Fugitives, Warren recalls that this "was my education. . . . I got the feeling that poetry was . . . related to ideas and to life."

As a student, Warren received many honors, culminating in a Rhodes Scholarship. As a teacher, first at Louisiana State University and then at Yale, he has had an immeasurable influence. His texts, *Understanding Poetry* and *Understanding Fiction*, written with Cleanth Brooks, have, according to some scholars, revolutionized the teaching of literature. Although the label "new criticism" has been attached to Warren's approach, he is a catholic critic, asserting that any criticism is good which gives a "deeper insight." His description of the elements of good criticism perfectly depicts his own: dependence on intelligence, tact, discipline, honesty, and sensitivity.

The variety and complexity of Warren's poetry make any generalization insufficient. It has been suggested that he is primarily concerned with the drama of the spirit; one might add, as *Brother to Dragons* shows, that he is equally engaged by the human spirit confronting its limitations, resisting the drive to abstraction, fragmentation, or annihilation, searching for self-knowledge.

These are the thematic threads of his fiction as well. Permeated by the material of his southern heritage, Warren's novels transform history and social criticism into art. The night-riding tobacco farmers; modern southerners consumed with the diseases of an urban culture; the political and moral realities of concentrated political power; the implications of an antebellum Kentucky murder; the complexities of social and personal relationships inherent in the experiences of a beautiful mulatto slave; a series of dramatic self-confrontations focused on a death in a cave; a Bavarian immigrant's spiritual journey through the Civil War—these are the subjects from which Warren spins his tales. Some readers are disturbed by the violence in Warren's fiction, or by a frankness bordering on coarseness; others criticize his work for its "Hollywood" appeal, or for its melodramatic elements, its "bloated rhetoric." Yet Warren's fiction remains serious, intelligent, expressive of a symbolic imagination.

In recent years Warren has returned to his interests in drama and social criticism. *All the King's Men*, first produced as *Proud Flesh*, has been acclaimed by critics both here and abroad for its formidable moral challenge. His earlier frank defense of segregation in the Agrarian symposium has been repudiated in *Segregation* and *The Legacy of the Civil War*. A southerner justifying segregation is resorting to the Great Alibi, he asserts; the events of a Little Rock "are nothing more than an obscene parody of the meaning of his history."

Since 1962, Warren has continued to publish extensively.

There have been three new volumes of poetry—*Incarnations* (1968), *Audubon: A Vision* (1969), and *Or Else Poems* (1973)—and editions of his *Selected Poems* appeared in 1966 and 1976. Three novels have been added to his canon: *Flood* (1964), *Meet Me in the Green Glen* (1971), and *A Place to Come To* (1977). There have also been new books on such literary figures as John Greenleaf Whittier and Theodore Dreiser. And some of Warren's most fundamental ideas appear in the 1975 publication of his Jefferson Lectures, *Democracy and Poetry*.

Warren remains a southern writer, but his work is infused with rather than dominated by his southernness. The "great moral drama" in Warren's body of writing has centered on man's loss of innocence in a timeless world, his growing involvement with the human condition. In this sense Warren's work is "historical," for his characters live into the basic patterns evolving in time and space. History, he has said, "is the big myth we live, and in our living constantly remake."

Stark Young (1881–1963)

Born in Como, Mississippi, the son of a doctor, Stark Young grew into the humane qualities of living expressed in a rare sensibility and a commitment to tradition, order, and the family. His background and activities contributed significantly to the development of an aesthetic both practical and creative, moral and organic. In his many careers, spanning half a century, Young was a teacher, playwright, literary journalist, novelist, translator, painter, and critic of the theater. "Art," he believed, should be "nostalgic with all we love and follow after life," its realism should be "so real and so precisely true and close that it becomes poetic."

As a boy Young was sent to private schools; at the age of fifteen he entered the University of Mississippi from which he graduated in 1901. Like a number of other southerners of his class and generation, he went north for graduate study, completing a Master's program at Columbia the following year. He remained in the academic world, a distinguished, popular professor of English, for some fifteen years. He began teaching at his *alma mater* in 1905, then moved to the University of Texas in 1907. There he established the *Texas Review* and the Curtain Club, a group offering an unusual fare of plays in Texas cities. This activity was an important catalyst in his developing interest in all aspects of theater. In 1915 he moved northeast to accept a professorship in English at Amherst College. During his five years there Young came to realize that his "bent" was not toward scholarship but toward a freer life in the arts—writing and seeing plays, going to art galleries and special exhibitions, reviewing and sharing his responses, traveling and living abroad from time to time. A year's leave of absence from Amherst gave Young an opportunity to experience firsthand something of the quality of Italian and Spanish culture. The pull of these interests and experiences led him to decide at the age of forty to give up the security of an academic post and to try free-lancing in New York. He resigned from Amherst in 1921.

Having contributed to a number of journals for five years before he left teaching—his articles and reviews had been appearing in *New Republic, Nation, North American Review,*

Theatre Arts Magazine, *Yale Review*, *Dial*, and *Bookman* —Young was already known in publishing circles when he settled in New York. Within a few months he was appointed an editor at *Theatre Arts Magazine*, and he was offered the position of drama critic for the *New Republic*, as well as a place on its editorial board; both of these were affiliations that lasted for more than a quarter of a century. The interruption of one year (1924/25), while he was drama critic for the New York *Times*, convinced Young that he was temperamentally unsuited to newspaper reviewing, with its deadlines and its expectation of a direct, relatively uncomplicated style. From 1917 to 1947 he published more than eight hundred articles and reviews in the *New Republic*, the New York *Times*, *Theatre Arts Magazine*, and a number of other journals. As a reviewer of the arts and an informal essayist, Young was a uniquely distinguished drama critic, noted for his uncompromisingly high standards, his seriousness, and his sensibility attuned to every element of the theater. He was always concerned about the organic unity, the relation of the parts to the whole: the quality of the play or the translation, the interplay of the actor, director, sets, costumes, lighting, sound—all areas in which Young himself had been involved during his Curtain Club productions in Texas. From his hundreds of essay-reviews about the theater, a number were selected for publication in five collections—*The Flower in Drama, Glamour, Theatre Practice, The Theater*, and *Immortal Shadows*— which are considered a model compendium of rare criticism, useful to actors as well as readers and audiences.

Young's involvement with the theater was unique in this century. In addition to his criticism, he published a number of one-act and full-length plays in journals and in book form. *Theatre Arts Magazine* was an important exposure for his work. Two of his plays were produced professionally by the Provicetown Players in Greenwich Village and the London Stage Society. As a translator Young achieved a reputation of great distinction. Early and late in his career, he translated for production works by Regnard, Molière, Machiavelli, and Pirandello, and his versions of four Chekhov plays were acclaimed for their sensitivity, the power of their directness, their grace and felicity.

For Young the effect of the totality of a work of art was basic —whether it was a play, a painting, a novel. Young's "organic aesthetic" was evident not only in his criticism and his own plays, with their romantic themes projected in nuance and a nostalgic delicacy of emotion, but also in his four southern novels published from 1926 to 1934. His last, *So Red the Rose*, reissued in 1953 with an appreciative introduction by Davidson, drew upon family experiences, letters, recollections of Mississippians, and "an immense amount of historical material" from the Civil War period. Considered his most perfect rendition of a traditional culture and the historical continuity of an antebellum society, *So Red the Rose* was in effect the novelist's effort to realize—like an image in art—a possible contemporary counterpart to destructive elements of industrialism.

Art existed, Young believed, not for its own sake but "to recreate, emphasize, mold and perpetuate the qualities of its society." This fundamental conviction explains, in part, his willingness to contribute to *I'll Take My Stand*. Although he disavowed a personal commitment to the Agrarian cause (even though he had a long, warm correspondence with both David-son and Tate), he saw himself among all of the Agrarians as "most truly expressing the Southern idea." In stories, essays, and sketches, some of which were rooted in other locales or cultures, the same assumptions about values in a coherent, organic society—based on land, family, and tradition—are implicit. Conscious of his heritage as a southerner, Young continued through the 1930s to draw upon his tradition and region for shorter fiction, essays, journalistic articles, and lectures: *Feliciana*, a collection of stories, was published a year after *So Red the Rose*; in the same year he decided to begin his memoirs with the first of the projected two volumes to focus on "loved things, loved people"; he lectured in the South and wrote (for the *New York Times Magazine*) on things southern; and in 1937 *A Southern Treasury of Life and Literature*, under his editorship, appeared.

In the 1940s an even more direct expression of Young's aesthetic emerged: he turned to painting and began his autobiographical reminiscences. Largely a self-taught artist, Young had two one-man exhibitions in New York (1943 and 1945) and a showing of his paintings in four important galleries, including the Chicago Institute of Art, the director of which purchased a large canvas for the permanent collection. Young's paintings, according to reviewers, attest to a "haunting and intensely personal mysticism," to his skill, and to his knowledge of art developed from years of travel and frequent reviews of exhibitions and books about painting. His own canvases—dreamlike flower studies and other strong representations of the elusive, whose titles were inspired by literature or religion—reflect his organic aesthetic. For Young "the actuality of

(408)

real things has no solidity as compared to the reality of our illusions and the precision of our emotions." Just as "art was to
extend life into dream," according to Young, his recording of
his memories in *The Pavilion* (1951), dedicated to Tate, was
to pay homage to the things he heard and saw, that his "elders
had seen and talked about," the foundations of whatever education he acquired, of whatever understanding of life or of art
—up to his twenty-first birthday. It was, in short, "a reaffirmation" of his desire to preserve "the finish of a pattern of culture." The title, contained in the Thirty-first Psalm—"Thou
shalt keep them secretly in a pavilion from the strife of tongues"
—reveals Young's hope to preserve the past in art. *The Pavilion* was his "child of endless memory and effort," a "definition
and nourishment of one's self," a representation to the tension
between a "consciousness of [one's] own separateness" and a
simultaneous acknowledgment of the role of the succession
from a known past to a future."

In his lifetime Young was accorded accolades unique in the
history of a southern American man of letters. Lectures on the
American theater, given in Italian while he was the Westing-
house Lecturer in Italy, were acclaimed with an award of the
highest title in the Order of the Crown of Italy; he was named
one of the distinguished Americans to New York University's
Hall of Fame and served on its board. He was a member of the
Institute of Arts and Letters, a recipient of the Creative Arts
Medallion of Brandeis University; and near the end of his life
he was chosen to receive the first "Distinguished Career Award"
from the South Eastern Theatre Conference. Solicited letters
written to Young in 1960 by thirty-nine of his colleagues and
friends—performers, critics, directors, teachers of drama, and

playwrights (among them John Gielgud, Maurice Evans, Katharine Cornell, Brooks Atkinson, Harold Clurman, Eric Bentley, Paul Green)—praised him for his rare gifts and unmatched achievements in theater. Passionate, fastidious, yet warm and human, a theater critic whose graceful and felicitous translations gave Chekhov "new breath and soul in the contemporary theatre," he holds "a special place," said Eric Bentley, precisely because "he was never in the swim."

Throughout his life and in his art, Young realized what was for him the special character of creativity, that "very last and ultimate flowering of all human experience"—"its sharing and revelation."